Sugar, Spice, and the Not So Nice

Sugar, Spice, and the Not So Nice

Comics Picturing Girlhood

Edited by

Dona Pursall and Eva Van de Wiele

LEUVEN UNIVERSITY PRESS

This edited volume is an outcome of the COMICS project funded by the European Research Council (ERC) under the European Union's Horizon 2020 research and innovation programme (grant agreement no. 758502).

erc
European Research Council
Established by the European Commission

Also published with the support of the KU Leuven Fund for Fair Open Access.

ISBN 978 94 6270 361 2 (paperback)
ISBN 978 94 6166 497 6 (epdf)
ISBN 978 94 6166 498 3 (epub)
https://doi.org/10.11116/9789461664976
D/2023/1869/7
NUR: 617

Typesetting: Crius Group
Cover design: Johan Van Looveren
Cover illustration: Original cover art by Valentine Gallardo

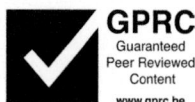

GPRC
Guaranteed
Peer Reviewed
Content
www.gprc.be

To Valentine Gallardo for her image,

To Joe Sutliff Sanders, Julia Round and Mel Gibson
for their commitment to the conference

Contents

Contents

Preface

This volume brings together some of the papers presented at the digital symposium Sugar and Spice, and the Not So Nice: Comics Picturing Girlhood, organised on 22 and 23 April 2021 at Ghent University. It also features some research initiatives that followed, inspired by our conference.

To learn about all of the papers that were presented, some of which did not end up in this collection, we refer to Julia Round's afterword in this volume, and to our digital report for Comics Forum, which features graphic renderings by John Miers and Dragana Radanovic: https://comicsforum.org/2021/06/14/symposium-report-sugar-and-spice-and-the-not-so-nice-comics-picturing-girlhood/. For inspiration from what was interchanged in the lively discussions during the conference, we wish to direct readers to our Padlet: padlet.com/eva_vandewiele/ComicsPicturingGirlhood. To keep the conversation going, we invite readers to use the hashtag #Comicspicturinggirlhood on Twitter.

Both the Girlhood Conference and this volume are an outcome of the COMICS project funded by the European Research Council (ERC) under the European Union's Horizon 2020 research and innovation programme (Grant agreement No. [758502]). We warmly thank every artist and author involved in this editorial adventure.

Finally, we are grateful to the directors of the series for considering our volume, and to the editors, reviewers and editorial staff at Leuven University Press for their support and feedback. The KU Leuven Fund for Fair Open Access also made it possible for us to publish this volume and circulate it widely.

Dona Pursall and Eva Van de Wiele

Introduction

Dona Pursall and Eva Van de Wiele

The term 'girl' is profoundly evocative. It can be used as endearment or abuse, with pride or derision. Moreover, it might be used to refer to a newborn, an adult, or anyone in-between. This non-specificity is a consequence of how social ideas about childhood and gender vary in different cultures and through history. Although notions might change, the word 'girl' does not seem to shed earlier, traditional or old-fashioned associations and replace them with the new, but it rather adds and accumulates, making 'girl' an increasingly complex, contradictory and problematic term. Girls learn to be girls by negotiating their way through the ambiguous, contradictory, judgemental and impossible ideals constructing the othered definitions of girls. Girls are not old, not knowledgeable, not independent, not strong and not unmediated.

This collected edition elaborates on the complexity and multifaceted nature of girlhood as represented in comics. Contemporary theories of feminism acknowledge a multiple or subjective theory of identity. "The feminist protagonist need not squelch her individuality in order to fit into society. Instead, her agency, her individuality, her choice, and her nonconformity are affirmed and even celebrated" (Trites 6). In line with this embodied, lived appreciation of being-as-character, feminist studies of literature and culture are concerned with voice, self-expression and agency. Multiplicity and flexibility are similarly essential traits of comics storytelling. Comics use image and text in tension; this opens possibilities of "unsynthesized narrative tracks" (Chute 108). The stylistic elements peculiar to comics therefore offer great potential for expressing the contemporary feminist concerns of voice, self-expression and agency. Between images, captions, speech and thought balloons, the medium's form invites polyvocal storytelling. This is furthered by the ways in which visual devices interplay through framing and perspective. Each artist, moreover, leaves traces of the act of expression (like the literal lines, and the chosen contours, and colours of both letters and words), which "give an idea of what the graphiateur and his or her graphiation is like" (Baetens 147). Those traces are clearer when the narratee is confronted with a sketch or a rough copy from a single artist or otherwise has the impression that this artist's *graphiation* (mediation through technique) is intensely present. Furthermore, the focus on visual storytelling foregrounds bodily expression. We "read" the characters' individual experience of the narratives through movement, emotion and those funny squiggles which say so much. By reading the gestures of both the characters within the narrative and the hand drawing of that narrative, readers re-experience the enunciative work of the artist (Baetens 150). Applied to our volume, this means that reading multiple representations of girls and girlhoods in comics can broaden a readers' experience of girlhood.

Beyond their specific formal devices, comics' nonconformity can be emancipatory, rebuking propriety and authority-through-singularity. Comics question and undo boundaries, power constructions and limitations. They only require pencil and paper and are thus accessible to all; they are popular culture and can therefore move beyond "high" art constraints of aesthetics and taste. Comics are always self-aware to some extent, as their panels continually acknowledge their own construction. To sum up, comics' sequence, seriality, flexible perspectives and polyvocality make retelling, reconsidering and critical reflection a normal quality of comics storytelling. As Theresa Tensuan argues, comics' abilities to question dichotomies and "make visible the ideologies that frame experiences, script actions, and shape identities" (141) makes them ideal for negotiating identities.

The personal experience of girlhood is unique. The cover image by Valentine Gallardo captures that uniqueness. Colours or categories like "pink" and "cute" are easily overthrown by girls' appropriations of the products created for their entertainment. Placing girls within the centre of a scholarly debate is the aim of this volume; correspondingly, Gallardo's girl is sitting in Het Pand, Ghent University's prestigious conference venue. The diversity represented in this collection offers a beginning, a first consideration of how comics' expression and liberty can and does (or does not) celebrate individuality. In such a project, it is informative to consider unique examples not as exceptions, but rather as typical examples of subjective identity. With this in mind, this introduction lays out some of the central tensions related to girlhood through specific examples. We contemplate the implications of "child" identity constructed in tension with "adult", explore how "girl" as a term is weighted with roles and categories, and ponder how embodied action and activity is flavoured by social ethics and expectations. This introduction uses comics to study judgements about normative behaviour and aesthetics of girlhood and what this means for how we view departures or exceptions as beyond or outside the constructed 'girl'.

Rethinking Growing Up

The "mythical status" of childhood (James 256) is first and foremost constructed in tension with adulthood. Divisions between the stages of child and adult relate to power. Power requires continual renewal and affirmation; it is not fixed. Therefore, the adult–child dichotomy is similarly unfixed, rather constantly changing. "Change, indeed, is the air that children breathe, which may be why they are more flexible than adults." (Halberstam 15)

If, as Mayall argues, the study of childhood "is essentially the study of child-adult relations" (21), the contradictions Cross highlights in adult behaviour towards children are informative.

> We see childhood as timeless, yet we shower the young with fads and innovation. We delight in the dependent, sweet child and despair when our indulgences seem to create the independent, jaded teenager. We buy more things for the little ones at birthdays and holidays than research shows they want, and then we fret when older children seem so insatiable. (Cross, 2004, 13)

The child simultaneously piques nostalgia for a pure, innocent, unsullied notion of goodness, and hope for an idealised, potential future. The personal grief for lost childish wonder inspires a desire to protect and recover the fictional "unspoiled" child.

The power of the notional child, and particularly the abstract girl, to disrupt adult rationality is not a new idea. Winsor McCay's 1905 comic *The Story of Hungry Henrietta* compresses these ideological constructs. The serial ran from 8 January until 16 July.

> Comic strip characters of the period [...] were typically ageless; however Henrietta noticeably ages from week to week. [...] In the premier episode she is three months old, but by the last – less than seven months later) she has aged eight years. (Roeder 39)

There is an irony in this journey of the child's growth contrasted with the adult characters' lack of development. In each strip opinions about idealised girlhood create "a commotion" of "frantic adults"; "people cluster around her, the child understandably begins to fuss and squirm, eliciting a torrent of advice and increasing attempts to regulate her behaviour" (Bukatman 40). The adults' propensity for offering opinions rather than

Figure 1 Winsor McCay, *Hungry Henrietta*, Chapter 2, image source: https://www.barnaclepress.com/comic/Hungry%20Henrietta (black and white).

any actual action or compassion ridicules discrepancies between appearance and reality, between performing and being. This narrative of child confinement through overbearing adult interference routinely concluded with a panel showing her "alone, horrifically (and only partially) pacified" (Bukatman 43). This strip echoes a wider social commentary about emancipation from the time. In a society of status and decorum, Henrietta's entire disempowerment forces her to have to ask for the most basic things (food and respect, for example), only to be met with entirely unhelpful opinions and behaviours. In the strip (**fig. 1**), the "sweet", "darling", "cute"[1] girl unacceptably cries. Her tears are interpreted by the adults as a great range of feelings, as flirting, fear, crossness, hunger, etc. Ridiculously, they try to resolve her emotional needs through distraction and entertainment. Our reading here contrasts with Alexander Braun's description of her as obnoxious and demanding, an image of "compulsive" gluttony (71). Rather, the strips mock adult reliance on consumption as a solution to emotional needs, drawing attention to how distraction is a flawed substitute for supressed emotional expression (Zornado 206). Jolly songs and dances can't feed Henrietta's hunger for reassurance. Their own beliefs about the child's wants leads each of them to fruitlessly perform different nursery rhymes and jigs; however, her distress only subsides once she is left alone. Although more peaceful in the final panel, her need for emotional reassurance remains unappeased. *Hungry Henrietta* is just one example of the idealised girl as passive, disempowered consumer. The adults offer contradictory judgements in regard to what Henrietta needs or wants. They are united in seeking to silence and pacify her, thereby maintaining her position as idealised. Adult involvement in constructing girlhood, as exemplified here, can be overt, prejudicial and unjust, damagingly constraining the potentially flexible child through opinion and tradition.

Gendered Expectations

The labelling of gendered genres and formats (romance comics, paper dolls) has enforced the containment of girls into physically safer and less politicised space. Curiosity and ambition were not completely rejected by these narratives, but the areas of interest were confined to aesthetics and intimate social spaces. In such constellations girls particularly were objectified as malleable, thereby both insubstantial and vulnerable. Not only the illustrated stories in magazines were gendered; the publicity also worked towards a segmentation of the sexes. In 1744, London publisher John Newbery included a toy with *A Little Pretty Pocket-Book*: girls were supposed to desire a pincushion, while boys got a ball to play with (Tarbox 18). Another powerful illustration of how this malleability played out in children's magazines are popular paper cut-outs. Like a fashion show, magazines would publish a collection of "looks" which children could cut out and fold around a generic body, thereby re-prescribing the characters' identity purely through image. Most of these DIY pages in the magazines provided girls with paper dolls, paper mascots, embroidery or knitting patterns with floral decoration to put on gendered objects such as knitting baskets and aprons. Paper dolls demand from girls that they understand fashion and know how to combine different pieces together or what to wear on what occasions, but paper dolls also require them to take up affectionate, motherly roles and nurture them as though they were their babies. In short, aesthetics meets ethics.

Although children can resist or ignore both these aesthetics and ethics, the message their toys proclaim is that there is a clear discrepancy between sexes and, with the repeated consumption of and prolonged exposure to these toys, comes an incorporation into the mind and body (Cross, 1997, 80). Before 1900 most of the toys for girls were learning or sewing tools. In the first decade of the twentieth-century girls' play paralleled the mother's work, as miniature domestic machines entered the doll houses; as a result, domestic labour and social rituals dominated play. Gradually, other affects became more important, such as friendship (a doll could replay a sibling or friend), and increasingly also the fun of spending and being fashionable took the dominant position (Cross, 1997, 80). Thus, the consumerist approach intermingled with the roles of friend or surrogate/future mother and became far removed from the 1900–1920s DIY ethos of making your own toys and sewing your own dolls' clothes. Instead, girls were pushed to buy and keep up with the latest trends.

Through repetition of such trends, what were once "youthful neutral details", as Abate has shown, gradually formed a way to separate genders and frame them as oppositional, underscoring heteronormativity: "including flowers, dainty trim, and the color pink – were relegated to girls and women" (69). Girls protagonists have granted independence to other female characters within the strips, whether through liberation from their conventional role in the family such as in the case of orphans, feral children or even tomboys, or through their powers of independent thought (as is the case of girl characters like Mafalda). Often these have been tied together and thereby create confrontation. One early incarnation of this trope can be seen in "the Dickensian melodrama and astringent conservative politics of Harold Gray's *Little Orphan Annie* (from 1924)" (Hatfield 5). Her iconic blank eyes due to an absence of eyeballs have been critiqued as a kind of void of conscience by Art Spiegelman (Spiegelman and Gaiman).

The same qualities that the critical thinking strips about innocent girl characters evoke have later evolved into the social commentary strips about "feisty" girls. As Michelle Ann Abate has discussed there have been many popular icons from the first half of the twentieth century in the US: funny, feisty, feminist girls that make readers laugh and think about independence, agency and autonomy (7). We could add to these examples the Argentinian *Mafalda* (1964–1973 by Quino) or the Italian *Bambina Filosofica* [Philosophical Girl] (2000–2013 by Vanna Vinci[2]), who exposed consistently how patriarchal society downplayed women (Paoppi). In the excerpt from this strip (**fig. 2**) Mafalda comments on the acceptance of prescribed domestic roles by mothers.

She questions the fatigue of housewives having to live up to their domestic role, laying aside their possible own aspirations: "Mom, what would you like to be if you were to live?" The mother's domestic confinement – she is shown literally up to her elbows in washing – emphasises her limited opportunities and possibilities. Her physical restriction is echoed by the philosophical question which pitches simply existing against "living" as a space of ambitions, hopes, dreams and self-fulfilment. Mafalda draws attention to the tension between lived experience and idealised constructions, a tension key to 1960s–1970s *Mirabelle*, as discussed by Joan Ormrod in Chapter 7.

Figure 2 Quino. *Mafalda. 5: tiras de Quino,* De La Flor, 2005, n.p.

Whilst girl characters powerfully notice such intractable constructs, comics characters demonstrating the embodied action and activity of living with, accepting and embracing the tensions, choices and limitations which shape girls also have an important role to play. Running since 1997, the Norwegian comic *Nemi* (originally *The Black Side*) is about a childlike twenty-year-old philosophical goth. Lisa Myhre's popular comic has been critiqued both for not representing typical females and for the ways in which the comic undermines typified expectations for what women should be and how they should behave. Although often angered by hypocrisy in the world, by acknowledging her own contradictions, such as being a humanitarian, pacifist fan of heavy metal, Nemi importantly affirms, and values as normative, a self-aware, complex, individual identity. She acts aware of, and yet despite, the layers of expectation, judgement and opinion. These examples share an overt acknowledgement, a voicing of, the complex pressures applied to girls and the importance these ideals are given within a social context.

Looking the Girl

The pervasive notion enforced by cut-outs, that there is such a thing as an appropriate outfit for specific occasions, speaks more broadly to the importance of girls' dress and decorum. The signifying power of clothes is representative not only of self-identification but of assimilation, belonging and conformity. The look of girls is further problematised because judgements of girls' taste and deportment are closely bound to discourses of morality.

Lalla and Lola, a short-lived comic series by Antonio Rubino for *Corriere dei Piccoli* in 1913 (**fig. 3**, fifth year of publication), opposes a simple girl (Lalla) to a bourgeois coquette (Lola), whose social class does not coincide with moral or ethical superiority. Lola is dressed impeccably, in one sense the ideal of a little girl. However, she commits the cardinal sin of vanity, showing awareness of her own good looks and lording over Lalla. The final panel of this gag comic always shows how Lalla's misfortune turns into fortune, as she ends up wearing a stunning natural outfit, provoking Lola's comparison and jealousy. Comparison alludes to the sin of pride. Here, arrogance is rewarded with jealousy through two negatively judged actions. Lola is unkind; she puts Lalla down, demonstrated by Lalla literally falling in the strip. Lola's comeuppance, her loss of status, is that she no longer has the finest outfit. She is outshone by Lalla's less conventional, accidental beauty. However, the attractiveness of the dress is enhanced by her moral goodness. She is humble and passive; she does not retaliate against Lola, nor does she ask for her new clothes. It is not just the outfit she models in the final panel, it is the ideal balance between beauty and innocence, modesty emphasised by her closed eyes.

Figure 3 *Lalla e Lola*, Antonio Rubino, *Corriere dei Piccoli,* no. 4, 26 January 1913, p. 1.
Image source: www.bsmc.it.

That girls should not have mean thoughts but rather be vessels of love and affection is a pervasive notion. Even today, nostalgia in contemporary comics made by women artists reflects a dominant position of the "cute" and the "romantic". Eliana Albertini's ironically titled *Good Girl* (**fig. 4**) engages with typical roles of the "good girl" who is easily led to tears, has an urge to care for teddy bears who state I love you, wants to own a Winnie-the-Pooh diary, and wear socks with hearts.

However, whilst some comics reinforce stereotypical ideas of cute and lean girls,[3] comics also have the power to show the tension between thoughts and behaviour, and, as a result, incorporate social commentary. Ida Neverdahl's depiction (**fig. 5**) of the disruptive power of eating disorders personified by a bright-pink giant leech-type creature is one such example.

The presence and weight of the creature, literally wrapped around her mind, creates behaviour which the reader realises is not entirely the girl protagonist's own. Our insight into her own dilemma strengthens the hurt caused by her friend's, innocent but accidentally raw, joking reply.[4] Image and words in tension layer meaning here, exemplifying how comics have the potential to unravel, redraw and question beyond being girls into the intricacies of thinking and feeling girlhood, such as Martha Newbigging's essay (Chapter 2) or Selina Tusitala Marsh's comic *Mophead* as discussed by Marine Berthiot (Chapter 11).

Figure 4 Eliana Albertini, *Good Girl*, Brescia: Maledizioni, 2020, bottom strips, p. 7.

Figure 5 Ida Neverdahl, *I'm a girl, it's fantastic*, Oslo: Jippi Forlag, 2014, p. 30.

Negotiating Socialisation

Social judgements about gendered bodies, actions and morals construct the girl as a cultural effigy. Relevant for this negotiation of socialisation is Judith Butler's idea of gender as an act. All subjects reproduce and actualise scripts of behaviours that have existed and have been rehearsed before they were born (Butler 272). These acts are thus historical constructs which can be troubled by the embodied existence of actual girls who find themselves negotiating these judgements. This is not only a tension between constructions of girl as not boy, but also girl as ideology. Boys are risk-takers, so girls should be sensible, but foolishness inspires a protective instinct, so they shouldn't be too sensible, because then they would be independent. Boys are independent, so girls should be dependent, want social interaction, appease and listen to others, need to be cared for, but not be needy or demanding because that would mean behaving actively. Boys are active, so girls should be passive, gentle, not competitive, nor should they sweat because that would show effort and strength. Boys are strong, and so... the list goes on. These contradictory illusions revolve primarily around the physical body, how it looks, how it is decorated and how it moves; however, it also stretches to encompass what girls should show interest in. Still, according to Butler, "alternative performative acts" can challenge and alter the way gender is constructed (278).

The gendering of genres of storytelling developed alongside increasingly commercial trends in publishing. This coincided with emergent literacy of the general population. Perhaps inspired by the very concerns about emancipation at the turn of the century, and the tension this created around the different social roles men and women should play, popular literature segregated genders increasingly overtly: independence, ambition and adventure for men; romance, acceptance and domesticity for women. This sentimentality filtered into children's literature. Viviane Alary, reflecting on comics magazines from Spain, states that all girls' comics magazines descended from a publication by Consuelo Gil *Mis Chicas* [My Girls], which created "a sheltered female world. As much through their graphic style as through the story lines, the girls' comics were a place where violence and adventure were not admitted" (2009, 270). This segregation began in Spain with Joaquín Buigas's short-lived girls' comics magazine *BB*, inspired mainly by French examples such as *Le Poupée Modèle*. The magazine imitated the format and techniques of the general comics magazine *TBO*. Eight pages were created out of a folded page: four black and white, four with two colours. When both periodicals' formats became bigger in 1922, *BB*'s price rose to 15 cents for a twice monthly periodicity yet *TBO* still cost 10 cents and remained a weekly. These editors were seeking to reach a broader readership and to expand their market. A contemporary reader might be surprised by the age range Buigas wanted to cater to: between three and twenty. *BB* represented a new, but unsuccessful, current in the Spanish publishing industry. Girls' magazines did not triumph until after the Spanish

Civil War when Franco's dictatorship exaggerated the conviction that society should be asymmetrically organised. One clear example of this in practise was the rigidly separate "girl" and "boy" sections in the Falangist youth organisation (Manrique Arribas 234). Gil chose to fill the girls' magazines with fantasy, fairy tale and a naive amiable style, whilst adventure, realist and spectacular style was absent from the girls' comics (Alary, 2016, 9).

Just like the temporary, disposable nature of cut-outs, designed to be swapped and replaced, comics' seriality creates opportunities for redesigning and reinventing the image of girls. As with McCay's Henrietta, the relationship between seriality and temporality has been extensively explored by a variety of comics. Many comics' girls eternally stay the same age, such as Little Lulu, Nancy, Mafalda and the Philosophical Girl, to name just a few. The ideological fallacy of a girl as frozen in a perpetual childhood alludes to other timeless stories. Fairy tales and folk characters are a rich source of inspiration for comics. There is an inevitable overlap between the girls of these traditional stories and a plethora of comic characters. More than just the characters though, the ideologies of folk stories filter through. As Pascal Lefèvre argues, prankster stories rewrite the "god, spirit, adult or anthropomorphic animal" of myth and folklore, into "a child that disobeys normal rules and conventional behaviour" (8). Although "naughty" in a traditional sense, the creative, playful, clever and unconventional trickster behaviour affords these characters an immunity from normal rules. Lefèvre argues that, consequently, trickster characters go unpunished. Although some are punished, there is a strange ambiguity about such characters that, despite their rule breaking, they are adored. There is a strong tradition of girl trickster characters, those who do not conform or those who are intentionally mischievous. Grace Drayton's Toodles (who later became Dolly Dimples), *Betsy Bouncer and Her Doll* by Tom Tucker (who was possibly E. W. Kemble), and *Madge the Magician's Daughter* by W. O. Wilson are just some from the turn of the century, whilst later incarnations of these characters are *Peanuts'* Lucy Van Pelt by Charles Schulz or Ernie Bushmiller's Nancy.

In British comics for children, this trope of trickster girls has led to a raft of characters whose names tell their stories; Beryl the Peril, Minnie the Minx and Ivy the Terrible are just a few examples. As characters of serial strips, what all of these characters share is their confinement to rules and morals. Although mostly humorous and therefore not intended to be taken seriously, such characters, by being continually naughty, draw over time clear demarcations around what is and what is not acceptable, good, nice, kind, thoughtful, correct or appropriate behaviour for girls. Whether their actions result in punishment or laughter, the strips themselves offer a wider social commentary about expectations, a commentary especially enforced through their repetition due to seriality. There is a curious tension worthy of exploration between how serial comic characters are frozen in their strip worlds, often with a dogmatic persistence (British girls were still spanked as punishment in comics in the 1980s, even though it was generally frowned upon in real life). At the same time, naughty girls in comics have an endless potential for repetition, for adjustment, change, replaying and rewriting the stories. Most frequently though, the children do not learn, develop or grow, but neither does the strips' social, contextual frame change. For these fixed girl characters, our expectations of who they are and how they will behave is fixed by our admiration for them as tricksters; their role is to draw attention, through their fun, to our own judgements about what is good or bad. The punchline of these gags is often laughter at the reader's misjudgement of normality or convention. The "trick" they play is that, like folk tales, they ensure the readers all agree about the boundaries of right and wrong, good and bad, or appropriate and inappropriate. The laughter they therefore evoke unites us in our agreement upon shared social codes, but also in our acknowledgement of how such codes are often silly. Such prejudices discussed in this volume are our ideas about time (Chapter 4), about what girls ought to look like (Chapter 2) or how they ought to behave (Chapter 5).

Stereotypes and generalisations about what girls are or should be have never been wholly true or appropriate to anyone. This collection is about appreciating and enjoying the rich multiplicity of flavours, colours, styles and tastes that reflect the real diversity of what it can possibly mean to be a girl, and to celebrate how comics offer a platform for expression and discourse about complex child identity and agency. The broad historical and cultural breadth of examples here attempts to illustrate complexity. Although these "one-off", particular examples of unique girls might on the one hand illustrate exceptions, rather, by collecting together what might be thought of as a underrepresented or othered narratives about "girls", we hope to affirm, that, in fact, through their persistence and pervasiveness, the widest, most different, most embracing definition of what it is to be a girl is actually a preponderance of exceptions. Girls as defined by what they are not can be found in the graphic essays by Newbigging, Purcell and Conard (Chapters 2, 4 and 10 respectively) or in Berthiot's analysis of Selina Tusitala Marsh's young avatar (Chapter 11).

Chapter Outlines

The following chapters introduce critical and graphic essays which engage with our broader notion of questioning girlhood and demonstrating diversity. The first two chapters offer perspectives on the child–adult tension. Mel Gibson's autoethnographic chapter reflects on her own career and the ways in which expectations failed to account for the richness and multiplicity of her lived selfhood. As the title, 'It's *the* girl!', alludes to, the narrowness of definitions related to expectations of what girls should be construct harmful notions of isolated and non-normative identity. Gibson's personal account rewrites the history of comics as a journey through shame and otherness. She reinforces how the defining lines drawn around girl identity not only shape girlhood but also followed her into adulthood. Martha Newbigging's practice-based research explores how the stories we tell ourselves, and those we tell about ourselves, relate to lived identity. In reframing perspective, judgement and power through drawing comics about lived experiences, Newbigging's work validates unique, individual queer experiences as articulations of gender and sexuality discourse through minority voices.

Continuing the biographical theme, the third chapter, by María Porras Sánchez, explores refugee experiences through comics, and the ways in which space, place, journey and transition allow the comics to tell the stories of voices often unheard. The fictional and factual lived experiences of girl refugees can result in reader's empathy and even political activation. Adding to the biographical theme is JoAnn Purcell's intimate family biography (Chapter 4), where she uses the process of comics making as reflective seeing. Comics as personal documentary invites a compassionate reading through appreciation of how a uniquely individual perspective draws attention to assumed notions of normativity. Purcell takes time to illustrate how her daughter's relationship to time differs from her own. By noticing, valuing and not judging, a sense of understanding evolves. Illustration of a subjective personal experience is powerfully significant here, not only because of how the comics offer insight to a reader but also in Purcell's discussion of the process of comics making as a socially bonding and reflective process.

The following two chapters cover a corpus of French-language comics and discuss gender roles. Sylvain Lesage and Benoît Glaude study how roles and norms are simultaneously underscored and questioned in comics series featuring girl characters. Lesage investigates the series *Corinne et Jeannot* by the male artist Jean Tabary in the context of the second feminist wave (Chapter 5). He analyses how the entire magazine containing the gag series, *Pif Gadget*, loyalised its mixed-audience readers through direct address in the editorials, in the series itself and through vivid discussions regarding gender roles and the "naughty" girl in the correspondence section. His chapter offers reader-response analysis as well as close readings of the series. Benoît Glaude discusses a contemporary comics series on a girl and her dog, *Margot & Oscar Pluche / Sac à Puces* (Chapter 6). Glaude contextualises this girl protagonist as a remediation of the form of the *franco-belge* family strip that addresses contemporary themes whilst showing that the series retains typical female traits and treats the subjects of girlhood and motherhood ambiguously. Glaude's chapter is, moreover, an example of how comics scholars can use quantitative analysis in addition to their qualitative close readings.

Continuing Lesage's historical perspective on comics, Joan Ormrod's analysis of active[5] female bodies in *Mirabelle* from the 1960s and 1970s explores the feedback loop between cultural change and popular culture's exploration of these sociocultural changes (Chapter 7). The diversity of ways in which the magazines interact with ideas about young women's bodies, actions, activities and movements demonstrates the tensions related to embodied experience. Joan Ormrod particularly draws attention to the ways in which comics can address multilayered, unresolved, changing cultures, engaging with contemporary discourse through exploration, mimicking the social, political, economic and development changes through fictionalising their impact on subjective experience. Aswathy Senan's contextualising discussion of *Bobanum Moliyum* (Chapter 8) considers not only how historical context but also publishing context affects comics storytelling and girl character identity. Through a comparison of changing ideologies in one strip in two different publications, Senan considers the construction of appropriate, mediated child- and girlhood.

Michel De Dobbeleer's chapter (9) offers yet another research approach to comics picturing girlhood. His chapter is a conversation with two feminist scholars in light of their re-reading of the Belgian comics series *Jommeke* and focuses on culturally constructed ideologies of girls in comics through key terms such as "symbolic annihilation" and the "male gaze".

The last two chapters consider how comics tell stories, and the ways in which formalist and aesthetic discourses about the medium of comic can be explored by the comics themselves. Sébastien Conard's graphic essay (Chapter 10) responds to art as storytelling and biography as inspiration. He considers the importance of the female voice through the work of Charlotte Salomon in light of his own graphic response. Marine Berthiot considers autobiographical comics in relation to the significance of voice (Chapter 11). Through analysis of *Mophead*, Berthiot explores how Selina Tusitala Marsh merges qualities of the Pasifika storytelling traditions with the comics form, to produce a unique, culturally discursive form of telling. Marsh's girl self-avatar voices a narrative about prejudice and difference, shifting the resistance evoked by fear of difference to empowerment created by cultural affinity. By paying attention to how the interweaving of storytelling forms echoes the gradual assimilation of identity, Berthiot's analysis alludes to how format is story.

In a volume that aspires to a plurivocal panoply of voices of and on girls, we end with more than a conclusion. We invited girl comics' specialist Julia Round to reflect upon the conference and the resulting volume in an afterword. Her text draws together the strands of all the chapters and reflects on the process which brought this collection together. This is one of the first critical collections which focuses on girls in comics.[6] As such, it is only the beginning of a conversation, an opening for more discussion, and a pointing out of what is already going on. Our intention for this collection is that by focusing on a few, diverse examples, we might begin to fill the huge gap in our knowledge of the past (and present) of comics, and of the place of female readers and artists in the history of comics (Guilhaumou and Dermenjian).

Notes

1. For a comprehensive study of the aesthetic category "cute", see Sianne Ngai, *Our Aesthetic Categories: Zany, Cute, Interesting*, Harvard University Press, 2015.
2. Vanna Vinci published the series first in 2000 in *Mondo Naif*, from 2001 in *Linus*, from 2008 on Facebook, and in 2013 Rizzoli published an anthology.
3. Jacqueline Danziger-Russell unwittingly uses the word "diet" to refer to girls' reading in her first chapter, which sketches a brief history of girls in American comics, when she states to want to "understand the importance of the comic book in the literary diet of girls, as well as its establishment as an art form" (2).
4. The translation of the Norwegian dialogue: "Crisps?" "..." "No thanks, I have, like, given up snacks."
   "Are you trying to give me an eating disorder or what? You are so thin." /// "Did moving out go well?" "It is going so well." "That's good."
5. Jacqueline Danziger-Russell shows similarly how in the American magazine *Calling All Girls*, already in 1942, a "you can do it" attitude was promoted in girls (23).
6. Kimberley Reynolds focused on early popular children's fiction in Britain for girls and not in *Girls Only? Gender and Popular Children's Fiction in Britain (1880–1910)*. Trina Robbins published in 1999 *From Girls to Grrrlz*, a history from 1940s to the 1990s of comics for girls. Jacqueline Danziger-Russell brought out *Girls and Their Comics* in 2013; her focus is on female protagonists from the US comic book market. In 2019 Julia Round dedicated a volume to *Gothic for Girls, Studying Misty and other British Comics*.

Bibliography

Abate, Michelle Ann. *Funny Girls: Guffaws, Guts, and Gender in Classic American Comics*. University Press of Mississippi, 2019.

Alary, Viviane. "Chicos, Revista Infantil y Tebeo Para Después de Una Guerra". *Une Enfance En Métamorphose (Espagne 1920–1975) La Infancia y Sus Metamorfosis (España 1920–1975)*, edited by Marie Franco and Begoña Riesgo-Martin. Université de la Sorbonne Nouvelle, 2016.

—. "The Spanish Tebeo". *European Comic Art*, vol. 2, no. 2, June 2009, pp. 253–276.

Baetens, Jan. "Revealing Traces A New Theory of Graphic Enunciation". *The Language of Comics: Word and Image*, edited by Robin Varnum and Christina T. Gibbons. University Press of Mississippi, 2001, pp. 145–155.

Braun, Alexander et al., editors. *Jahrhundert der Comics: die Zeitungs-Strip-Jahre*. DruckVerlag Kettler, 2008.

Bukatman, Scott. *The Poetics of Slumberland: Animated Spirits and the Animating Spirit*. University of California Press, 2012.

Butler, Judith. "Performative Acts and Gender Constitution: An Essay in Phenomenology and Feminist Theory". *Performing Feminisms: Feminist Critical Theory and Theatre*, edited by Sue-Allan Case. Johns Hopkins University Press, 1990, pp. 270–282.

Chute, Hillary. "Comics Form and Narrating Lives". *Profession*, 2011, pp. 107–117.

Cross, Gary S. *Kids' Stuff: Toys and the Changing World of American Childhood*. Harvard University Press, 1997.

—. *The Cute and the Cool: Wondrous Innocence and Modern American Children's Culture*. Oxford University Press, 2004.

Danziger-Russell, Jacqueline. *Girls and Their Comics: Finding a Female Voice in Comic Book Narrative*. Scarecrow Press, 2013.

Gibson, Mel. "Comics and Gender". *The Routledge Companion to Comics*. Routledge, 2016.

—. *Remembered Reading: Memory, Comics and Post-War Constructions of British Girlhood*. Leuven University Press, 2015.

Guilhaumou, Jacques, and Geneviève Dermenjian, editors. "La Bande Dessinée : Un Nouveau Chantier Pour l'histoire Des Femmes". *Bulletin d'information – Association Pour Le Développement de l'histoire Des Femmes et Du Genre*, 2006, pp. 21–39, http://www.mnemosyne.asso.fr/uploads/Journee-etudes/2005/BD_dermenjian_guillaumou.pdf. Accessed 1 July 2022.

Halberstam, Jack. *Gaga Feminism: Sex, Gender, and the End of Normal*. Beacon Press, 2012.

Hatfield, Charles. *Redrawing the Comic-Strip Child*. Oxford University Press, 2011, https://doi.org/10.1093/oxfordhb/9780195379785.013.0009. Accessed 2 Feb. 2021.

James, Allison. "Life Times: Children's Perspectives on Age, Agency and Memory across the Life Course". *Studies in Modern Childhood: Society, Agency, Culture*, edited by Jens Qvortrup. Palgrave Macmillan, 2005, pp. 248–266.

Lefèvre, Pascal. "Of Savages and Wild Children: Contrasting Representations of Foreign Cultures and Disobedient White Children during the Belle Epoque". *The Child Savage, 1890–2010: From Comics to Games*, edited by Elisabeth Wesseling. Routledge, 2016, pp. 55–70.

Manrique Arribas, Juan Carlos. "Juventud, Deporte y Falangismo. El Frente de Juventudes, la Sección Femenina y los Deportes del 'Movimiento'". *Atletas y ciudadanos. Historia social del deporte en España 1870–2010*, edited by Xavier Pujadas Martí. Alianza Editorial, 2011, pp. 233–272.

Mayall, Berry. *Towards a Sociology for Childhood: Thinking from Children's Lives*. Open University Press, 2002.

Ngai, Sianne. *Our Aesthetic Categories: Zany, Cute, Interesting*. Harvard University Press, 2012.

Paoppi, Cecilia. "Mafalda: La Representación de Una Década". *A Contracorriente: Revista de Historia Social y Literatura En América Latina*, vol. 13, no. 2, 2016, pp. 264–286.

Reynolds, Kimberley. *Girls Only? Gender and Popular Children's Fiction in Britain, 1880–1910*. Temple University Press, 1990.

Robbins, Trina. *From Girls to Grrrlz: A History of Women's Comics from Teens to Zines*. Chronicle Books, 1999.

Roeder, Katherine. *Wide Awake in Slumberland: Fantasy, Mass Culture, and Modernism in the Art of Winsor McCay*. University Press of Mississippi, 2014.

Round, Julia. *Gothic for Girls: Misty and British Comics*. University of Mississippi Press, 2019.

Tarbox, Gwen Athene. *Children's and Young Adult Comics*. Bloomsbury, 2020.

Tensuan, Theresa. "Difference". *Comics Studies: A Guidebook*, edited by Charles Hatfield and Bart Beaty. Rutgers University Press, 2020, pp. 138–150.

Trites, Roberta Seelinger. *Waking Sleeping Beauty: Feminist Voices in Children's Novels*. University of Iowa Press, 1997.

Zornado, Joseph L. *Inventing the Child: Culture, Ideology, and the Story of Childhood*. Garland Pub, 2001.

Chapter 1

'It's *the* girl!': Comics, Professional Identity, Affection, Nostalgia and Embarrassment

Mel Gibson

Introduction

This chapter explores relationships between gender, professional identity and personal history in relation to the comic strip medium. I take an autoethnographic approach to this topic, outlining my uniquely individual perspectives as a female British library professional intensely engaged with graphic novels in the 1990s, a contemporary development in the medium at that point, and that of being a girlhood comics reader from the 1960s onwards. In discussing both I look at tensions between child and adult, but also my experience of the conflicts between ideological and lived identities. This links the chapter with the others within this volume and in some ways sets the scene regarding individual remembered experience. The chapter goes on to locate the tensions I experienced around gender and comics in a wider context in which I played a significant role, that being the development and promotion of graphic novel collections in British public libraries during 1990s and into the twenty-first century.

After that I analyse why there were uneasy or uncomfortable responses from other female librarians when they encountered graphic novels in the training courses I ran. It was needful to acknowledge and support the exploration of the emotions that informed these responses, as they might otherwise hinder professional engagement, knowledge of the form and, in turn, collection development. Unpacking this discomfort often involved investigating forgotten memories of girlhood memories of reading comics as few were (or would admit to) reading contemporary comics as adults.

These memories typically centred on gendered (and age-related) understandings of the medium and included both a deep affection for the genre of British girls' comics which the majority had read, embarrassment about the stereotypes of those comics and their readers (including their younger selves) and a nostalgic response that was understood as both enjoyable and discomfiting. I next offer a case study about the editing, content and marketing of a nostalgia reprint that exemplifies one way that girlhood and publications for girls have been positioned. Whilst the way that girlhood is framed changes slightly according to time period and generation, this nostalgia reprint for adult women suggests that embarrassment and nostalgia about girls' comics were often intertwined due to negative cultural constructions of both girlhood and girls' popular culture.

Why Autoethnography?

According to Garance Maréchal, "autoethnography is a form or method of research that involves self-observation and reflexive investigation in the context of ethnographic field work and writing" (43), and Carolyn Ellis defines it as "research, writing, story, and method that connect the autobiographical and personal to the cultural, social, and political" (xix).

I must admit that I am uncomfortable when using autoethnography, exploring anecdotal and personal experience and then connecting it with wider cultural, political and social meanings and understandings. This discomfort is possibly because my peers and I were told as children not to draw attention to ourselves or make our experiences central to conversation. It could also be because, as an academic, I tend to write about subjects where I am not personally involved, in an attempt to maintain objectivity. Even in making that comment I flag up one of the criticisms of the approach, which is that it has been seen as self-indulgent or narcissistic. As Andrew C. Sparkes states, "The emergence of autoethnography and narratives of self [...] has not been trouble-free, and their status as proper research remains problematic" (22).

Nonetheless, I felt this approach was useful in unpacking cultural views about comics and gender, and around profession and comics. This is because I played a part in the history of librarianship and comics. Given my insider knowledge, using an autoethnographic approach means that personal elements of that history are retained. This approach is also key in Thierry Groensteen's analytical account of his publishing house experience. Equally, as a girl reader of comics, I experienced key incidents which I share to give insight into how I thought I was seen and understood. I consequently reflect on having passed, or visited, formative cultural stations (whether objects, texts or activities) in the past and so consider comics, graphic novels, comic shops and their staff, along with libraries and training courses, as cultural stations in this chapter (Bolt). This links with, as Andrew F. Herrmann wrote, the way that "[o]ur identities and identifications with popular culture artifacts assist in our creation of self. Our identities and pop culture have a long-term recursive relationship" (7).

I am also aware that in this chapter I apply an academic lens to historical events and objects, and in editing and selecting narratives about the culture of groups of which I have been a member. Here, then, I use autoethnography to describe and critique cultural beliefs, practices and experiences whilst also acknowledging my relationships with others.

Alongside this I employ critical discourse analysis, a method which argues that social practice and linguistic practice constitute each other (Fairclough). In exploring gender, age and comics and how they intersect with professional roles, I investigate how power relations in society are established and reinforced through language use (Fairclough). In doing so I highlight power imbalances in normative metanarratives about gender and comics which meant that my personal experience, and those of other women, were downplayed or dismissed.

On Failing to See Oneself as a Valid Comics Reader, Fan or Professional

I begin by talking about my experience over time as a reader, and my practices, thus partly exposing a history of comics and gender.

My first comics were a mixture of monthly superhero comics (and other comics from the United States), British *Girl* annuals (published by Hulton Press in the 1950s and 1960s), gift books and annuals focusing on newspaper strip characters Rupert Bear and Teddy Tail, and albums of classic *bandes dessinées* focusing on Tintin, Asterix and Lucky Luke. All but the first were either gifts from family and close family friends or passed down from older relatives. The albums, gift books and annuals were robust bound volumes, most of which I still have today. These formative cultural stations served to suggest that comics existed in several formats, came from many places, that they were for both male and female readers and that they had a history going back before my birth. How they came to me also suggested that I was part of a community of readers, albeit a junior member given the power imbalance between adult and child, as I did not choose the texts but had them chosen for me.

However, ownership and purchase being attached to agency in childhood, it was the former category, the more fragile monthly floppies, that I was most attached to. In addition, I liked them because they were a point of contact with my father, who shared his enthusiasm about the medium with me, seeing it, in Michael Thompson's (273) terms, as creating objects, art and narratives that were "durable" rather than "transient", or "rubbish". This was not a common view at the time. All the same, my ownership was compromised, for despite his enthusiasm for comics, my father would sometimes cut elements out of "our" comics for use in the collage-based artworks he created early in his career (Gibson, 2018, 38–39). I would keep the remainder, reading around the gaps, as it were. So, although these were texts that we shared, the older male partner had control of the physical comic. This emphasised that these were texts for adults, although children might also access them.

To address these gaps and to follow my developing interests, I started to buy my own comics when funds allowed. These initially came from two sources. In England in the 1960s and 1970s, comics were available in newsagents' shops, which, as their name suggests, sold newspapers along with periodicals of all kinds, sweets, cigarettes and sometimes a few household supplies like tea and biscuits. One of Benjamin Woo's respondents talked about a similar system in North America in that period, where new comics were sold through news stand distribution, a system

> which had significant drawbacks for dedicated readers [...] [for, as the interviewee states, it] was usually a little bit difficult because you couldn't get all the comics you wanted, or you had to go to several places, or they wouldn't get very many and they would sell out. (127)

This chimes with my memories of having to visit a lot of shops to find titles I wanted and creates another formative cultural station in embedding, informally, the idea of collecting and acquiring comics as a major project demanding commitment. It was also a solitary experience, although that could also be read as independence, which moved away from the notion of community that the bound volumes implied.

Comics were also available in Britain from covered markets like Jacky Whites Market in Sunderland and Grainger Market in Newcastle. In these spaces a broad range of stalls would sell goods of all kinds, from food to furniture. Both markets contained second-hand book stalls, which stocked long boxes of older editions of comics. These may not have been second-hand in the sense of having been owned by an individual (although some were, as evidenced by owners' names being written on them), but instead may have been sold on to the second-hand shops by newsagents. Given that these were titles which had not sold in that first set of shops, more obscure titles featured quite heavily. Searching through these boxes took time and necessitated carrying a list of what (ideally) one would want. This, too, might be recognised as proto-collector behaviour.

These behaviours were also accompanied by a commitment to travel to locations, so travel costs might be involved as well as the cost of the comics. This was a major undertaking, especially for a ten-year-old. I had a bicycle and would use that to get from my village (about four miles away from Sunderland) to the various newsagents and Jacky Whites. However, going as far as Newcastle (about eight miles in the opposite direction) meant making a bus journey.

This collecting tendency continued in later years, although how I accessed comics changed. As a young teenager in the mid-1970s I witnessed the start of the shift from sales via newsagents to specialised comics shops. The specialist shop I would visit was in Newcastle and was called either Timeslip or Son of Timeslip. I was mostly reading Marvel at this point and had a particular love of the X-Men. This shift to direct marketing via specialty retailers developed in the 1970s in North America too, and as Woo states, "the system was firmly entrenched by the 1980s" (127). I also very occasionally visited what quickly came to be seen as iconic comic shops, such as Dark They Were and Golden Eyed and Forbidden Planet, both located in London (either on school trips or on family holidays).

However, my engagement was cautious, as when I went into Timeslip/Son of Timeslip, the owner would always address me by saying "it's *the* girl!", with a heavy emphasis on the word "the". To be so singularly addressed was embarrassing, and whilst I persisted with buying comics from the shop, the impression that the medium was not for me became part of that formative cultural station. It was not age that was important in terms of accessing comics, I learnt, but gender. In addition, my understanding of comics as an inclusive community evolved into one where being female was problematic, particularly, although not exclusively, in relation to the superhero genre. This was also noted in the research about female readers that emerged in the 1990s. Amy Kiste Nyberg's study of female comic book fans, argued that they perceived themselves as "trespassers" within the male-coded culture of comic books. As Nyberg states, "[w]omen readers try alternately to fit into the role constructed for the predominantly male comic book reader and to resist that construction" (205). Similarly, Stephanie Orme, writing in 2016 of the experience of later female readers and the depiction of comic stores in popular culture, states that they "are portrayed as a male space where female patrons are an anomaly" (403). Whilst she adds that this did not fit the reality of 2016, her comment nonetheless is in line with my historical experience.

Being told that I was singular, and that I was "wrongly" gendered, plus the fact that I knew of no other girls of my own age who read superhero comics (or even *Asterix*), meant that I came to have an increasingly uncomfortable relationship with the medium, as the normative metanarrative seemed to imply that I either did not, or should not, exist. This lack of comfort remained an issue for later readers, for as Orme reports, one of her interviewees, Doreen, stated that going into a comic shop "definitely felt like something that I wasn't supposed to do. I think being a girl is a big part of that" (411), adding that she stayed away from the local comic shop, as "I don't wanna be talked down to. I don't want them to assume I know nothing, which is what happens" (411). Despite the different time periods and geographical space, gender stereotypes and assumptions about media and gender are in play in both accounts.

What also comes into play at this point is a feeling that if I were to stay involved with comics, I should keep quiet about liking superhero titles. This self-silencing and reluctance to be visible was historically common in female readers. This could be seen as linked with Orme's theory that "many female comic book fans render themselves invisible in the comics community out of fear of stigmatization, from both non-comics fans as well as male members of comics fandom" (403).

Simultaneously, I shied away from the weekly British comics for girls, such as *Bunty* (DC Thomson, 1958–2001), despite having enjoyed reading *Girl* annuals. This genre was a popular one, and many girls would have their comics delivered to their homes, in a vastly different kind of engagement with the medium. It meant that such reading tended to be tied to what Angela McRobbie and Jenny Garber identified as girls' bedroom culture (and so was invisible in other ways, a point I will return to). I was aware from comments made in comic shops that some staff felt I should be reading those comics and not reading superhero titles. In addition, these shops typically did not stock material like *Wimmen's Comix*, or indeed comics aimed at women in general, which I only discovered in later visits to specialist feminist bookshops in London, so that was not part of my formative cultural station. This is in line with Orme's assertion that "Stereotypical representations of what a comic book reader looks like and acts like, gendered language, such as fan*boy*, [...] codes geek culture as something belonging to men" (404). This was accompanied by value judgements about British girls' comics, as the staff considered them less important and of poorer quality. This was not hostility, exactly, but was a kind of gatekeeping via an assertion of an assumed superior male cultural capital about comics, male ownership of genre and medium, and related spaces, and a condemnation of anything coded female (including me). Thus, in my formative encounters with comic shops and their employees, I came to understand that I was not seen as a valid fan or reader.

Jumping forwards a few years, when I studied librarianship in the early 1980s, comics were not mentioned (this also applied to students training to be teachers and typically is still the case in training for both professions today). This silence in librarianship about comics may have been linked to historical constructions of comics as a stigmatised low or mass culture (Brown). That meant that after qualifying as a librarian, my internalised feeling of being "other" regarding comics culture, combined with professional cues, meant that I did not connect my private comic reading with my professional self or talk about what I read. One might occasionally hear of comic swap boxes in libraries where children could bring in what they had read and exchange it free for something new, but that was typically the full extent of the intersection of libraries and the medium.

In contrast, there was mention of work with children and young people on the programme, although that only consisted of one module. This led to a desire to work in that sector. However, later I was often asked by other professionals and the public, when in post as a children's librarian, what I wanted to be "when I grew up". The implication was that working with children meant one was childish and, again, lesser, in this case in relation to those librarians who were based in the adult, reference or local history sections of the library. This was a different normative metanarrative, but one which also served to locate power and control with another group of professionals (one that was, much as the comics shop staff were, much more dominated by male personnel). There was, then, a kind of stigmatisation around working with young people and their texts, which comics were assumed to be in wider cultural discourses, even whilst they were unmentioned in a professional context, something I was aware of throughout my library career in the 1980s and into the 1990s.

Why, and against What Background, Did Library Graphic Novel Collections Develop in the 1990s?

In the 1990s public services were under threat due to central government cuts to local government funding. Public libraries had been perceived as inessential by central government for years, given the neoliberal ideology of the Conservatives between 1979 and 1997, and had become seriously underfunded as a result. Indeed, Nick Moore's research shows that in 2000 "the total expenditure on the public library service per thousand population was no greater than it had been in 1985" (Ayub and Thebridge 66). Consequently, as Moore argued, "if the public library service had been stagnating during the 1980s, during the 1990s it began to seriously decline" (64).

Simultaneously, libraries were under pressure to prove their relevance to all groups within communities, given a very valid high priority being placed on social inclusion. One of the groups seen as poorly served given this agenda were young people, despite the existence of specialist librarians and stock. Historical assumptions of libraries as a valuable aspect of community coherence, and of education in the broadest sense, were discarded given inconsistent commitment to these ideals in favour of validation via statistical data, combined with the need to provide proof of value. This created a tension that was challenging to manage, in that attracting new users, especially younger ones, often meant having to take risks on stock that might not prove popular, whether in the form of new formats or technologies, so potentially increasing pressure on limited funding.

However, even given the financial issues, there were positive developments and initiatives, for, as Ayub Khan and Stella Thebridge argued, in the 1990s libraries had, "an almost unique opportunity to 'legitimize' a mass of cultural material and the interest of many publics" (61). There was also a shift towards librarians demonstrating that they were, as Rachel Van Riel stated in 1993, "proactive and educative in their approach to fiction" (81). Van Riel's initiatives around reading fiction, along with those of other partners working with libraries, were the start of the reader development movement, which asserted that fiction was valuable. These two arguments are indicative of a quite dramatic change, as libraries were seen as having previously failed to positively promote fiction stock, instead favouring non-fiction.

The emergence of graphic novels, a format more suitable for library stock, enabled the development of collections. This was one of the ways in which fiction was foregrounded, along with, amongst other initiatives, the increased purchase of paperback novels. This returns us to Thompson's (273) argument, in that these were versions of comics that were coming to be seen as culturally "durable", as well as physically so. The arguments about legitimisation and fiction mentioned above were widely discussed in the early 1990s and were empowering for some library staff, including myself. Further, given assumptions about young people's lack of library use, material like graphic novels was seen as potentially addressing issues around social inclusion. This assumes a link between comics and younger readers which was, of course, itself problematic, but was a useful threshold concept regarding professional engagement with the medium. As someone who was a branch librarian, working in an area where library use was not necessarily part of family or community culture, in a service point attached to a high school as well as serving the general public, I felt I could seek permission to develop a collection. I did so in conjunction with a member of school staff and some pupils who were interested in comics, which meant "coming out", as it were, as a comics fan. The pupils involved, who were all male, declared me an "honorary male" in my role as librarian, which was meant kindly, although this still pointed to ideas of difference and ownership of the medium.

The popularity of that collection, and my involvement with the local branch of the Youth Libraries Group (YLG), a national network of librarians working with young people that was part of the Library Association (now the Chartered Institute of Library and Information Professionals), meant that I began to talk professionally, for the first time, about comics and graphic novels. The success of the collection and the need to address the agenda outlined above meant that I was not primarily seen as an oddity, but as someone who might have useful professional knowledge. This amounted to another formative shift in my understanding of self, one in which professional identity and comics started to coalesce.

The next step was accidental, if fortuitous. I was told at a local YLG branch meeting that there was an opportunity to be a contributor to a possible national publication on graphic novels in libraries. Eventually, this became *Graphic Account* (1993), edited by Keith Barker, and published by the YLG. However, I recall there was a tension in the meeting and that one person said, disparagingly, "why don't you do it? You like that sort of thing..." – a quite dismissive statement. In effect, some of my professional peers were unsure that they wanted to be associated with what they considered problematic texts. Here, the comic medium, to non-readers, was stigmatised, and there was a concern that there might be a dual stigmatisation of working with comics (as low/mass culture) and with children, possibly undermining their professional status.

In the end, *Graphic Account* (1993) had an impact upon library services nationally and resulted in an increased interest in the medium. In personal terms this resulted in my professional identity becoming further intertwined with comics and graphic novels, as I was invited to run training for YLG branches. The demands of keeping the training fresh and my knowledge up to date meant that I needed to buy a lot of material and read widely, leading me to describe myself as an advocate for the medium, rather than a fan of a specific genre, in effect a return to my original childhood identity in relation to comics when I had engaged with a wide range of titles.

However, the growth of a wider interest in graphic novels was accompanied by increased tensions regarding professional identity, something which became apparent in training sessions. Some staff, particularly the female ones, who formed the majority of staff in YLG and other youth-focused library sectors, felt threatened or insecure. This could have been related to this being another new initiative in a period of funding cuts, but seemed to have other roots, as I will shortly discuss. The first round of training sessions led to more, and I got to work with the School Libraries Association (SLA) and School Libraries Group (SLG), literacy charities, museums, art galleries and educational umbrella organisations like the British Educational Research Association. Consequently, between 1993 and 2000, I ran over two hundred trainings and other events, developed bibliographies and wrote for various professional journals. This reflects the slow growth and spread of an acceptance of the medium in non-comic reader circles.

In effect, I came to be seen as an expert, although I preferred the term "advocate", as I was more comfortable with the connotations of the latter. Thus, even as I became considered by some to be a national authority, the issue around gender and expertise continued to have an impact upon me, leaving me unwilling to challenge the idea of comics as male space. To position myself as expert would have led, I felt, to continuous challenges from male comic fans, whether within fandom, or within libraries and being labelled, as Orme says of later female readers, as a "fake geek girl" within comics culture (412).

How Might Emotions, Professional Role and Gender Be Linked in Relation to Graphic Novels and Comics?

Working with my largely female peers in YLG, SLA and SLG in building library collections and developing their understanding of and familiarity with graphic novels (and later manga in translation) involved engaging with powerful emotional responses linked to constructions of self. As mentioned, there was often an uneasiness about graphic novels. Fear was often apparent at the start of training sessions, with a typical argument being "we are word people, not picture people", or stereotyping the graphic novel as either inherently sexist, or "nasty", or "violent". This was because of the perception of the comics medium as unfamiliar, hostile and, above all, a male preserve, with there being minimal understanding that comics had been created for women or could be feminist. Acknowledging and unpacking these responses revealed echoes in their adult and professional selves of understandings around formative cultural stations regarding gender and medium.

In part this was about the history of cultural ambivalence about comics. Although, as I mentioned earlier, a movement emerged in libraries in the 1990s about engaging with fiction and a wider range of materials was becoming seen as appropriate library stock, the commentaries on comics in Britain from the 1950s onwards had often labelled comics as invalid or even dangerous. The librarians I worked with would have, in many cases, come across this normative metanarrative in childhood, one which reflected the hostility on the part of some in Britain towards popular culture. In part the uneasiness, then, was tied to understandings of libraries as preserving and protecting significant aspects of knowledge and culture, another kind of cultural gatekeeping. One might be seen as failing as a gatekeeper if popular materials were included in collections.

However, there was another significant element – that of gender. The concerns around comics in Britain in the 1950s and 1960s were tied in with ideas about appropriate reading for girls. This was clear in librarian and campaigner George H. Pumphrey's *What Children Think of Their Comics*, where girls were seen as particularly morally vulnerable to what they read (a blank slate model of girlhood encouraging adult censorship or control of both girls and any media texts they might encounter). Consequently, he praised titles which he saw as promoting useful information and occupation, such as cookery, home decoration and dress patterns, such as *Girl*, as mentioned earlier. This helped to create a discourse in which comics and girlhood could only be linked if the comic focused on the performance of traditional femininity, because otherwise the connection would be stigmatising. Thus, anything except comics specifically for girls was inherently a problem, although the problematic status of the medium itself meant that even these titles were compromised.

Consequently, for some of my professional peers, graphic novels reminded them that as children the comic medium was considered inappropriate for them and that reading comics could be seen as contaminating or immoral. This creates multiple reasons why comics might be seen as problematic, something that continued to resonate with the adult self. This was rarely extreme, although I met two individuals during training for whom comics were associated with Satan and so they felt that reading them imperilled people's souls. Whilst that was not a position that offered any hope of compromise, it became my aim to get most people past their unease and help them negotiate emotional responses tied to years of experiencing anti-comic rhetoric. Few had read superhero comics as children or read comics as adults, so they had journeys quite different from mine, although on the rare occasions that someone else who liked the medium attended training, participants seeing a colleague (rather than an outsider like myself) who had knowledge and expertise would extend and deepen discussion.

Yet with my increasing awareness of comics history, especially about how popular girls' comics had been, I was faced with a puzzle. It seemed unlikely that any of the female professionals I was working with had never read a comic before, yet this genre was not mentioned, and there appeared to be a gap in memory (like the literal gaps in some of my childhood comics) where they should be. There was another form of silence and invisibility here, where memories of girlhood reading had been lost, replaced by dominant cultural and professional discourses about comics. This act of forgetting could also be seen as a gendered and quite literal interpretation of the injunction to "put away childish things" (1 Corinthians 13:11). Yet in this context this seemingly only applied to women and girls, as male collecting of both historical and contemporary titles was firmly in place and seen as a valid, if odd, cultural activity.

To try to address this puzzle, I tentatively began to mention titles of girls' comics in training, hoping to chart whether British girls' comics were familiar texts in my professional peers' childhoods. I hoped that remembering these comics and having a sense of ownership of them would remind them that they had knowledge of the medium. This was intended to build their confidence to explore other aspects of it and appreciate that contemporary comics and graphic novels might have a similar significance for readers.

Whilst my practice was to use contemporary texts in training, over time I began to include older titles too, largely publications from the 1950s to early 2000s, to connect past and present via medium. I would now identify this as object elicitation, engaging directly with what Anna Moran and Sorcha O'Brien describe as the "emotional potency of objects in our lives and the relationships that exist between people and objects" (xiv). It can also, as Wesseling suggests, reflect how "childhood nostalgia has come to depend on the availability of tangible memorabilia" (4).

Mentioning girls' comics, and examples of the actual historical texts, was productive. It became apparent that, despite frequent claims of never having read comics, few training participants had no familiarity at all with the medium. This only occurred when reading comics had been forbidden and the girl had accepted this cultural and familial control of her reading. I would add that others who had not been allowed comics found ways around this stricture (Gibson 2015).

However, whilst this strategy was successful in supporting engagement and understanding, invoking girls' comics also had risks. This was because, given the points above and the historical male denigration of girls' titles, alongside a deep affection for girls' comics once remembered, there was also embarrassment (as well as nostalgia) about them (Gibson

2015). Using aspects of historical girls' material culture, realia, in training, relates to Henry Jenkins's comment about "the emotions, sentimental attachments and nostalgic longings that we express – or hold at bay – through our relationship with physical objects" (15).

On Visibility, Embarrassment and Nostalgia

The conversations in training sessions about girls' comics were positive, and people frequently discovered shared titles or narratives. This training, unintentionally, had become a public recognition of British historical girls' bedroom culture (as well as of print culture). The discussions made visible female knowledge of comics and engagement with the medium. This was a good outcome, in addition to the positive impact of the actual graphic novel training. All the same, whilst embarrassment is much easier to work with than fear, it, too, is a powerful emotion.

Embarrassment appeared to relate to several distinct aspects of women and girls' relationships with the comics medium. Although my choice of comics was different, I very much understood that emotion. The first variant, which I had experienced, was about being a female reader of comics seen as part of male-coded comics culture. Reading graphic novels, for the participants in training, could have evoked similar feelings, but in labelling this as reading for professional purposes, the potential for this to be embarrassing became neutralised.

In contrast, the second type of embarrassment was specifically about comics for girls. Here stereotypes of girls' comics and their readers were central, along with the idea of girls' culture as lesser. Whilst this might not have reflected the reality of the content of the titles, the dominant discourse around girlhood and girls' comics culture contributed to both silence and forgetting.

To give an indication of what dominant discourses around girls' comics might look like, I turn to how nostalgia publishers of girls' comics presented and marketed texts, as they exemplify them. Prion Press, an imprint of Carlton Publishing, were the main publishers of such material in the 2000s. Prior to that girls' comic nostalgia publishing, like the idea of women collecting comics or being part of fandom, was not widely part of comics culture. On the Prion Press website (since taken down[1]), whilst reprints of boys' comics were promoted in a straightforward way, as a celebration of boyhood and re-engagement with texts marked as significant, there was considerable ambivalence around titles for girls.

To begin, titles for girls were placed in the humour section, which implies that the texts should not be taken seriously. One example, *Mother Tells You How: Essential Life Skills for Modern Young Women – Girl 1951–1960* (Russell) focuses on a short weekly strip that appeared in *Girl*. It was a colour strip consisting of six to nine panels, which focused on a specific topic. It was bound up with the performance of middle-classness and domestic femininity. On the website the marketing began by stating, "Each week Mother would teach her exemplary-in-every-way daughter, Judy, one of life's essential skills, such as how to decorate biscuits, how to prepare a grapefruit or how to do the washing up" ("Mother Tells You How"). The choice of task and juxtaposition with the term "essential" serves to imply triviality and a kind of prissy conformity.

This does not reflect the material elsewhere in the actual publication, which incorporated working-life comic strips, adventure, school, comedy and mystery narratives and a considerable number of depictions of independent girls. However, Prion chose this strip in constructing a narrative about a historical version of girlhood, one that is homogenised and lacking nuance. The site added that whilst it appears to be a "spoof [...] [it is] a wholly genuine period piece, and it's its authenticity that provides such high comedy" ("Mother Tells You How"). In effect, the historical constructions of girlhood that girls were offered, the women who are assumed to be the main readers of the volume, and the texts of the period are all to be laughed at, rather than with. The implication is also that the adult reader should be a "good sport" and recognise the ridiculousness of their girlhood.

This is also emphasised in other marketing comments, which describe the publication, and the readers, in patronising terms. For example, the site stated that "*Girl* readers weren't to have their little heads filled with science they didn't understand [...] [instead] they were kept busy sorting out their small odds and ends into a shelf-tidy, and experimenting with unusual sandwiches" ("Mother Tells You How"). Again, the emphasis is on the small world girls inhabited, a patronising assumption that does not reflect the overall tenor of the publication or the range of girlhood experiences it contained in non-fiction items. Additionally, the use of the word "little" serves to imply a lack of intellect.

Further, the idea of these titles as lesser compared to boys' print culture was clear from the rest of the initial marketing, which directly and disparagingly compared *Girl* to the comparable title for boys, *Eagle* (Hulton, 1950–1969). For example, the site stated that whilst

> *Eagle*, featured new inventions and clever conjuring tricks, *Girl* had Mother telling Judy how to make a shelf-tidy. *Eagle* subscribers read about shark fishing off the coast of Australia, while their sisters would turn to *Mother Tells You How* for wise words on how to care for goldfish. ("Mother Tells You How")

Here the emphasis is on the limited nature of what girls were and of what they were offered. There is also a focus in the marketing on *Eagle* as a whole and an emphasis on its diverse content, whereas *Girl* is reduced to a single strip presented in an essentialist manner.

Moving on from how nostalgia publishing replicated and extended negative views about girlhood and girls' culture, a final element of embarrassment was about the dominant discourse of comics as for children and so a discourse about adults reading them being seen as somehow childish, or non-professional (a link established in relation to my professional experience earlier in the chapter). Orme, in interviewing female comic readers in the United States, for instance, noted that one of the participants reported that her "desire to be taken seriously in her profession [...] makes her conscientious about participating in an activity perceived as frivolous and inappropriate for adult women" (410). This clearly articulates what might be at stake regarding comics and female professional identity. This could be seen as compounded (as noted earlier) by being a librarian who worked with children and young people, resulting in a form of professional stigmatisation based on both medium and role.

There were also, for those who had read girls' comics, cultural concerns about appearing nostalgic. Nostalgia has, as Elisabeth Wesseling notes, "not fared well with the critics and that is putting it mildly" (2), adding that "most discussions of this disreputable sentiment pivot around a truth-falseness dichotomy, relegating nostalgia to the negative pole of the opposition" (2). However, she goes on to argue that it need not be solely read in that light, pointing to the work of Svetlana Boym, who argued that two types of nostalgia exist, with very different connotations, and that one type could be seen as productive. Boym divided nostalgia into "restorative" and "reflective" types, stating that the former "does not recognize itself as nostalgia [...] but mistakes itself for truth or tradition" and so links with critiques of nostalgia as an imaginary past (Wesseling 3). The latter, in contrast, "does not want to return to a past that never was, but it likes to dwell on alternatives to the present, out of fundamental discomfort with the idea of linear historical progress" (Wesseling 3), troubling the status quo.

Encouraging a form of reflective nostalgia, then, was something I had accidentally stumbled into. The discussions amongst the librarians, once historical reading and contemporary texts were linked, tended to be playful and humorous rather than conflicted, also in line with notions of reflective nostalgia. What they additionally did, through a recognition of girls' culture and comics that challenged dominant discourses about both, was encourage questions about why silence and invisibility, even at the internal level, was dominant regarding girlhood. In effect, this was a recognition that embarrassment and nostalgia were often mixed due to negative cultural constructions of girlhood and girls' culture.

To Conclude

Tony Adams, Stacy Holman Jones and Carolyn Ellis write of reflexivity as part of autoethnography that it "includes both acknowledging and critiquing our place and privilege in society and using the stories we tell to *break long-held silences* on power, relationships, cultural taboos, and forgotten and/or suppressed experiences" (103). In this chapter stories of identity and power are linked with emotions and memory and reveal the complexity and pressure of holding conflicted identities. In looking at forgotten memories the chapter also explores various forms of silence around comics and girlhood, the idea of comics as taboo, and the resonances that had for women professionals in the 1990s when engaging with potential library stock that was linked via medium with that silence.

Additionally, I outline that I broke my own silence about the challenges of being a girlhood reader of comics and a professional working with them as an adult. As a last point I would like to flag that working with comics in libraries enabled me to invite creators into my space, but also allowed me to avoid being involved in fan culture. This was because, as a young library professional, I assumed that comics fandom (which was depicted as male-dominated) would be unwelcoming. This fear, then, resulted in another form of invisibility, and it was only after my career in librarianship had ended that I felt confident enough to engage with fandom.

Given that I have been able to contribute to establishing and developing major comics-focused events that are female-friendly and family-friendly, my experience of fandom in the last fifteen years has been largely positive. However, I have sometimes met older male fans, even recently, whose normative narratives about comics have meant that I have experienced assumptions about what I have read and attempts to correct my understanding of it. A particularly striking encounter was with a male comics fan who insisted that the British girls' comics genre, given the erotic art created elsewhere by artists who drew strips for them, was pornography for boys and had nothing to do with girls at all, an excessive way of insisting on a male-coded comics culture. This is not unlike the experience of one of Orme's interviewees, of whom it was reported that they had met male fans who, "would assume that, as a woman, Carol lacked the geek credentials to understand and appreciate comic books" (412).

More importantly, however, in this chapter I have also started to unpack how emotional states around media and childhood might, through policing of girlhood comics culture, have had an impact upon the later professional identities and the development of graphic novels collections. Here the cultural coding of comics culture as male created tensions for the adult female professionals attempting to create services that they hoped would support contemporary young people's reading needs.

This, then, is the background in the mid-1990s against which I encouraged librarians to engage with the medium. It can be hard to make decisions to stock material like graphic novels and advocate for the medium when lacking confidence because of having historically seen oneself and one's texts positioned as lesser. However, having positive acknowledgements of girlhood knowledge of the medium, and hands-on experience of contemporary titles, enabled librarians to integrate their historical comics reading into their professional identities and come to terms with the challenge of graphic novels.

Notes

1. I downloaded much of the publicity from the site in 2007 before it was taken down and have kept the material on file. I can confirm that the text on the Amazon site is that which originally appeared on the Prion website.

Bibliography

1 Corinthians 13:11, Holy Bible: King James Version.

Adams, Tony E. et al. *Autoethnography: Understanding Qualitative Research*. Oxford University Press, 2015.

"Mother Tells You How", *Amazon*, 2021, https://www.amazon.co.uk/Mother-Tells-You-How-Essential/dp/1853756172. Accessed 24 May 2021.

Barker, Keith. *Graphic Account: The Selection and Promotion of Graphic Novels in Libraries for Young People*. Library Association Youth Libraries Group, 1993.

Bolt, David, editor. *Finding Blindness: International Constructions and Deconstructions*. Routledge, 2023.

Bowman, John H. *British Librarianship and Information Work 1991–2000*. Routledge, 2006.

Boym, Svetlana. *The Future of Nostalgia*. Basic Books, 2001.

Brown, Jeffrey A. "Comic Book Fandom and Cultural Capital". *The Journal of Popular Culture*, vol. 30, no. 4, 1997, pp. 13–31.

Ellis, Carolyn. *The Ethnographic I: A methodological novel about autoethnography*. AltaMira Press, 2004.

Fairclough, N. *Critical Discourse Analysis: The Critical Study of Language*. London: Longman, 1995.

Gibson, Mel. *Remembered Reading: Memory, Comics and Post-War Constructions of British Girlhood*. University of Leuven Press, 2015.

—. "'It's all come flooding back' Memories of childhood comics: narratives, practices and objects". *Comics Memory: Archives and Styles*, edited by Maaheen Ahmed and Benoît Crucifix. Palgrave MacMillan, 2018, pp. 37–56.

—. "Memories of a medium: Comics, materiality, object elicitation and reading autobiographies". *Participations*, vol. 16, no. 1, 2019, pp. 605–662.

Groensteen, Thierry. "De l'An 2 à Actes Sud, une alternative à l'alternative Témoignage d'un éditeur". *Comics in Dissent: Alternative, Independence, Self-Publishing*, edited by Christophe Dony, Tanguy Habrand and Gert Meesters. Presses Universitaires de Liège, 2015, pp. 167–174.

Herrmann, Andrew F. "Daniel Amos and Me: The Power of Pop Culture and Autoethnography". *The Popular Culture Studies Journal*, vol. 1, no. 1–2, 2013, pp. 6–17.

Jenkins, Henry. *Comics and Stuff*. New York University Press, 2020.

Khan, Ayub and Thebridge, Stella. "Public Libraries" in Bowman, John H., editor. *British Librarianship and Information Work 1991-2000*. London: Routledge, pp. 61-82.

Maréchal, Garance. "Autoethnography". *Encyclopedia of case study research*, edited by Albert J. Mills, Gabrielle Durepos and Elden Wiebe. Sage Publications, 2010, vol. 2, pp. 43–45.

McRobbie, Angela, editor. *Feminism and Youth Culture from Jackie to Just Seventeen*. Macmillan, 1991, pp. 12–25.

Moran, Anna, and O'Brien, Sorcha. *Love Objects: Emotion, Design and Material Culture*. Bloomsbury, 2014.

Nyberg, Amy Kiste. "Comic books and women readers: Trespassers in masculine territory?" *Gender in Popular Culture: Images of Men and Women in literature, visual media and material culture*, edited by Rollins, Peter C. and Susan W. Ridgemont Press, 1995, pp. 205–225.

Orme, Stephanie. "Femininity and fandom: the dual-stigmatization of female comic book fans". *Journal of Graphic Novels and Comics*, vol. 7, no. 4, 2016, pp. 403–416, https://doi.org/10.1080/21504857.2016.1219958. Accessed 1 May 2021.

Pumphrey, George. H. *What Children Think of Their Comics*. Epworth Press, 1964.

Russell, Lorna, editor. *Mother Tells You How: Essential Life Skills for Modern Young Women – Girl 1951–1960*. Prion Press, 2007.

Sparkes, Andrew C. "Embodiment, academics, and the audit culture: a story seeking consideration". *Qualitative Research*, vol. 7, no. 4, 2007, pp. 521–550.

Thompson, Michael. *Rubbish Theory: The Creation and Destruction of Value*. Oxford University Press, 1979.

Van Riel, Rachel. "The case for fiction". *Public Library Journal*, vol. 8, no. 3, 1993, pp. 81–84.

Wesseling, Elisabeth. *Reinventing Childhood Nostalgia: Books Toys and Contemporary Media Culture*. Routledge, 2018.

Woo, Benjamin, "The Android's Dungeon: comic-bookstores, cultural spaces, and the social practices of audiences". *The Journal of Graphic Novels and Comics,* vol. 2, no. 2, 2011, pp. 125–136.

Chapter 2
Looking for Queerness

Martha Newbigging

(re)search

looking for queerness
MARTHA NEWBIGGING

or...

experiments in drawing

turned to

queerness in childhood

as the puzzle of an unintelligible subject

practice-based methodology or graphic autotheory, making autobio comics opens allowances for remembering situations silenced, ignored or forgotten

cultural intelligibility is contingent on normative "coherence & continuity among sex, gender, sexual practice & desire" (Butler)[1]

an affective quality of experience I had no words for

HOW MIGHT DRAWING POINT US IN QUEER DIRECTIONS?

(Re)orient
I made a list of queer sorts of stories...

· five-year-old crush
· cornering the girls
· was that sex?
· cutting my hair
· girls' team
· prom dress
· are you a boy or a girl?

queer object

WORKMANICS

I'M THINKING ABOUT DRAWING PICTURES AND MAKING COMICS AS A PEDAGOGICAL ENCOUNTER WITH THE PERFORMATIVITY OF MY OWN SUBJECT FORMATION...

I LOVED MY NUMBER NINE T-SHIRT

IT HAD TWO BLUE STRIPES ON THE SLEEVES

THE NUMBER WAS IN A SPORTS STYLE

WEARING IT MADE ME FEEL STRONG

AND THE IMPLICATIONS OF AUTOBIOGRAPHICAL DRAWING FOR MY CAPACITY TO THINK, TO IMAGINE, AND TO BE, OUTSIDE OF NORMATIVE FORMS THAT SUGGEST OR IMPOSE A PREDETERMINED TYPE OF GIRLHOOD ON A CHILD.

VIEW OF THE LAKE (BAY) FROM THE COTTAGE LAWN

THE CULVERT

LOOK!

I CAUGHT A FROG!

TOUCH IT

"THERE IS A STATE OF MIND THAT COMES ABOUT WHEN WE LET A LINE LEAD US ALONG ITSELF. IT CAN LOOSEN THE STRAIGHT-AWAY OF THINKING AND HELP US GET WHERE WE ARE GOING" (BARRY)[2]

BY DRAWING THIS ENCOUNTER, AND OTHER FRAGMENTS OF MEMORY, THESE QUEER MOMENTS ARE GIVEN A CONCRETE, VISUAL REALITY THAT VALIDATES THE EXPERIENCES OF MY CHILD SELF – EXPERIENCES THAT WERE NOT TALKED ABOUT, OR BARELY GIVEN SIGNIFICANCE, AT THE TIME.

THE DRAWING PRACTICE BRINGS THIS SUPPRESSED SUBJECTIVITY TO LIGHT, OFFERING A COUNTER-NARRATIVE TO NORMATIVE READINGS OF MY OWN "GIRLHOOD"

DRAWING IS AN ACT OF TOUCHING AS MUCH AS SEEING

I HAVE A BOYFRIEND

DO YOU?

WHY NOT?

NO

I DUNNO

DRAWING IS SENSING — TO FEEL MY WAY — OUT OF THE KINESTHETIC, PROPRIOCEPTIVE, AND VISUAL PROCESSES OF MAKING FORM

HOW DOES THE CHILD MAKE SENSE OF THEIR FELT EXPERIENCE WITHIN THESE PRESSURES AND DEMANDS TO BE CULTURALLY INTELLIGIBLE?

DRAWING MY LIVED EXPERIENCE AFFORDS A SENSORY, AFFECTIVE WAY TO EXPLORE AND ENACT GENDERED SUBJECTIVITY, A WAY TO MANIFEST OPEN FORMS OF INTELLIGIBILITY WITHIN CHILDHOOD.

HOW MIGHT DRAWING POINT US IN QUEER DIRECTIONS?

Acknowledgements

Parts of this graphic essay were produced as a research-creation project to fulfill the requirements of the Master of Environmental Studies, York University, 2017.

Thought developed, alongside drawing, from the writing of many others before me, including; Sara Ahmed, Lynda Barry, Kathryn Bond Stockton, John Berger, Michael Taussig, Jack Halberstam, and Jen Gilbert.

Thank you to my mother, arts educator, Eva Ardiel, who told me that drawing is more than seeing. Gratitude to nancy viva davis halifax who ensures that the "telling deepens narrative imagination and empathic presence in the world".[3] Gratitude to Aparna Mishra Tarc who observes that "the storied process by which the child becomes an active self is critical to her capacity to make meaningful relations between her self and others".[4]

Endnotes

1. Judith Butler, (1990). *Gender Trouble.* Routledge. p.23.
2. Lynda Barry, (2010). *Picture This.* Drawn & Quarterly. pp.68-69.
3. nancy viva davis halifax, (2009). *Disability and illness in arts-informed research: Moving towards postconventional representations.* Cambria Press. p.1.
4. Aparna Mishra Tarc, (2015). *Literacy of the Other: Renarrating Humanity.* State University of New York Press. p.13.

Chapter 3

Harrowing Rites of Passage: Refugee Girlhood in the Wake of Syrian Migrant Crisis

María Porras Sánchez

Introduction

Humanity has always been in transit, but migration has become central for the dynamics of globalisation in the last decades. The late twentieth and early twenty-first centuries constitute what De Haas, Miller and Castles have defined as the "age of migration" (2020). Restrictive policies regarding refugees and migrants in general are intrinsic to the logic of the age of migration, as they have been increasingly considered a threat to the sovereignty of states (De Haas, Miller and Castles 5, 17, 65). In the age of migration, the Mediterranean has become the frame of a heterogeneous modernity, "a sea of migrating cultures, powers, and histories [which] continues to propose a more fluid and unstable archive, a composite formation in the making, neither conclusive nor complete" (Chambers 39). The Mediterranean area is an example of how world population is by definition heterogeneous and coexists in "unchosen cohabitation" (Butler 145).

In parallel, migration has become a defining motif in contemporary culture (Said). In the case of comics, many *autographics* (Whitlock) describe the experience of migration, for instance Thi Bui's *The Best We Could Do* (2017). Descendants of migrants have also reproduced those experiences, as in the case of the graphic memoir *Baddawi* by Leila Abdelrazaq (2015). Likewise, refugees' lives have been approached from the witness perspective of the volunteer worker, as in Kate Evans's *Threads from The Refugee Crisis* (2017) or that of a journalist, like Sarah Glidden's *Rolling Blackouts: Dispatches from Turkey, Syria, and Iraq*

(2016), Carlos Spottorno and Guillermo Abril's *La Grieta* [The Crack] (2016) or the Pulitzer-winning comic strip *Welcome to the New World* (2017), by Jake Halpern and Michael Sloan. Other examples include graphic narratives involving no direct exchange between creator and protagonist(s), such as Reinhard Kleist's *An Olympic Dream: The Story of Samia Yusuf Omar* (2015). In other instances, the narratives are based entirely on fictional refugees, such as the graphic poem *Como si Nunca Hubieran Sido* [As if They Have Never Been] (2018), by Javier and Juan Gallego.

Although the potential of comics for addressing trauma and memory has been largely explored (Chute; Romero-Jódar; Nabizadeh; Davies and Rifkind), the term "refugee comics" has been adopted by Rifkind and Mickwitz (2020b) to highlight their contrapuntal nature in counteracting predominant political and media discourses (278). They also succeed by interrupting "the photographic regime of the migrant as Other" that dominates the visual record of globalisation (Rifkind 649).

This chapter focuses on the graphic representation of Syrian girl refugees in Morten Dürr and Lars Horneman's *Zenobia* (2017), a fictional graphic narrative originally published in Denmark; Samya Kullab, Jackie Roche and Mike Freiheit's *Escape from Syria* (2017) published in Canada, introducing another fictional character; and an Italian documentary comic, Giulia Pex's *Khalat* (2019), based on an eponymous short story by Italian author Davide Coltri. Factual or fictional, these narratives represent girls as transient beings caught between innocence and experience, girlhood and womanhood, East and West, violence at home and precariousness and vulnerability at their destination.

In many of these narratives, the migrants' transit is evoked by representing the crossing of the Mediterranean Sea. Sea-crossing as a narrative motif calls forth notions such as quest and travel, threat and hope. The traveller is represented as someone with expectations, fears and presuppositions about the other side. Someone who has left a life behind and starts a new one. When migration is involved, sea-crossing evokes a flight from economic, political or cultural realities that threaten the individual, comparing them to the dangers of the sea and the uncertainties of the other shore. Such uncertainties are framed within the constraints and coercions of border policies in European shores of the Mediterranean, according to Paul Gilroy, "a war against asylum seekers, refugees, and economic migrants" (xi). Wherever they go, they are redundant humans, "unwanted and left in no doubt that they are" (Bauman 42). But refugees also lack a solid identity as long as they are on the move, at least as perceived by non-refugees. Their precarious existence becomes their only identity feature: "that of a stateless, placeless, functionless and 'papers-less' refugee" (Bauman 39–40). They are almost invisible, only moving into visibility "when they die in this way, or when they are arrested by border police or when they suddenly appear in their thousands fleeing war" (Young 26).

Representations of migrants that do not reproduce the prejudices of mainstream media and the belligerent role of European authorities might help to challenge from within the notion of an "embattled European region as a culturally bleached or politically fortified space, closed off to further immigration, barred to asylum-seeking, and wilfully deaf to any demand for hospitality made by refugees and other displaced people" (Gilroy xii). Thus, any glimpse or recreation of migration helps to "illuminate much of the landscape we inhabit" and mitigates the negative framing of migrants (Chambers 2). In addition, the length and intermedial form of the comics medium admits detailed and multiple extended narratives "that can act as counterpoints to decontextualized, single images and the soundbite simplicity of rolling news headlines" (Mickwitz, 2020a, 463).[1]

The graphic narratives addressed in this chapter "span a factual-fictional continuum" (Mickwitz, 2020b, 279). The corpus is a sample of recent Danish, Italian, Canadian and US "refugee comics" (Rifkind; Mickwitz, 2020a; 2020b). Three of these works were created by women authors and one by men. Also, *Khalat*, *Escape from Syria*, and *Zenobia* present two central young female protagonists, whereas in *Drawn to Berlin* young migrants are secondary characters. This comparative perspective addresses the multiplicity of approaches to refugee comics through the representation of Syrian girls: *Zenobia* and *Escape from Syria* are fictional narratives, *Drawn to Berlin* a witness account of a US volunteer in a refugee shelter, and *Khalat* a secondary witness account, an adaptation of a short story based on interviews with a refugee. The range of sources also serves as a sample of the multiplicity of experiences and life stories populating the age of migration. These defy a monolithic interpretation of migrant lives, which are turned into public enemies by virtue of fear, prejudice and racism, frequently presented by mainstream media as a flood of "unwanted invaders" (Parker 1) and even "non-persons" (Dal Lago 27).

Visualising Migration and Refugees in Comics

Although this chapter explores girl refugees in comics, it is noteworthy mentioning that comics are also a migrant medium. Comics are a transnational endeavour in terms of publics, markets and genres. "On any given day, graphic narration rides currents traversing the globe" (Smith 61). Migrants also traverse the world any given day, usually from South to North, fleeing war, prosecution, hunger, poverty, environmental conditions or simply looking for a chance to change or improve their future. Many of these migrants are children and youths. According to a recent report, 52 per cent of the global refugee population is underage (*World Migration Report 2020* 57). Out of a total of the 6.6 million Syrian refugees worldwide, 5.7 remain in the region, and half of them are women and girls. Their vulnerability is also gendered: according to UN Women, "Syrian women and girls have higher rates of poverty than men; they face increased risk of gender-based violence; and they shoulder the responsibility of caring for their children and other family members" (Mlambo-Ngcuka and Kanem). Child marriage targets Syrian refugee girls. In

Lebanon, for instance, 29 per cent of Syrian girls between the ages of fifteen and nineteen were married in 2018. Only 2 per cent of them were enrolled in school or worked (*2018 Vulnerability Assessment for Syrian Refugees in Lebanon* 37). The percentages were similar in 2019 and 2020.[2]

In spite of these chilling statistics, figures fail to convey personal stories. Or, as Fitzgerald writes in *Drawn to Berlin*, "the contours of [the refugees'] personhood [remain] hidden behind paperwork and headlines" (65). They are inevitably partial, reductive, dehumanising. Images, such as the photo of Aylan Kurdi, a 3-year-old Syrian who drowned crossing the Mediterranean, taken by Turkish photojournalist Nilüfer Demir on 2 September 2015, on the other hand, "talk" to spectators. This image, reproduced graphically by Kullab and Roche in *Escape from Syria*, circulated throughout the globe and changed the tone of the press coverage of the Syrian refugee crisis.[3]

It seems that images bring spectators and readers closer to "the pain of others" (Sontag 2004). They are moved or outraged, their preconceptions are challenged, perhaps they are even compelled to act. Images carry personal stories and their force "draws the crisis near to us in proximity, perception and empathy, instilling a cosmopolitan conception of this as the moral responsibility of humanity" (Landon 92).

Notwithstanding the power of images to bring into focus certain crises, raising empathy and moral engagement, they can be easily turned into stereotypes. In Aylan's photo, many Europeans saw their own offspring. They were not compelled by his personal story, what promoted identification was his death. As suggested by El-Enany, the fact that Aylan was a light-skin minor could explain the surge of compassion and identification, since similar images of black African bodies or "coded images of Muslims" such as women with hijab had not provoked a similar reaction (14).

Comics share with photographs their visual power. However, unlike photographs, they are not static, they develop a narrative through the combination of words and images. Unlike photographs, they do not try to capture the real in a supposed objectivity. On the contrary, they embrace the very subjectivity of the medium, in which the author's gaze manifests itself through their style. Comics authors such as the ones included in this analysis address the refugee crisis in the Mediterranean from their personal perspective; their works are examples of what Chute defines as "the rich visual-verbal form of comics to be able to represent trauma productively and ethically" (*Graphic Women* 3).

As Chute states, comics visualise themes that challenge representation, such as war and death: "Graphic narratives, on the whole, have the potential to be powerful precisely because they intervene against a culture of invisibility by taking [...] the risk of representation" (*Disaster Drawn* 5). Refugee comics deal with war and death and other forms of atrocity such as violence and exile. As such, they "use the form to interrupt static media images with the plenitude, fragmentation, and unruliness of the comic's page" (Rifkind 649). The question at stake is not whether atrocity should be represented but how to represent it.

Therefore, it points at an ethics of representation. In this chapter, we analyse the ethics of representation by choosing examples of how refugees have been represented in fictional and non-fictional comics. That is, how refugees are framed by these "Western" comics authors and what their representation denotes about their own biases and mindset.

'Ethics in the gutter': Strategies for Raising Empathy

Graphic narratives can be a "provocative resource" for engaging readers with complex realities such as migration (Boatright 468). For Judith Butler, images and accounts of suffering have the power to compel "our concern and moves us to act, that is, to voice our objection and register our resistance to such violence through concrete political means" (135). In this sense, refugee comics may function as examples of such "ethical solicitation" (Butler 135). That is, they elicit an ethical response from the reader that goes beyond borders and the national / regional / cultural paradigm. Similarly, Susan Sontag argues that works presenting the pain of others should allow for a political and social "intensity of awareness" (106). Through graphic narratives readers can learn about the experience of migration in order to understand the past of the refugees better and to welcome them into their joint present, building up more egalitarian communities which avoid a prejudicial framing. In the same line, LaCapra reflects that a traumatic event in the past "must be worked through in order for it to be remembered with some degree of conscious control and critical perspective that enables survival and, in the best of circumstances, ethical and political agency in the present" (69).

Refugee comics and crisis comics in general participate in this ethical solicitation. As Chute (2016), Davies and Rifkind, Mickwitz (2020a; 2020b) and Polak (2017) argue, the form of comics, based on fragmentation, multiple points of view and gutters, makes them especially apt to illustrate atrocity, trauma and memory. In *Ethics in the Gutter*, Polak suggests that comics "fictionalized treatments seek to comment on representational ethics, the ethics of spectatorship, and how point of view creates pathways for identification" (1).

One of the most effective strategies for engaging is creating an empathic response, as Mickwitz (2020a, 462) and Smith point out. As I argue in the next section this ethics of recognition and identification holds certain limitations. A comic such as *Zenobia*, which presents a passive character whose reality is mainly illustrated by her death at sea, surely provokes compassion, but it also turns readers into privileged subjects outside the narrative. They become "safe subjects [whose] reading rehearses a form of rescue of the other through the invitation to empathetic identification and outrage" (Smith 64).

There are also other potential dangers of this ethical approach to migrant lives, mainly the commodification of life-writing by resorting to stereotypes or the decontextualisation of larger sociopolitical realities, for instance overlooking the migrant experience, the context of the Syrian Civil War or the prosecution of the Kurdish minority in Syria. Also, by turning to empathic identification, refugee comics and crisis comics in general may overlook structural inequities and forms of exploitation (Smith 65). As Alfarhan states, many comics embedded within a universal human rights rhetoric promote "empathy-fuelled reading practices that do not force the reader to question or contend with their own role or subject position" (155).

Smith argues that many graphic narratives which describe violations of human rights emphasise the positions of "victim", "perpetrator" or "rescuer" in an attempt to offer agendas for change (Smith 62). In the case of *Zenobia*, the authors opt for presenting just the victim, eluding perpetrators and rescuers. *Khalat*'s and *Escape from Syria*'s main characters are recognisable victims too, but there are also textual allusions and visual representations of perpetrators (soldiers and smugglers). The case of *Drawn to Berlin* offers a wider plurality of perspectives, since it is the memoir of a volunteer working for a refugee centre in Berlin. There is an absence of perpetrators, but the author questions her own role as "rescuer" and witness to the refugees' stories throughout the narrative. *Zenobia* encourages victimisation by focusing exclusively on the death of a refugee at sea-crossing. I argue that empathy is limited to the outrage felt when witnessing a tragedy. However, the identification with the character(s) might be partial, since this narrative obscures the life of the main character before the crossing. At best, readers might become symbolic saviours of these lives by reading about their deaths, but this hardly promotes an ethical representation.

Representing and Documenting Girl Lives in Transit

The four works chosen for this chapter illustrate refugee girlhood before, during and after the girls' transitions. They recreate fictional and real lives, from the perspective of the refugees themselves (*Khalat*, *Escape from Syria*), from a third-person perspective (*Zenobia*) and from the perspective of a first-person witness (*Drawn to Berlin*). *Zenobia*, *Escape from Syria* and *Khalat* focus exclusively on a single girl character, while *Drawn to Berlin* is more polyphonic, including a plurality of young male and female characters.

Zenobia and *Khalat* show young female protagonists, a young girl and a university student. The first book is a marketed as a "middle grade graphic novel"; the second is an adaptation of the eponymous short story by Italian author Davide Coltri.[4] Dürr and Horneman's story is entirely fictional. Coltri, a humanitarian worker living in Beirut, based his short story "Khalat" on a real Syrian refugee he had personally met, introducing a first-person narrator to tell the story from the girl's perspective.

Zenobia (Triangle Square, 2018) tells the story of Amina, a girl who lives in a village in war-torn Syria. After her parents disappear she embarks on a flimsy boat and perishes at sea from the blow of a wave. Little is known about Amina's inner life, her tastes or her personality, apart from her enthusiasm for Zenobia, the third-century queen of the Palmyrene Empire and emblem of Syrian culture; she daydreams of becoming like her, a strong woman capable of riding horses, fighting men and leading armies (Dürr and Horneman 37–41). However, Amina has little opportunity to show her alliance to Zenobia as a symbol of strength and endurance. Most of the comic involves her death: thirty-one of the ninety-one pages show the fall from the boat and, mostly, Amina's body underwater (7–16, 26–27, 32–34, 68–69, 76–91). In all, a third of the graphic novel involves the death of the girl. This is further emphasised by the circular structure of the graphic novel, which starts and ends with the tragic sea-crossing, interspacing it with flashbacks to her previous life in Syria and her daydreams about Zenobia, but also with flashforwards including Amina's drowning. The rhythm of the narrative is slow in many of these repeated scenes, involving page-size or large panels. The structure, the rhythm and the repeated drowning motif overemphasise Amina's tragic end. Her facial expression while drowning is unchanging, an alternation of the same surprised and sleepy face. The result is Amina's death recreated in slow motion.

Throughout the narrative, Amina is a passive subject: she waits for her parents to return home, she is taken by her uncle to the boat, she embarks and she dies. Queen Zenobia as a symbol of empowerment does not add any heroic dimension nor does it enfranchise Amina. It rather becomes a metaphor of Amina's crushed dreams in the Mediterranean, the last thing she sees when drowning, the name of a sunken boat.

What is the ethical purpose of presenting a middle grader as a symbol of refugees whose only function in the story is dying? What is the symbolic intention of recreating her death repeatedly and extendedly? What kind of response does it elicit? Probably Dürr and Horneman did not intend to create further trauma among their readers, but they surely add to the construction of the migrant as someone who is only visible in their dying (Young 26). Furthermore, it is unlikely that readers may feel identified with a passive character without any emotional or personal development. The ethical potential of this refugee comic is therefore undermined. *Zenobia* becomes yet another representation of migrants whose life is reduced to their deaths, adding to the "callousness" of readers already saturated with images of suffering through television or internet (Sontag 105–106).

One of the effective strategies for raising sympathy and engaging readers is that of presenting young characters and their development through a crucial period of their lives, the transit from childhood/youth to adulthood. In the case of *Zenobia*, Amina's coming of age is interrupted by her early death, but *Khalat* follows this motif. Coming-of-age stories commonly involve narratives of education with an egalitarian imagery in which trauma, exclusion, resilience and recovery are recurrent themes. Slaughter and Smith have pointed out that the genre of Bildungsroman or coming of age interacts with human rights through fictions in which full personality development and a humanist social vision coalesce. In addition, many coming-of-age stories make use of the motif of life as a journey to emphasise the transition from adolescence to adulthood.

Giulia Pex's *Khalat* (Hoppípolla Edizioni, 2019) also focuses on a single protagonist, an eponymous Kurdish girl. Her entrance to university in Damascus coincides with the early days of the Arab Spring prior to the Syrian Civil War. For Khalat, the death of her brother Muhsen is the traumatic event that changes her life and expectations of studying of becoming a poet or a journalist. Muhsen's death prompts the family to flee Qamishli and migrate with thousands of refugees to Europe through Iraq, Turkey, the Mediterranean, then Greece, Macedonia, Serbia, Hungary, Austria and, finally, Germany.

Like Dürr and Horneman, Giulia Pex presents a young character carried by external circumstances, but, even if Khalat has to renounce her dreams of studying and working as an independent woman, we still get a glimpse of her rebelliousness, her unwillingness to become a submissive woman. Unlike Amina in *Zenobia*, Khalat has a personality, she has dreams, she has a life before, during and after becoming a migrant. Her life is not reduced to crossing an expanse of water.

Most of the texts in *Khalat* are adjoined texts, in other words, narrative captions "in which text is visually integrated, though not directly connected to some element within the Representational Plane" (Cohn 19). These captions offer a first-person narrative: it represents Khalat telling her own story through her own words. Even in the infrequent cases in which Pex includes word balloons, they do not include a tail connecting them to a particular speaker. They are words voiced by the people surrounding Khalat (her French professor, her father, her husband, the smugglers at the frontier), but they float on the page; even if they are part of the narrative, the focus remains on Khalat. This narrative choice also creates the impression of an interior monologue in which Khalat's story is interspaced with her memories of past conversations. This narrative perspective facilitates an identification with the protagonist: Khalat is a storyteller who narrates her story exclusively for the reader, not to any other character. In fact, she renounces answering truthfully to an anonymous speaker asking her "What did you do before moving to Iraq?" (Pex 116, my translation). The tone is also revealing, fluctuating between melancholy and repressed anger.

Pex's graphic style is delicate and precise, matching the narrative voice: she draws with soft pencils and uses subdued tones, focusing mostly on faces and specific objects instead of recreating large vistas or detailed backgrounds. Although the story told in words is linear, Pex's style is not entirely sequential: she opts for aspect-to-aspect transitions and non sequitur, albeit symbolically related, combinations of images. Even if melancholy is evident, Khalat's story is not commodified into a cute portrait of migration. Pex draws objects which synthesise part of the written text: four books, to explain that the protagonist has entered the library (18); her brother's hands holding hers, when she begs him to be careful (28–29); an abandoned shoe, to illustrate the hurried escape from Syria (50). Alternatively, other objects and details hold a symbolic meaning, such as the distant birds flying in a pink sky while Khalat asks herself what is going to happen with her after her activist brother dies; this melancholic image foreshadows the loss of freedom she will endure as a migrant. The combination of these graphic techniques results in an intimate narrative full of lyricism, which fuses Khalat's inner journey as a young woman and her real journey as a refugee.

As opposed to *Zenobia*, Khalat's crossing is just a small fraction of the graphic novel, barely four out of 120 pages. The migrant's experience is told from the protagonist's perspective. The full-page and double-page panels recreate her gaze: a mute crowd of bodies huddled together, a sea landscape without any text, a pitch-black double page to illustrate the night on board. This double page symbolises the uncertainties and fears of those on board without resorting to naturalistic representation. When Khalat explains "We listened to the sound of the <u>sea</u>" (Pex 101, my translation), the reader shares the uneasy darkness that engulfs the protagonist and the threatening presence of the Mediterranean.

Khalat also describes the "frozen transience" of the refugees, caught in an impasse of not belonging. Bauman defines this state as an "ongoing, lasting state of temporariness, a duration patched together of moments of which none is lived through as an element of, let alone a contribution to, perpetuity" (46, my translation). Pex echoes this transience when Khalat reaches a camp in Iraq: "[The worst] was not the houses nor the tents. Not even the bombs. Even worse than that was <u>the wait</u>. Living in a paralysed time but also losing the days, months, years" (79, my translation).

Khalat's fierce dignity and the recreation of her inner life through the abovementioned narrative and visual techniques build a round character with undoubtable appeal. Readers might feel compassion with her ordeal, but they would never pity her. Her transition from youth to adulthood is definitely unwanted and unwelcomed, and the protagonist stresses that she never chose to become a refugee, to lose her brother, to get married to an older man she barely knows, nor to become a young mother nor caregiver for her father in Germany. All these changes mark a present that bears little resemblance with her teenage dreams, but she still is a proud survivor.

Escape from Syria by Samya Kullab and Jackie Roche (Firefly Books, 2017) presents the coming-of-age story of Amina, a girl whose dreams of adult life are thwarted from the outset. Kullab, a reporter covering the refugee crisis in Lebanon, wanted to create a fictional protagonist "inspired by the strength and determination of the Syrian youth I've encountered. The grim reality of Amina's life in Lebanon is the same one that thousands of young Syrians have involuntarily met" (4). Therefore, the author's intention is very clear: to create an artefact of social denunciation to illustrate the disgraceful figures of official statistics. Although Kullab does not specify why she chose a girl instead of a boy as a protagonist, we can assume she wanted to give visibility to real-life girls because their vulnerability is also gendered: while lack of access to education and healthcare, child labour, violence and discrimination target both boys and girls, the latter face child marriage and higher rates of sexual abuse and harassment.

Amina's girlhood is abruptly interrupted by the war. She is about to tell a neighbour about her projects for adulthood when her house in Homs is destroyed by a bomb explosion. Roche's layout is very effective: she uses a full-page panel followed by ragged, irregular panels evoking Amina's shattered dreams, a technique she uses for dramatic, violent passages. In fact, readers never have the chance to learn about those dreams: the process of coming of age is radical and sudden, from schoolgirl to refugee and bread earner, from girlhood to womanhood. On the next page there is a flashforward: through a set of panels, we see an episode of Amina's daily life in Canada four years later. Roche follows a technique of superimposed panels to connect future and past to illustrate the change in Amina's life. From the comfortable and carefree life of a schoolgirl to her role as a mediator for her father in a foreign culture. The passage from girlhood to womanhood is reinforced by the visual metaphor of the shredded teddy bear that she carries, which is replaced by the image of Amina wearing a hijab. Many Muslim girls start wearing it in puberty, but Amina starts wearing it as soon as she starts her refugee life.

Like Khalat, Amina is the narrator of her own story. She tells us how her life changed when her house exploded, how the family fled to Lebanon, where they spent three years in a refugee camp. Increasingly indebted, her parents believe marrying Amina will ensure her safety. Everything changes when she tells her story to a UNHCR worker and the family is resettled in Canada. Although their most urgent needs are met – Amina's brother is given the medical care he could not get in Lebanon, they are all safe and well fed and she starts to attend high school – the cultural shock and a constant feeling of alienation never abandon Amina and her family. The end of the graphic novel is bittersweet: they might have improved their situation, but other family members are still trapped in Syria.

Even if Amina is the narrator of her own story, from the outset she speaks as an informed narrator, as an adult with the necessary background knowledge on the political situation in Syria before the war, the social unrest and political upheaval. Since the comic is narrated in the past tense, a grown-up Amina could be responsible for such remarks. However, the general impression is that Kullab and Roche have created a comic of ideas to offer as much context as possible, reinforcing it through the use of paratexts at the end of the book, including specific data, statistics and photographs. As a result, *Escape from Syria* partakes of Polak's representational ethics by contextualising the refugee crisis from the point of view of a vulnerable girl, but its informative treatment undermines the identification of the reader with the protagonist.

In turn, Ali Fitzgerald's *Drawn to Berlin: Comic Workshops in Refugee Shelters and Other Stories from the New Europe* (Fantagraphics, 2018) is a multifaceted document full of fragments of personal stories. The graphic memoir is told from the perspective of the author, a US volunteer in a refugee shelter in northern Berlin who teaches comics to children and adults. A considerable part of *Drawn to Berlin* consists of the drawings and comics made by Fitzgerald's students and her commentaries on them.[5] The first to appear, the teenagers

Haya and Amira, reflect a "harrowing, transient girlhood" (Fitzgerald 11), marked by the Mediterranean crossing. Both girls describe how an inflatable boat capsized when next to theirs. The event is similar to the fictional account in *Zenobia*. But Fitzgerald's recreation, presented in four pages (9–12) is brief, unpassionate, non-traumatic. The result is less dramatic but emotionally moving, as readers have the chance to know more about Haya and Amira: namely, that they are mediators between their families and the new surroundings, translating for them with their halting German.

Like Amira and Haya, most girls appearing in *Drawn to Berlin* are teenagers, but they are not a homogenous presence. For instance, their appearance is not codified: there are Syrian girls with and without hijab, girls wearing more traditional attire and girls wearing trousers and T-shirts. When referring to the drawings of different girls, regardless of whether they are Syrian, Fitzgerald focuses on the differences between them rather than on their similarities. Even if most of the girls' stories are not told in detail – unlike the stories of Saker and Michael, two young refugees who befriend Fitzgerald – they are differentiated through their artistic works, their style, their preferences and the objects they choose to draw.

At a visual level, *Drawn to Berlin* is a mirror narrative: Fitzgerald asks her students to draw, they draw their experiences and she, in turn, redraws them and recreates their own conversations in her memoir. She does not include the original drawings made by the students in her book. Both options – including the originals or redrawing them – can be considered a direct and indirect form of appropriation, and therefore an unethical choice. This ethical conundrum plagues the author, as we will see in the next pages, since Fitzgerald is concerned about the possibility of becoming the "colonizer" of the migrants' stories (Fitzgerald 185). From my point of view, the process of redrawing the originals is part of the process of retelling the migrants' stories. Fitzgerald took some notes, but she did not use a tape recorder to rewrite the refugees' exact words either. Their stories and their drawings are mediated by Fitzgerald's drawing style and conditioned by her recollections. After all, *Drawn to Berlin* is a memoir, not an example of comics journalism, so the author interprets the stories she has heard through her own lens, bias, memories and experiences.

Also, these mirror drawings evoke mirror realities: girls and boys sketch "innocent" images (flowers, landscapes, boats, reproductions of cartoon characters, football team shields, etc.), which frequently reveal the underground, traumatic reality of the refugee experience (inflatable boats which capsize, air forces dropping bombs, destroyed homes). The very idea of drawing also has two sides: drawing is for Fitzgerald a means to communicate with her students, most of whom struggle to communicate in English and German. In turn, she needs to filter those drawings through her own style and present them to readers. Also, the title has a double meaning: who is drawn to Berlin? Fitzgerald, attracted by the literary and decadent aura portrayed by Christopher Isherwood in his writings, and the refugees, drawn to the promise of a safe haven within Europe. But, while the author's transit is unproblematic thanks to her US passport, any refugee has to endure a journey full of hardships and dangers.

This strategy of mirrors turns the graphic memoir into a meta-memory artefact: there are memories of the refugees within the drawings recreated by Fitzgerald, memories of Fitzgerald and also recreations of pre-WWII Berlin through captions and illustrations of Joseph Roth's *The Wandering Jews* (1926–1927). By including references to how Jewish refugees were perceived and treated in Berlin in the 1920s as a "peril from the East" (20), Fitzgerald draws a parallelism of the past and present refugee experience linking historical and recent memory.

In a note at the end of her graphic memoir, Fitzgerald reveals her working process: all names are modified for discretion, and she documents the encounters with refugees through notes, sketches and photographs that she does not include in her comic:

> for the portions of this book that take place in shelters, I sought to record the people and environment of these workshops faithfully. To that end, I tried to only use quotations culled from my notes. I used sketches and the few photographs I took to help fill in my visual memory. (Fitzgerald 197)

Her "collection of illustrated observations" is undisguisedly subjective (197) and shows her engagement with an ethics of representation.

However, Fitzgerald questions her role as a witness and keeper of those memories: "I just [...] don't want to colonize those people's stories" (185). "But this is your story too, isn't it?", replies her interlocutor, possibly a therapist (Fitzgerald 185). The author concludes: "The exact ethical contours of the question still elude me" (Fitzgerald 185). The struggle to understand, describe and draw the refugees she meets is transferred to the pages. It is a struggle to represent and visualise ethically those who are invisible. The elusive ethical contours of the story might be impossible to determine, but the fact that the author/narrator questions her own position as such transfers the question to the reader. I argue that *Drawn to Berlin* is an example of "ethical spectatorship" (Kozol 166). Kozol applies the term to Joe Sacco's graphic journalism in which the reporter/author invites the reader to share a similar ethical stance. By questioning her own position as a "colonizer" of the refugee's stories, by presenting herself as vulnerable through her own doubts, Fitzgerald draws a collective portrait of the people she encounters. It is a sketch rather than a portrait because she acknowledges the limitations of her own experience, but in those limitations lies its effectiveness: she acknowledges her lack of objectivity, her mood changes, her partial knowledge of the people she encounters, her impotence when they tell her about their problems, her own biases. Readers probably learn more about Fitzgerald than about the rest of characters, but the fragments of the lives told in the story raise the reader's empathy because the author manages to recreate an honest account. The suspended condition of refugees is defined as a "breezy transience" (Fitzgerald 23). It is mirrored by Fitzgerald in relation with her students, who enter and abandon her life, leaving a feeling of loss that "always felt like losing a friend" (23). By being transparent about her own feelings towards the refugees, the author evokes empathy in the reader.

In *Drawn to Berlin*, the refugees' rite of passage does not take place at sea, but once they reach their destination. As Fitzgerald writes, "The shelter was a surreal, liminal place" (43). The in-betweenness of the refugee's life is exemplified by this space, a symbolic standstill that marks the arrival to a destination that only offers uncertainties at first. But for Fitzgerald, the refugees achieve visibility at the shelter: the place where they meet with each other, where they learn German or get relevant information. Most of the time, they wait and attend workshops, such as the one taught by Fitzgerald. The wait is unheroic and unremarkable; it is not as visually engaging as the moment of the sea-crossing, but it is not uniform and undifferentiated. Therefore, characters achieve visibility in this defining stage through the stories told to Fitzgerald, through their drawings and through the portraits they constantly ask her to draw: a lasting symbol of their presence, "of this desire to be reflected" (Fitzgerald 64). Inevitably limited by her own subjectivity, Fitzgerald offers an empowering visual homage to those who were her students by documenting their lives and including herself within the narrative as an unreliable narrator.

Conclusion

Surely, any given day Syrian refugee girls are subject to some kind of systemic violence, whether they are victims of the atrocities of the war, restrictive frontier policies or the difficulties, discrimination, harassment and poverty along the road and once they reach their destination. Ensuring their visibility might seem a laudable enterprise. However, reinforcing their visibility through death is ethically questionable and supports the same stereotypes already overly present in mainstream media. Thus, in *Zenobia*, ethical solicitation is undermined by the focus on Amina's failed crossing, since it dehumanises her by reducing her existence to a static and harrowing impasse. Amina's death is objectified and commodified, dramatically interrupting the rite of passage from girlhood to youth. Strategies such as sentimentalisation, instrumentalisation of trauma or romanticisation of death offer little insight into the singularities of the refugee experience. Therefore, these kinds of refugee comics tread the "thin line between trauma and propaganda" (Romero-Jódar 71) to the extent of objectifying young migrants as voiceless and passive symbols of suffering.

Instead of focusing on death or the Mediterranean crossing, Kullab, Pex and Fitzgerald illustrate more powerfully than *Zenobia* the wait, what Bauman called the "frozen transience" of refugees, the suspension of life in the in-betweenness of here/there, home/

exile, war/safety. As Butler shows, the location of suffering as a "here" and "there" is reversible (138). The earth population moves and needs to negotiate the "unchosen cohabitation", since "we are all [...] the unchosen, but we are nevertheless unchosen together" (Butler 146). These comics go beyond these binary oppositions problematising the girls' arrival to their destination. This and their gendered vulnerability is what shapes their unwanted coming of age, a traumatic passage from girlhood to womanhood.

Readers contemplate different positions when engaging with refugee comics. When reading about a character like Amina in *Zenobia*, they might become symbolic rescuers, but this position does not promote an ethical representation of girl refugees. *Escape from Syria* and *Khalat* present multifaceted girl characters that make possible an identification with the reader. Both illustrate an unwanted transit from girlhood to womanhood, an unrequested process of self-discovery. The motif of coming of age is reversed, but it retains its engaging potential. In *Drawn to Berlin*, the girls' transit to adulthood is marked by their role as mediators between cultures, like Amina in *Escape from Syria*. These three narratives fulfil an important ethical obligation, that of mitigating the othering of migrants.

In addition, Fitzgerald humbly documents the pain of others in the context of her own pain and experience and related to European historical memory. Her work does not offer a real insight into the lives of girls. However, Fitzgerald's ethical spectatorship provides a more ethical and engaging approach to refugee lives, creating an empathic mirror to look at those lives from a non-hegemonic, non-homogenising perspective. Graphic narratives like *Drawn to Berlin* go a step beyond ethical representation, working towards an "ethics of cohabitation" (Butler), giving examples of peaceful and productive coexistence. Even in their differences, these refugee comics invite complementary compassionate readings. To a greater or lesser degree, they expand our critical perspective of the situation of Syrian girl refugees and the refugee crisis, offering a wider and plural perspective which might contribute to a cosmopolitan reframing of the representation of girl refugees and migrant young lives in general.

Notes

1. Of course, there are other media apart from graphic narratives that might contribute to this task: documentaries or immersive reportages may also offer a more ethical representation than a short piece on the press or a clip on TV news.
2. See UNHCR reports *2019 Vulnerability Assessment for Syrian Refugees in Lebanon (VASyR)* (https://data2.unhcr.org/en/documents/details/73118) and *2020 Vulnerability Assessment for Syrian Refugees in Lebanon (VASyR)* (https://data2.unhcr.org/en/documents/details/85002).
3. See, among others, Gunter, Kingsley and Timur, Langdon, and El-Enany.

4. "Khalat" is included in Davide Coltri's *Dov'è Casa Mia: Storie oltre i Confini* (Edizioni minimum fax, 2019).
5. The Brazilian journalist André Naddeo carried out a similar initiative in Greece: "Drawfugees" (2016–2018) shows photos of refugee children and their drawings. They are published with their testimonies on a Facebook page: https://www.facebook.com/drawfugees/. In *Threads*, Kate Evans also recreates a similar experience with art therapy in the precarious refugee camp of Calais (33–35).

Bibliography

Alfarhan, Haya Saud. "Visual Detention: Reclaiming Human Rights through Memory in Leila Abdelrazaq's *Baddawi*". *Documenting Trauma in Comics: Traumatic Pasts, Embodied Histories, and Graphic Reportage*, edited by Dominic Davies and Candida Rifkind. Palgrave MacMillan, 2020, pp. 153–171.

Bauman, Zygmunt. *Liquid Times: Living in an Age of Uncertainty*. Polity, 2013.

Boatright, Michael D. "Graphic Journeys: Graphic Novels' Representations of Immigrant Experiences". *Journal of Adolescent & Adult Literacy*, vol. 53, no. 6, 2010, pp. 468–476, https://doi.org/10.1598/JAAL.53.6.3. Accessed 4 Mar. 2021.

Butler, Judith. "Precarious Life, Vulnerability, and the Ethics of Cohabitation". *The Journal of Speculative Philosophy*, vol. 26, no. 2, 2012, pp. 134–151. www.jstor.org/stable/10.5325/jspecphil.26.2.0134. Accessed 4 Mar. 2021.

Chambers, Iain. *Mediterranean Crossings: The Politics of an Interrupted Modernity*. Duke University Press, 2008.

Chute, Hillary L. *Disaster Dawn: Visual Witness, Comics, and Documentary Form*. Harvard University Press, 2016.

—. *Graphic Women: Life Narrative and Contemporary Comics*. Columbia University Press, 2010.

Cohn, Neil. "Beyond Word Balloons and Thought Bubbles: The Integration of Text and Image". *Semiotica*, no. 197, 2013, pp. 35–63.

Davies, Dominic, and Candida Rifkind. *Documenting Trauma: Traumatic Pasts, Embodied Histories & Graphic Reportage in Comics*. Palgrave Macmillan, 2019.

De Haas, Hein, Mark J. Miller and Stephen Castles. *The Age of Migration: International Population Movements in the Modern World*. Red Globe Press, 2020.

Dal Lago, Alessandro. *Non-Persons*, translated by Marie Orton. Ipoc Press, 2009.

Dürr, Morten, and Lars Horneman. *Zenobia*. Triangle Square, 2018.

El-Enany, Nadine. "Aylan Kurdi: The Human Refugee". *Law Critique* no. 27, 2016, pp. 13–15. https://doi.org/10.1007/s10978-015-9175-7. Accessed 4 Mar. 2021.

Evans, Kate. *Threads from the Refugee Crisis*. Verso, 2017.

Fitzgerald, Ali. *Drawn to Berlin: Comic Workshops in Refugee Shelters and Other Stories from a New Europe*. Fantagraphics, 2018.

Gilroy, Paul. "Migrancy, Culture and a New Map of Europe". *Blackening Europe: The African American Presence*, edited by Irial Glynn and J. Olaf Kleist. Routledge, 2004, pp. ix–xx.

Gunter, Joel. "Alan Kurdi: Why One Picture Cut Through". *BBC*, 4 Sept. 2015, http://www.bbc.co.uk/news/world-europe-34150419. Accessed 4 Mar. 2021.

Kingsley, Patrick, and Safak Timur. "Stories of 2015: How Alan Kurdi's Death Changed the World". *The Guardian*, 31 Dec. 2015. https://www.theguardian.com/world/2015/dec/31/alan-kurdi-death-canada-refugee-policy-syria-boy-beach-turkey-photo. Accessed 4 Mar. 2021.

Kozol, Wendy. "Complicities of Witnessing in Joe Sacco's Palestine". *Theoretical Perspectives on Human Rights Literature*, edited by Elizabeth Swanson Goldberg and Alexandra Schultheis Moore. Routledge, 2012, pp. 165–179.

LaCapra, Dominick. *History in Transit: Experience, Identity, Critical theory*. Cornell University Press, 2004.

Langdon, Nicola. "Syria's Refugee Crisis in the British Press". *Critical Perspectives on Migration in the Twenty-First Century*, edited by Marianna Karakoulaki, Laura Southgate and Jakob Steiner. E-International Relations, 2018, pp. 91–112.

Mickwitz, Nina. "Introduction: Discursive Contexts, 'Voice,' and Empathy in Graphic Life Narratives of Migration and Exile". *a/b: Auto/Biography Studies*, vol. 35, no. 2, 2020a, pp. 459–465, https://doi.org/10.1080/08989575.2020.1738079. Accessed 4 Mar. 2021.

Mickwitz, Nina. "Comics Telling Refugee Stories". *Documenting Trauma in Comics*, edited by Dominic Davies and Candida Rifkind. Palgrave Macmillan, 2020b, pp. 277–296. https://doi.org/10.1007/978-3-030-37998-8_16. Accessed 4 Mar. 2021.

Mlambo-Ngcuka, Phumzile, and Natalia Kanem. "Op-ed. Put women at the centre of Syria crisis response". UN Women, IV Syria Conference (Brussels), 2 July 2020. https://www.unwomen.org/en/news/stories/2020/6/op-ed-joint-women-at-the-centre-of-syria-crisis-response. Accessed 4 Mar. 2021.

Nabizadeh, Golner. *Representation and Memory in Graphic Novels*. Routledge, 2020.

Parker, Samuel. "'Unwanted invaders': The representation of refugees and asylum seekers in the UK and Australian print media". *eSharp*, vol. 23, no. 1, 2015, pp. 1–21. http://orca.cf.ac.uk/id/eprint/79108. Accessed 4 Mar. 2021.

Pex, Giulia. *Khalat*. Hoppípolla Edizioni, 2019.

Polak, Kate. *Ethics in the Gutter: Empathy and Historical Fiction in Comics*. Ohio State University Press, 2017.

Rifkind, Candida. "Refugee Comics and Migrant Topographies". *a/b: Auto/Biography Studies*, vol. 32, no. 3, 2017, pp. 648–654, https://doi.org/10.1080/08989575.2017.13394 68. Accessed 4 Mar. 2021.

Romero-Jódar, Andrés. *The Trauma Graphic Novel*. Routledge, 2017.

Said, Edward W. "Reflections on Exile". *Reflections on Exile and Other Literary and Cultural Essays*. London: Granta Books, 2001, pp. 173–183.

Slaughter, Joseph R. "Enabling Fictions and Novel Subjects: The 'Bildungsroman' and International Human Rights Law". *PMLA*, vol. 121, no. 5, Oct. 2006, pp. 1405–1423, https://doi.org/10.1632/pmla.2006.121.5.1405. Accessed 4 Mar. 2021.

Smith, Sidonie. "Human Rights and Comics: Autobiographical Avatars, Crisis Witnessing, and Transnational Rescue Networks". *Graphic Subjects: Critical Essays on Autobiography and Graphic Novels*, edited by Michael A. Chaney. University of Wisconsin Press, 2011, pp. 61–72.

Sontag, Susan. *Regarding the Pain of Others*. Picador, 2004.

United Nations High Commissioner for Refugees, United Nations Children's Fund, World Food Programme. *2018 Vulnerability Assessment for Syrian Refugees in Lebanon (VASyR)*. Lebanon, 2018. https://www.unhcr.org/lb/wp-content/uploads/sites/16/2018/12/VASyR-2018.pdf. Accessed 4 Mar. 2021.

Young, Robert J. C. "Postcolonial Remains". *New Literary History*, vol. 43, no. 1, 2012, pp. 19–42, https://doi.org/10.1353/nlh.2012.0009. Accessed 4 Mar. 2021.

Whitlock, Gillian. "Autographics: The Seeing 'I' of the Comics". *MFS Modern Fiction Studies*, vol. 52 no. 4, 2006, pp. 965–979, https://doi/org/10.1353/mfs.2007.0013. Accessed 4 Mar. 2021.

Chapter 4
Comics, Caregiving and Crip Time

JoAnn Purcell

a morning before school...

Rather than bend disabled bodies and minds to meet the clock, crip time bends the clock to meet disabled bodies and minds.

—Alison Kafer (27)

Crip time is time travel. Disability and illness have the power to extract us from linear, progressive time with its normative life stages and cast us into a wormhole of backward and forward acceleration, jerky stops and starts, tedious intervals and abrupt endings.

—Ellen Samuels (n.p.)

My comics practice is a reflective exercise I lean on to slow down and make sense of the incomprehensible or the unknowable and can impart a deeper, perhaps more compassionate, understanding of events and the people involved in them. In September 2020 we were already a few months into the Covid-19 pandemic. I was both optimistic and worried for my daughter Simone as she began high school, but only in part because she was born with the genetic difference Down syndrome. She started high school with dramatically modified routines, classes were sometimes in person but more often on a computer in a virtual classroom with peers whose range of learning styles was considerable. The adjustment to high school life was difficult. She missed the familiarity of routine at her elementary school and her old friends, all of whom had gone to other high schools. I also struggled – I cancelled my anticipated travel, my daily commute and gatherings with family and friends. I thrive in and thought I enjoyed living in what Hartmut Rosa calls the accelerated "temporal structures and horizons of modernity" (22). At the launch of the pandemic, I was resentful of the stay-at-home restrictions for both of us. In time, Simone seemed to fall into the new school routine and I gave in to the new rhythm that replaced the often frenetic pre-pandemic pace. A contained and predictable pace, it was decidedly slower – for me. I returned to creating comics to consider how the pandemic constraints were affecting Simone in the short sequence titled *A morning before school*.

A few years ago, as part of my PhD in Critical Disability Studies, I revived my art practice after many years of teaching and administration. I love to draw with an un-erasable pen, simple lines directly onto paper, to transpose thoughts and observations without the mediation of rational intent or purpose. So with that foundation, I began a daily comics practice that lasted three years, beginning when Simone was ten years old, to the accumulation of 1095 pages. The commitment to a daily entry worked on many different levels. I found shorthand ways to draw, and my rusty drawing skills improved given the time, space and purpose to develop again. The need for content in the nightly transcription forced me to observe Simone more closely. I regularly paid attention to the small and seemingly meaningless details of our routine and repetitive life together. I could see her, hear her, sense her in a new way. These comics connections were relational, multifaceted and material. This new way of knowing came through my drawings and, as artist and critical theorist John Berger has illuminated, the action of drawing can be key to locating and internalising knowledge (p. 58). My perception of Simone's vulnerability gave way to understanding her profound human agency. She is the knower of her embodiment, and the comics impart a glimpse into her. And so during the Covid-19 pandemic, I returned to drawing comics alongside her – using the observation and comics skills I had honed.

I began to explore the manifestation of time and Simone's experience of it. Unquestionably, she navigates the world with a different rhythm than I do. Through my comics practice, I became acutely aware of this different pace. I discovered through the individual writings of Robert McRuer (200), Alison Kafer (27) and Ellen Samuels (n.p.) that it had a name – *crip time*. The word *crip* – reclaimed by disability movements from the pejorative cripple – combined with *time*, crip time serves to define the world through the cadences of the disabled person. Crip time is non-normative. It exists in the larger social arena to challenge the myth of progress and standardised life goals as well as in the different paces of everyday life. It is not on a clock; it does not adhere to expectations. Crip time does not follow a trajectory from beginning to end with a desired result; it can be just more of the same without closure or completion.

As an art form, comics are adept at imparting an understanding of the experience of time. They can linger in a moment, slow time down, speed it up, stop or go in reverse. Comics theorist Scott McCloud dissected the visual elements and concluded that in addition to the content, the shapes and sizes of panels, and the space inside and between the panels, visualise time duration. McCloud also states that the direction the panels are read in, from left to right as is expected in Western languages, can factor into a preconditioned expectation of a "linear progression" of time (99-101). Artist Chris Ware creatively employs the visual comics elements to disrupt and disorient the reader. He focuses on depicting time at a slow pace specifically as counter to the speed of modernity. Georgiana Banita in response to Ware's work states that his portrayal of "disrupted temporality [through] incrementalism and fragmentation [...] do not function identically, they converge to generate narrative slowness and critique modern practices of acceleration" (177). Ware employs empty panels, non-verbal panels, repetition of panels and a disruption of the reading logic through panel placement. These same strategies can also be used to depict crip time and the experience of it by those who navigate the world differently – like Simone. Comics make crip time materially clear.

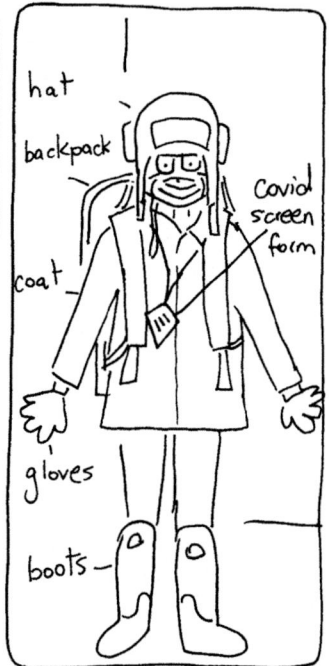

I learned through the creation of the comics sequence that Simone's pace during Covid-19 remains generally unchanged. She is oblivious to the demands of time, the arrival of the school taxi, the start of virtual school or online occupational therapy. Some days we are in sync; others, not so much. It leads me to reflect on my own connections to time by the clock and the stress it causes me when I perceive other people waiting. I race to cram in as many tasks as I can, in part because as a full-time working mother of three children, I perceive there is always so much to do. I hold my internal clock in high value, and like most normative experiences and embodiments, it can be invisible until a contrast materialises, as when normative time and crip time are experienced side by side. I sense the time intersections as a frustration expressed as hurry up, slow down, more time, time is up, etc. I am increasingly aware that caregiving requires an orientation to the pace of the person being cared for, often at a rate a little or a lot different from the caregiver's speed. I am beginning to learn to move, without resistance, at this different pace with my daughter. When I do, it enhances our bond and is a method to acknowledge and respect her difference.

Creating comics also slows me down, takes care of me, gives me a focus and a joyful outlet. Comics help me to challenge assumptions I might have about Simone, ones I make even after living with her for her fifteen years of life. They confront my preconceived beliefs about time and what is normative. Comics make material the dialogic exchange and force me to reflect on my responses. And while the Covid-19 pandemic has decelerated my life and forced me to adjust, I am aware I am still tied to a clock and its dictations of meetings, school and dinner, but Simone is not. The contrast between crip time and post-industrial modern time is manifested in my household on a regular basis, but underscored even more so during Covid-19. Crip time is her time orientation, and my attention to it is generative for both of us. *Crip time* makes time to take care.

Acknowledgements

In these pandemic years of loss and disruption, I have much to be immensely grateful for. My work would not be possible without the patience, kindness and care from my comics collaborator, Simone, and her older siblings, Madeleine and Luc.

I dedicate this paper to my dad – John J. Purcell (1933–2021) – who also lovingly compelled me to slow down, especially in his final months.

Bibliography

Banita, Georgiana. "Chris Ware and the Pursuit of Slowness". *The Comics of Chris Ware, Drawing is a Way of Thinking*, edited by David M. Ball and Martha B. Kuhlman, University Press of Mississippi, 2010.

Berger, John. "To Take Paper, to Draw: A world through lines". *Harpers*, Periodicals Archive Online, 1 Sept. 1987.

Kafer, Alison. *Feminist, Queer, Crip*. Indiana University Press, 2013.

McCloud, Scott. *Understanding Comics: The Invisible Art*. Harpers Collins Publishers, 2013.

McRuer, Robert. *Crip Theory: Cultural Signs of Queerness and Disability*. New York University Press, 2006.

Rosa, Hartmut. "Social Acceleration: Ethical and Political Consequences of a Desynchronized High Speed Society". *Constellations*, vol. 10, no. 1, 2003.

Samuels, Ellen. "Six Ways of Looking at Crip Time". *Disability Studies Quarterly*, vol. 37, no. 3, Summer 2017, https://dsq-sds.org/article/view/5824/4684%20.%20 Accessed%2012. Accessed 12 Oct. 2022.

Chapter 5
Discussing Gender in a Communist Comics Magazine: *Corinne et Jeannot*, 1970

Sylvain Lesage

Bande dessinée: A Masculine History

At the end of 1970 the weekly magazine *Pif Gadget* published an advertisement for the publication of an album in the series *Corinne et Jeannot* by Jean Tabary. The image showed the two heroes of the series in a posture characteristic of the series: Corinne threatens Jeannot with a giant book, and Jeannot cautiously flees the harassment he receives from Corinne, shouting: "Don't buy it, it's an insult to the man ... that I am", to which Corinne retorts: "Shut up, you *publiphobe!*".

This advert (**fig. 1**) raises a whole series of questions. On the one hand, it questions advertising strategies in a rapidly changing market, and the way in which the book depicted in it is invested with an ambiguous role. The album certainly appears as a monument to the glory of the two heroes, but a monument that proves overwhelming. *Pif Gadget*, however, refrained from venturing into book printing. Few of the stories published in the pages of *Pif Gadget* were reissued as books: for financial as well as ideological reasons, the magazine refused to initiate a sustained policy of book publications, thus missing out on the major evolution of the comics market. If we take the image literally, and read into it an ambiguous monumentalisation, we cannot fail to read it as a reflection of the tensions that this editorial choice aroused.

On a second level, this image refers to the construction of the ninth art canon. This canon was largely built around the form of the comics *album* (Lesage, 2022), and the tension underlying this publicity image also questions the status of the *Corinne et Jeannot* series, which has long remained in a memorial in-between, between the complete canonisation of series such as *Iznogoud*, by the same Tabary – but initially published in the pages of the newspaper *Pilote*, which was far more active in the field of multimedia adaptations – and the relegation of *series* published in *Pif* and never reissued as albums.

Yet in this canon of comics, which is largely conveyed by the album, comics for girls are particularly rare. Like the cinema for a long time (Sellier), the history of comics was largely written in the "masculine singular". The question of girls in Franco-Belgian comics is largely understudied (Flinn), since for a long time the assumption was that girls did not really read comics, or that they consumed a type of comics that was not worth mentioning. The existence of *Bécassine*, the immensely popular heroine of a series of stories published in *Le Journal de Suzette* and albums published by Gautier-Languereau, is generally mentioned as an important phenomenon for the beginning of the twentieth century (Couderc). But apart from this extremely popular figure, comics for girls remain largely ignored in general comics histories. Mentioning *Bécassine* thus makes it easier to ignore publications aimed at girls.[2] The classic historical overview of female figures in comics then generally moves on to the 1960s with sexualised figures (*Barbarella* is the most famous, but also *Jodelle* and *Pravda*, among others), and then to the 1970s with the arrival of a new generation of heroines in the pages of illustrated comics for boys – for example, *Natacha* the stewardess or *Yoko Tsuno* (Reyns-Chikuma).

In short, there is a huge gap in our knowledge of the past of comics, and of the place of female readers and artists in the history of comics (Guilhaumou and Dermenjian). This historical misunderstanding has profound effects, as manifested – in a grotesquely caricatural way – by the 2016 edition of the Angoulême Festival (Girard et al.). Faced with the outcry over the absence of female authors in the official

Figure 1 *Pif Gadget*, no. 90, 9 November 1970.

selection, the festival director defended himself by arguing that historically there were few female artists, that for the Grand Prix (which rewards an entire career) there was not much that could be done about it, and that once Claire Bretécher and Florence Cestac had been awarded, there were not many artists left to award. The discussions that followed showed that, historically, women had always been present in the world of comics, but less recognised, because they were often confined to secondary roles (colourists, for example) or, above all, to less recognised publications, less collected, less reprinted: Catholic newspapers for little girls, and girls' magazines in general (Kohn).[3]

This chapter, however, does not focus on the work of a female author,[4] but on an album signed by a male author, and a relatively well-known one: Jean Tabary. Tabary gained fame not for *Corinne et Jeannot*, but for the series *Iznogoud*, which he created with René Goscinny in 1962 for the weekly magazine *Record*, and reprinted in *Pilote*. *Iznogoud* stands out as a pioneering comics series in the use of a particularly unsympathetic hero, a manipulative and devious vizier, whose phrase "I want to be caliph instead of the caliph" (*je veux être calife à la place du calife*) quickly became a commonplace to qualify the cynicism accompanying a political (or simply careerist) ambition.[5]

This chapter focuses on female readers, and how these readers can interact with the identification figures offered to them. This is a work in progress, started through the readers' mail in *Pif Gadget* and based on the construction of the feminine and the masculine.[6] Despite the great interest that girls-oriented comics present (Gibson), it seemed relevant to me to question the construction of female roles, and the interaction between identification figures and readership in a mixed children's magazine, for several reasons.

First, and strikingly, the conditions of conservation and access are much easier for mixed publications than for specifically female publications. In itself, this imbalance speaks volumes about the asymmetric construction of the ninth art canon. But, above all, this choice stems from the hypothesis that the distribution of gender roles can perhaps be observed in a more refined way in a mixed magazine. On the one hand, male and female readers feel equally legitimate to react (whereas one can imagine that, in a female magazine, male readers will express themselves less, or their letters might be published less). Above all, for male and female readers, reading a mixed magazine and writing to it reinforces the need to strengthen their gender identities, to assert themselves as girls or boys in relation to the other sex. My approach is thus part of a perspective that aims to go beyond the description of normed roles, to focus on the actual appropriation of a magazine by its readers (Thiesse; Warner).

The few elements available in terms of readership surveys indicate that male and female readers play with gender assignments (magazines and heroes for boys on the one hand; magazines and heroines for girls on the other). Consequently, a magazine that advertises itself as openly mixed constitutes, from the outset, a space for the negotiation of gender identities. Yet the series stages and makes room for discussion of girl/boy relationships and, beyond that, of gendered roles and gendered codes in comics. More interestingly, in my opinion, the series constitutes a medium for intense discussion, of which there is a (meagre) trace in the readers' letters, and which the advert with which I started my chapter summarises.

Before getting to the heart of the question of a gender war going on in *Corinne et Jeannot*, it is worthwhile to present the publication that hosts it. Created in 1969 *Pif Gadget* is a weekly magazine that prolongs the weekly *Vaillant*, created at the Liberation. *Pif Gadget* was the biggest seller of the comics press in the 1970s, well above the average, with about half a million copies sold every week over the whole decade. The only paper that came close was *Journal de Mickey*, which did not publish readers' mail, or did so only occasionally. Conversely, letters played a big role in *Pif*. Throughout the decade, *Pif* maintained a close relationship with its readers, who regularly commented on and criticised the evolution of the newspaper. At first sight, this readers' mail seems much less gendered than in the pages of the *Journal de Spirou* or *Tintin*, where gender identity was more marked.

Pif not only prolonged *Vaillant* but also continued a whole series of illustrated magazines existing from the beginning of the twentieth century and aimed at the children's branches of the French communist youth: *Jean-Pierre*, close to the *Confédération Générale du Travail*[7] and whose first issue appeared at the end of 1901, then *Les Petits Bonhommes*, *Le Jeune Camarade*, *Mon Camarade* and *Le Jeune Patriote*, which was rebranded as *Vaillant* in 1945 (Medioni). The magazine is thus part of the history of the partisan press, even if entertainment takes precedence over political struggle (Rannou). Thus, at the Liberation, *Vaillant* was able to recycle openly collaborationist authors (Ory), a sign that graphic skills took precedence over political commitments. At the end of the 1960s, the transition from *Vaillant* to *Pif* was a clear indication of an ambition to broaden the readership and to become even more dedicated to entertainment. However, the moral framework proposed by this children's magazine differs markedly from that proposed by illustrated magazines of Catholic inspiration, such as *Tintin* or *Le Journal de Spirou*, whose history is better known (Dayez).

In the 1960s the organisation of communist youth movements moved from a communism of parallel movements (one branch for girls, another for boys) to a mass, mixed approach (Roubaud-Quashie). *Pif*, launched in 1969, promotes this coeducational facade. Thus, to understand the history of *Pif*, we can put forward a hypothesis: while *Spirou*, *Tintin* (two magazines linked to the heritage of the scout movement, which was powerful in Belgium) and *Pilote* explicitly targeted boys in their editorials, editorial choices and advertisements, *Pif* adopted a different strategy. The readership it targeted was more intergenerational (*Pif* being the newspaper that was exchanged between siblings) and, above all, more mixed. Moreover, because of its initial political anchorage, *Pif* targets a more popular readership than *Spirou* or *Tintin*, rooted in bourgeois values. Indeed, as Mel Gibson reminds us, "childhood can never be entirely divorced from class, gender, disability and ethnicity" (289).

In addition to its singular readership, *Pif* offers an original editorial model in the world of French comic book publications. Magazines such as *Tintin* or *Spirou* are structured around a continued story, the one-page or two-page division of a story always tending towards the suspense of the following week (Boillat et al.). Conversely, *Pif* favours complete stories, on a model closer to that of the American comic book: the episodes follow one another, but each issue offers a minimal closure, and can be read independently – although each issue also offers humorous, one-page series.

The second original feature of the magazine, which can be read in the title, is that every week, *Pif Gadget* offers its readers a gadget: an object to assemble, a toy or even a naturalist curiosity – like Mexican jumping peas ("*Pifitos*") in 1971, or fir trees in 1975 – to mention only the most famous ones. Where other comics magazines offered sections dedicated to the new commodities of the consumer society – electricity, radio, operation of electronic devices – *Pif* offered a more playful approach, based on DIY and direct observation, in line with the ethics of popular education to which the Communist Party was very close.

The third editorial characteristic is that the magazine is almost exclusively confined to the world of the press. While the other titles of the comics scene published a variation of the best stories in books (Lesage, 2018), *Vaillant*, like *Pif*, confined itself to magazines sold in news stands, for complex reasons – linked in part to the Communist Party's hold on the venture.

The "Yellow Kid" prize that the magazine received in Lucca in 1970 for its efforts to promote comics, and the abundant prizes awarded by the Société française de bande dessinée in the early 1970s, bear witness to *Pif*'s central place in the process of legitimising the ninth art (Lesage, 2019). Thus, in 1970, the newspaper was proud to receive four of the "grand awards" of the Société française de bande dessinée: Hugo Pratt (for *Corto Maltese*), Mattioli (for *M le magicien*), Mic Delinx (for *La Jungle en folie*) and finally Jean Tabary (for *Corinne et Jeannot*) were all published by *Pif*. Despite this recognition, despite the decisive role played by the magazine in the introduction of Hugo Pratt in France, *Pif* missed the market mutation towards the album, which, in the middle of the 1970s, was already transforming the landscape of the French comics industry.

Corinne et Jeannot is therefore an atypical series among the most important comic strip magazine of the 1970s. As an explicitly mixed magazine, *Pif* published with *Corinne et Jeannot* a series depicting the difficult relationships between boys and girls, at a time when the social roles of boys and girls were being redefined in depth by the social transformations in France (most notably mixed schooling, which gradually becomes the norm in the 1970s). Examination of the readers' letters published in *Pif*, which discuss the series *Corinne et Jeannot* at length, thus makes it possible to question – albeit indirectly and imperfectly – the reception and appropriation of a series by its readers. In other words, *Corinne et Jeannot* makes for a good case study in understanding how the experience of reading the magazine can contribute to the construction of gender roles (Pasquier; Biscarrat; Ang).

Displaying Gender Roles

The album *Corinne et Jeannot* bears the trace of these editorial singularities in its very materiality. It does not include a publisher's name on the cover (as is clear from **fig. 2**).

The cover displays the faces of the two main characters in an extreme close-up, facing each other, indicates a number one – without it being clear what this numbering refers to (a series? a collection?). Furthermore, the back cover does not include any inscriptions, a sign of an unfinished project. In French-language publishing, the space on the back cover is traditionally used to present the author and promote neighbouring albums, either from the same series or from other series published in the same magazine. This formal incompleteness bears witness to the manufacturing process. The publisher, who gathers episodes previously published in the press, clearly has no idea how to make a book out of them, except, intriguingly, by mobilising the most conventional form of book publishing: the preface, a sign, perhaps, of a classical school culture.

The cover proposes a confrontation. In fact, the narrative scheme of the series is based on one-page gags revolving around two kids, Jeannot Larose and Corinne Vons. Jeannot loves Corinne, but Corinne spends her time playing nasty tricks on him – unless it is the nasty tricks Corinne plays on him that make Jeannot fall so hopelessly and desperately in love. Jeannot himself is not the only one to try to trick Corinne, but this fails systematically – and miserably.

Corinne et Jeannot therefore has a special place in the magazine. It is indeed a series that features a girl as a main character, whereas the rest of the magazine is marked by masculine heroism: *Rahan*, the prehistoric man, is the archetype of this triumphant masculinity – a masculinity which is not only based on pure strength but also on intelligence, reflection and generosity, altruism. The rest of the content is similar, with WHO doctors fighting organised crime, Indian warriors, etc. The same goes for comedy series where, at best, women are extras, as for example in *Gai-Luron*, where Belle-Lurette is essentially reduced to her physical attractiveness (she is "belle-lurette", when her companion is cheerful) and to the fact that she is systematically late.

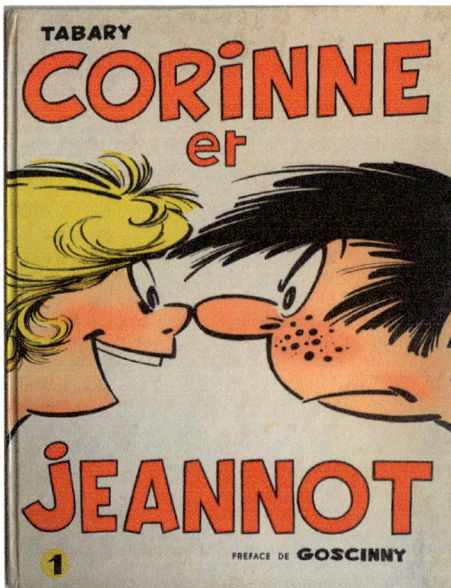

Figure 2 Jean Tabary, *Corinne et Jeannot 1*. Paris, Éditions Vaillant, 1970.

Figure 3 Jean Tabary,
Corinne et Jeannot 1.
Paris, Éditions Vaillant,
1970, p. 3.

The series thus features the confrontation of the sexes. The whole album is in fact marked by the confrontation between the passionate lover and Corinne's contortions to escape Jeannot's pressing advances. The opening page of the album (**fig. 3**) clearly places the series under the sign of a discussion – eminently problematic – of the question of consent: Jeannot is desperate to kiss Corinne, whom he pursues despite Corinne's repeated refusals. After ten frames of resistance from Corinne, in an aside that breaks the fourth wall, Jeannot addresses the readers: "Don't listen to her! She's trying to make you believe something else! In truth, I simply want to wish her a happy new year! And I will! Even if I have to spend the whole year!"[8]

In one page, this opening sequence perfectly sums up the stakes of the series: inscribed in a very French conception of the kiss as an ambiguous form, between a friendly relationship and the beginnings of a love relationship (Cahen), the series plays on the pluralities of interpretation of the same scene. Jeannot, who feels offended by Corinne's refusal to accept his kiss – which he insists is part of the custom of the New Year's kiss – is answered by Corinne's refusal. Corinne is frightened by Jeannot's insistence, but she is systematically able to thwart his ardour.

The rest of the series deals less directly with the issue of consent. However, it systematically stages the differences in perception in the ambiguous relationship between the two characters. Jeannot expresses this in "Des sentiments profonds": "If [Corinne] makes jokes to me, it's because she doesn't have the opportunity to express other feelings ... she should be put to the test". Thus, Corinne spends her time playing tricks on Jeannot, which he interprets as signs of the interest – without considering that she is trying to escape his advances, or to get back at him. In "Amour, quand tu nous tiens", Corinne has to react to the graffiti on a wall in the neighbourhood, in which Jeannot publicly professes his love for Corinne: "I want her to know how I feel about her ... and maybe she'll be nicer to me in the future". Corinne adds Jeannot's address to the graffiti so that the police officer can come get the boy and make him clean up all the graffiti in the neighbourhood. Obviously, Jeannot does not consider the possibility that Corinne is evading his insistent statement.

With slight variations, the whole series revolves around this framework: Corinne plays a trick on Jeannot; Jeannot expects Corinne to play a bad trick on him, but Corinne thwarts Jeannot's expectations and plays a more devious trick on him. A gallery of secondary characters accompanies the two characters – notably the police officer, who is convinced that Jeannot is trying to persecute Corinne, and is blind to the misfortunes of Jeannot.

One of the singularities of the series lies in the regular address to the reader: Jeannot often turns to the readers to share the fruit of his reflections: the readers are thus associated with Jeannot's pitiful machinations – which systematically turn against him. Less often, he also turns to the editor of *Pif Gadget* to get rid of Corinne, as in the episode "Corinne est un monstre! Mais...": walking down the street, the two heroes see a crying baby on a doorstep. Jeannot asks Corinne if he knows this child: yes, Corinne tells him, he lives on the corner. As Jeannot is driving the child away, Corinne rings the doorbell in front of which the baby was sitting, telling the child's mother that her child has been kidnapped. Caught by the police, Jeannot is thrown into prison. Put on a diet of bread and water, he writes to the editor of the magazine:

> Corinne is a monster! And I ask you to be kind enough to dismiss her from our Thursdays, sniff, and to find me another girlfriend! Snif, only, I would like her to be, snif, pretty like Corinne, smart like Corinne, cheerful like Corinne, cute like Corinne, snif, adorable like. (Tabary 30)

Apart from the metaleptic wink, we notice that Jeannot, to free himself from the torments that Corinne makes him suffer, asks for another girlfriend. Celibacy does not seem to be an option for the man-child. In other words, the series offers young readers an apprenticeship in toxic masculinity. Moreover, Jeannot's first concern is to have a girlfriend who is "pretty like Corinne", before any other characteristic.

In "Un amour de fou", Corinne pretends to repent for the bad things she does to Jeannot. On the telephone, she tells him of her despair and her desire to end her life. Madly worried, Jeannot runs to her house and, without any answer from Corinne, breaks down her door; Corinne, meanwhile, sets about calling the police, who arrive just as they see a madman trying to break into Corinne's house.

Thus Jean Tabary explicitly stages the troubles of masculinity in the early 1970s, and the way in which a young boy's developing virility is upset by the affirmation of powerful female figures like Corinne. In "On croit rêver" (Tabary 47), Jeannot goes to Corinne's father's house to ask for help. Eloquently, he is not asking for help from the mother, but from the father, calling for male solidarity in the face of Corinne's vileness. The father's reaction, however, is implacable. When Jeannot complains about the terrible and nasty jokes he is subjected to, the father interrupts him:

> You? A boy?! A male?! A man?! ... Listen to me, boy! I'll talk to you man to man! Of course, I could scold her, use my authority, even punish her. But your prestige as a man would still be affected! No! It is you alone who must impose your law on her! Your manhood! Your power! (Tabary 47)

This abrupt affirmation of manly values is, however, instantly defused by the water bowl the father receives on his head when opening a door, the third since he came home, and which is the work of his wife!

The series thus offers a reductive picture of heterosexual relationships, marked by asymmetrical ridicule: impotent men versus manipulative women. As a consequence, the discussion of what is at stake in male/female relationships is central to the series. The episode "La demande en marriage" published in *Pif Gadget* no. 39 (17 November 1969), and used as the final gag of the album, provides an eloquent illustration. After his visit to Corinne's parents, Jeannot is afraid of suffering the same fate as Corinne's father, and refuses to become a dominated man:

> Needless to say, given the well-known saying, "like mother like daughter", if I ever thought of marrying you, later on, it is now absolutely out of the question! To suffer such humiliations all my life? Not for me! You could beg me on your knees, Corinne! You could promise me, swear at me, but... But you are crying, Corinne!? You can cry, monster! Your crocodile tears do not impress me!! (Tabary 48)

When Jeannot sees the police officer who systematically takes Corinne's side, he is frightened: what will happen if he sees Corinne crying? It is the fear of retaliation that justifies Jeannot's backtracking – and not a regret for having pushed things too far with Corinne. He then tries to make up for it: "Listen, Corinne! Stop crying! I didn't say anything! I am marrying you! I am marrying you! I promise you that! I swear to you! Huh? You're pretty! Cute, nice...". The police officer, surprised to see Corinne crying, questions her – and Jeannot tries to defend himself, swearing to love Corinne with all his heart, and promising to marry her. To Jeannot's great incomprehension, this is the problem for Corinne: "I'm too small! I haven't finished my studies! And it's not normal to want to get married at your age!" Jeannot consequently becomes, in the eyes of the policeman, the "little monster", who thinks "about such things" that are not fit for his age. Thus Jeannot struggles to overcome his toxic relationship with Corinne. Although he regularly professes his love for her, he systematically does so out of time, and never listens to Corinne's reservations; Corinne's consent seeming secondary to him. He has no doubt that Corinne wants to move from friendship to girlfriend status, because she is "so pretty".

Tabary stages the reduction of women to their physical appearance in a highly ambiguous way. The ambiguity of the asymmetrical girl/boy relationship lies in the plurality of possible interpretations of these sketches. In the eyes of a male reader, Jeannot may well appear to be the victim of an implacable harpy pursuing him with her misdeeds. Many of the pranks Corinne plays are based on Jeannot's willingness to trust her: isn't the gift she gives him, for once, sincere? Can't she redeem herself? In "Piqué au vif" (*Pif Gadget* no. 7, 7 April 1969), he decides to systematically refuse all contact with Corinne. She offers him her hand as a sign of friendship – which Jeannot refuses to shake. In the face of her insistence, Jeannot agrees to shake her hand. But it was a cleverly prepared trick on Corinne's part to shake Jeannot's hand with a drawing pin in the palm of her hand.

In the manner of *Calvin and Hobbes*, *Corinne et Jeannot* thus stages the tough love between two children, a fool and a girl who is clearly more intelligent than him, thwarting his plans to bully her. But where Calvin's affirmation of his feelings for Suzy has to be mediated by his stuffed tiger, Jeannot's feelings for Corinne are omnipresent, even overflowing. It is Corinne's systematic refusal of Jeannot's advances that plunges him into a stubborn rage.

However, ambiguity remains central to the series, as the question of who is responsible for the misdeeds remains. Tabary seems to have more sympathy for Jeannot, but leaves the reading of the episodes open enough to be discussed. Indeed, *Corinne et Jeannot* evokes a lot of readers' letters in the pages of *Pif Gadget*.

Discussing Gender Roles: *Corinne et Jeannot* and the Readers' Mail

Letters from readers occupy an important place in the magazine – a place that is clearly greater than in other illustrated magazines published at the same time. The letters in *Pif Gadget* are published, but the magazine also mentions the names of correspondents whose letters were not reproduced in the issue. Moreover, there was a strong demand to see one's letter reproduced, as it was the subject of recurrent letters. The readers' mail is a crucial space in the magazine, occupying the second page with the editorial, and the penultimate page. Symbolically, the mail frames the reading of the illustrated magazine, and it is therefore the letters that give it meaning and participate in building a community (Esquenazi 2015). This construction of a community built through the mail goes beyond the framework of the mail. A permanent competition of riddles sent by readers, for example, shows that communication between the editorial staff and the readers is central.

As stated above, *Corinne et Jeannot* stages this communication much more than any other published series. The two characters regularly address the readers, invoking them as witnesses. In "La demande en marriage", Corinne justifies her call to the police force to the readers by referring to how Jeannot publicly humiliated her: "I'm going to teach him to humiliate me in front of the readers!" (*Pif* no. 39, 17 November 1969, p. 78). In the same way, Jeannot regularly addresses the readers, to whom he explains the dirty tricks he plays on Corinne; in "C'est horrible" (*Pif* no. 13, 19 May 1969, p. 82), Jeannot slips an old cheese into Corinne's rucksack: "Imagine what will happen when she takes that out in the middle of class!"

In a magazine that attaches such importance to readers' reactions, it is not surprising that a series explicitly addressing readers should provoke reactions, especially as it thematises the issue of child love, the learning of gender roles and the plurality of interpretations of love situations – all of which testify to the centrality of the magazine in the inculcation of social roles.

Before entering into the analysis of the mail devoted to the series, however, it is necessary to outline some (preliminary) quantitative elements. Of the first five hundred correspondents who wrote to *Pif Gadget*, over a third were girls (as well as a few women, since some mothers joined the movement). Compared to the presumption of masculinity that weighs on French comics magazines, this figure is far from negligible. But what is most striking is that only 26 per cent of girls had their letters published, compared to 35 per cent of boys. In other words, one in three male letters was published, compared to one in four for girls. Mail sent by girls was thus clearly considered less worthy of interest by a rather male editorial staff (Medioni).[9]

In the readers' letters, *Corinne et Jeannot* occupies a significant place, both in the letters published in the magazine and in the mail received by the editorial staff. In his history of the magazine, Medioni, who back then was editor-in-chief, mentions that at some stage two out of three letters received were about *Corinne et Jeannot*, which was the most popular series comic series among the nine- to fourteen-year-old readers (Medioni 378). Along with questions about gadgets and more practical questions (such as: how does *Rahan*, the prehistoric man, shave?), *Corinne et Jeannot* is one of the main topics of discussion, so much so that as early as issue 14, the editorial is devoted to the question:

> I would like to see "Corinne and Jeannot's Thursdays" [the full name of the series] change, because it is always Corinne who wins. I would like it to be Jeannot!
> This extract from a letter is no more from Pierre LASSAGNE in Paris than from Georges VILLINTE in Nice or Annie BERTHOU in Orléans, but rather from all those hundreds of letters that come to Jeannot's defence.
> But to be objective, and this is our role, we must quote the hundreds of other letters which say: "Bravo to Corinne, at last a girl who doesn't let herself be taken

advantage of and who is the strongest!" or: "Hurray for your editorial staff, at last a heroine in the newspaper. Until now, the only heroes were boys or men".

One conclusion can be drawn from all this passionate correspondence. This story is terribly appealing. Would it be the same if it was Jeannot who won one week and Corinne the other? Gone are the great discussions of the whole family gathered around Pif; gone are the bags of letters swollen to bursting point for our mailman (René – that's his name – wouldn't complain about it! and yet, you never know! Corinne manages to soften even the "toughest classes!"); no more "tussles", verbal of course! with Jean Tabary, the creator and cartoonist of "Corinne and Jeannot's Thursdays", who always ends with a "my story is a reflection of reality, that's how it is in life!" which plunges us into an abyss of reflection! Is it really so? We need to get to the bottom of the problem. Write to us (too bad for René!) Give us your opinion on this human drama![10]

A whole series of letters undertakes to defend poor Jeannot: "The poor Jeannot of M. Tabary's serial, too often the ridiculous victim of the abominable Corinne, will he never have a dazzling revenge?", asks Alain Jollain (*Pif* no. 47). The boys are not the only ones to come to Jeannot's defence; Armelle Prokop states "that Corinne's character improves, because Jeannot is too unhappy" (*Pif* no. 50). Similarly, Joëlle D. asks: "Why, in Corinne et Jeannot, is it always Corinne who makes the jokes? When in reality, we girls are adorable, while the boys" (*Pif* no. 64). Similarly, Jacqueline Lamarque "protests against Corinne, Jeannot is always subjected to stupid pranks" (*Pif* no. 49). Patrick Levy goes even further: "Corinne is a witch. But I've found a way to put an end to it. When I read it, I put Corinne in Jeannot's place and Jeannot in Corinne's place" (*Pif* no. 80). This extract is particularly striking in its use of the term "witch", summoned as a stigmatising epithet to qualify Corinne's misdeeds – while, at the same time, the feminist wave had reappropriated the figure of the witch. Above all, it testifies to the strength of resistance to the reversal of oppression that Corinne and Jeannot embody in their own way. To see the girl get away with it, even in the space of fiction, is clearly unbearable for many readers.

The letters published by the magazine in defence of Corinne are rare. Among these, there is this letter from a certain Brigitte X.:

Unlike the other readers, I say bravo to Corinne, the boys are so mean; they have to be taught a lesson from time to time. But Corinne mustn't always play nasty tricks on Jeannot. You mustn't think that we girls are devils. We are so nice. (*Pif* no. 71)

Several letters insist on asking whether Corinne and Jeannot plan to get married (*Pif* no. 79, *Pif* no. 80, in particular).

The magazine goes further, however, as the editors stage the feverish exchanges in the readers' letters, in particular by publishing fictitious letters from Jeannot as editorial material. For example, the editorial in issue 76 consists of a letter from Jeannot:

> I am writing to you in response to the many letters you have received about me. Reading our stories, some readers have a "proud opinion" of me. I would like to point out to you that I am not the poor Jeannot that they think I am, I am almost happy that Corinne plays tricks on me, it proves that she is constantly thinking of me, Sir, I love Corinne. But when she pushes the joke too far, I am able to foil her tricks. The proof is that in 1963 I managed to win and almost made a fool of her, but since my feelings towards Corinne run counter to this kind of reaction, I prefer to bow my head and suffer her.
>
> So, Sir, keep on making my stories appear as they are; one day she may realise that if I had wanted to, I could have. But if I didn't, it's because Corinne is much more than a girlfriend to me. (Pif no. 76, 3 August 1976, p. 2).

Thus, Jeannot reaffirms his agency in this fictitious letter. On a second level, it must be noted that Jeannot multiplies his attempts as he is faced with Corinne's repeated refusals. Nothing stops him, and the cruellest tricks Corinne plays on him are perceived as proof of interest. It is therefore a breviary of the toxic relationship that the series proposes in its narration as well as in the accompanying paratexts. The question of consent is completely sidestepped.

The readers' mail and the editorials are particularly rich instances of discussion of the series' content, as they offer a singular reading of the series. The most fascinating case is undoubtedly the editorial in issue 82, devoted to the start of the school year (**fig. 4**). Corinne and Jeannot both lament the announced return to school. Corinne, who is smarter, as shown here through her ability to anticipate the start of the school year, has already found a solution: she sends an electronic doll in her place. Jeannot is astonished that such a ploy is possible, and deplores the fact that there are no similar toys for boys. Corinne's reply is scathing: "Do the same with a monkey, Jeannot! I doubt your teacher will notice anything!" A monkey to embody a boy, and a doll to take the place of a little girl: it is difficult to explain more clearly how Corinne and Jeannot function as a metaphor for gendered relationships...

These mail exchanges, however, lie at the intersection of a discussion of gender roles with young readers, and the marketing construction of the series as an arena for debate. The magazine's editorial staff abundantly staged the conversation sparked by the series, passing on the spirited defence of one or the criticism of the other. In issue 80, for example, little Gina Troni writes to the magazine: "I like all the series except *Corinne et Jeannot*. I think you make Jeannot look too much like an idiot, a coward. Corinne always has the upper

Figure 4 *Pif*, no. 82, 14 September 1970.

hand. If at least, from time to time, it was Jeannot, it would be more fun". This marketing construction of the discursive object undoubtedly reaches its climax with the release of the album in 1970. The advertisements surrounding this release, as discussed, maintain this ambiguous dynamic of a thwarted couple and children playing at being a couple. The editorial paratext abounds in this sense, for example, in the editorial of issue 98:

> I don't quite understand anymore!
>
> Explain it to me!
>
> Not a day goes by without multiple protests reaching me concerning the Corinne-Jeannot Affair (for it has taken on the proportions of a real affair).
>
> Some complain about the deceitful, devious, heartless character of this abominable little monster called Corinne.
>
> Others pity this stupid, victim, martyr, sufferer, this "poor" little fellow Jeannot.
>
> But (and this is where I don't quite understand) both SOME and OTHERS are unanimous in considering this comics as a real masterpiece, Corinne and Jeannot as a real couple that would have to be invented if they didn't exist!
>
> Let's be frank! We like them both. Jeannot without his abominable Corinne is not Jeannot! And Corinne without a little bit of Jeannot to eat, she's not Corinne! We like them as they are! And it is no coincidence that the album Corinne et Jeannot, which has just been published, is a triumph with those who complain and those who complain.

The dynamic of the controversy thus fuels the construction of the series' editorial interest. The cover of the album with which I started my chapter plays on this dynamic by depicting in very close-up the confrontation between the two characters: a hilarious Corinne, and a scowling Jeannot (**fig. 1**).

In the midst of the second feminist wave (Thornham), *Corinne et Jeannot* testifies to the strength of the backlash that can manifest itself in the pages of children's and teenage comics. Under the guise of featuring a more assertive female character, Tabary depicts the emergence of feminism in a conservative way. Corinne is a horrible harpy, since she refuses to accept Jeannot, and this characterisation is not far removed from the hysterics that form the background of anti-feminist stereotypes (Bard). However, the series is more complex than this first reading, for two reasons. The first is the age of the protagonists: by depicting this scene of sexual relations at the level of children, Tabary complicates the dynamics of the couple, which plays with the codes of romantic relationships, but in a distanced way. The interest of the series lies in its capacity to provoke discussions on inculcating gender roles, in the way that television series have been able to provoke discussions on the learning of feelings in adolescence (Pasquier). More importantly, the vigorous critical reception of the series is a testament to the ability of readers to appropriate the series for personal relationships (Hoggart). As such, the series constitutes an arena for discussion of gender issues and boy/girl relations within a weekly illustrated magazine for young people, allowing for diverse readings of the respective roles of girls and boys.

Notes

1. A neologism designating someone who is anti-advertising.
2. For a critical discussion of that framework, see MacLeod.
3. The "Matrimoine" project, which started in 2021, aims to address this under-representation of women in the history of comics. See https://www.mshparisnord.fr/event/seminaire-matrimoine-de-la-bd/2022-03-18/.
4. To date, there are relatively few works devoted to French-speaking female comics artists. Among the exceptions is the publication of a dossier devoted to girls' comics in the magazine *Neuvième Art* (Groensteen), the pioneering work of Blanche Delaborde (Delaborde) or the study by Mira Falardeau (Falardeau).
5. To give an idea of the popularity of the phrase, a search for "calife à la place du calife" returned 55,800 results on Google in December 2021.
6. In this respect, I would like to thank Sébastien Laffage-Cosnier for his invitation to explore the corpus of publications linked to the *Pif* galaxy, following on from Henri Garric and Jean Vigreux who had organised a series of events dedicated to the series *Pif*.
7. The CGT is the main French labour union.

8. All translations are my own.
9. In the absence of editorial archives, it is difficult to assess precisely the proportion of male and female staff in the magazine. However, all the histories written on the matter (mostly by former employees) mention male-only editorial management, and women seem to be relegated to secretarial and correction tasks.
10. "Corinne ou Jeannot ?", editorial, *Pif Gadget* no. 14, p. 2.

Bibliography

Bard, Christine. *Un siècle d'antiféminisme*. Fayard, 1999.

Biscarrat, Laetitia. "Le genre de la reception". *Communication. Information médias théories pratiques*, no. 33, vol. 2, Dec. 2015, https://doi.org/10.4000/communication.5775. Accessed 1 June 2022.

Boillat, Alain et al. *Case, Strip, Action ! Les Feuilletons En Bandes Dessinées Dans Les Magazines Pour La Jeunesse (1946–1953)*. Infolio, 2016.

Cahen, Gérald, editor. *Le baiser : Premières leçons d'amour*. Autrement, 1997.

Couderc, Marie-Anne. *Bécassine inconnue*. CNRS éditions, 2001.

Dayez, Hugues. *Le Duel Tintin-Spirou : Entretiens Avec Les Auteurs de l'âge d'or de La BD Belge*. Luc Pire, 1997.

Delaborde, Blanche. *Le magazine Ah ! Nana: 1976–1978*. Université Strasbourg II, 2001.

Falardeau, Mira. *Femmes et humour*. Presses de l'Université Laval, 2014.

Flinn, Margaret C. *Drawing (in) the Feminine: Women and Bande Dessinée*. Ohio State University Press, forthcoming.

Gibson, Mel. *Remembered Reading: Memory, Comics and Post-War Constructions of British Girlhood*. Leuven University Press, 2015.

Girard, Quentin et al. "Festival d'Angoulême, la parité malgré eux". *Libération*, 6 Jan. 2016, https://www.liberation.fr/livres/2016/01/06/festival-d-angouleme-la-parite-malgre-eux_1424751/. Accessed 1 Aug. 2022.

Groensteen, Thierry, editor. "La Bande Dessinée Des Filles". *Neuvième Art*, no. 6, 2001, pp. 32–73.

Guilhaumou, Jacques, and Geneviève Dermenjian, editors. "La Bande Dessinée : Un Nouveau Chantier Pour l'histoire Des Femmes". *Bulletin d'information – Association Pour Le Développement de l'histoire Des Femmes et Du Genre*, 2006, pp. 21–39, http://www.mnemosyne.asso.fr/uploads/Journee-etudes/2005/BD_dermenjian_guillaumou.pdf. Accessed 1 Aug. 2022.

Hoggart, Richard. *The Uses of Literacy: Aspects of Working-Class Life, with Special References to Publications and Entertainments*. Chatto and Windus, 1957.

Kohn, Jessica. "Women Cartoonists, a New Avenue for Understanding a Little-Known Profession". *Drawing (in) the Feminine: Women and Bande Dessinée*, edited by Margaret C. Flinn. Ohio State University Press, Forthcoming.

Lesage, Sylvain. *Ninth Art. Bande Dessinée, Books and the Transformation of Mass Culture.* Palgrave Macmillan, 2022.

—. *Publier La Bande Dessinée. Les Éditeurs Franco-Belges et l'album, 1950–1990.* Presses de l'Enssib, 2018.

—. "Une bande dessinée adulte ? Usages et mésusages de la légitimation". *Belphégor. Littérature populaire et culture médiatique*, no. 17, 1, Mar. 2019, https://doi.org/10.4000/belphegor.1607. Accessed 1 June 2022.

MacLeod, Catriona. *Invisible Presence: The Representation of Women in French-Language Comics.* Intellect Books, 2021.

Medioni, Richard. *'Jean-Pierre', 'Les Petits bonhommes', 'Le Jeune camarade', 'Le Jeune patriote', 'Mon camarade', 'Vaillant', 'Pif gadget': l'histoire complète.* Vaillant collector, 2012.

Ory, Pascal. *Le Petit Nazi Illustré : Une Pédagogie Hitlérienne En Culture Française: 'Le Téméraire' (1943–1944).* Nautilus, 2002.

Pasquier, Dominique. "'Chère Hélène'. Les Usages Sociaux Des Séries Collège". *Réseaux*, vol. 13, no. 70, 1995, pp. 9–39, https://doi.org/10.3406/reso.1995.2665. Accessed 1 June 2022.

Rannou, Maël. *Pif Gadget et Le Communisme. 1969–1993, Un Hebdomadaire de BD et Ses Liens Avec Le Parti Communiste Français.* PLG, 2022.

Reyns-Chikuma, Chris. "De Bécassine à Yoko Tsuno : entre stéréotypes, oublis et renaissance. Réflexions sur les personnages féminins et leurs auteur(e)s en bande dessinée". *Alternative francophone*, vol. 1, no. 9, Feb. 2016, pp. 155–170, https://doi.org/10.29173/af27279. Accessed 1 June 2022.

Roubaud-Quashie, Guillaume. "La jeunesse dure longtemps. Quarante ans d'historiographie des organisations de jeunesse communistes françaises". *Cahiers d'histoire. Revue d'histoire critique*, no. 116–117, July 2011, pp. 195–227, https://doi.org/10.4000/chrhc.2396. Accessed 1 June 2022.

Sellier, Geneviève. *Masculine Singular: French New Wave Cinema.* Duke University Press, 2008.

Tabary, Jean. *Corinne et Jeannot 1.* Éditions Vaillant, 1970.

Thiesse, Anne-Marie. *Le roman du quotidien : lecteurs et lectures populaires à la Belle-Époque.* Le chemin vert, 1984.

Thornham, Sue. "Second Wave Feminism". *The Routledge Companion to Feminism and Postfeminism*, 2nd ed. Routledge, 2001.

Warner, Michael. "Publics and Counterpublics". *Public Culture*, vol. 14, no. 1, Jan. 2002, pp. 49–90, https://doi.org/10.1215/08992363-14-1-49. Accessed 1 June 2022.

Chapter 6

The Ambivalence of Girlhood and Motherhood in A Girl-and-Her-Dog Comics Series: *Margot & Oscar Pluche / Sac à Puces*

Benoît Glaude

Although this chapter does not draw on reader-response criticism, it follows on from the previous one, by Sylvain Lesage, in the sense that it studies the questioning of gender roles and norms in a corpus of French-language comics that appeared in the children's press. This chapter concerns a comics series published between 1990 and 2010 by Belgian authors De Brab (Carine De Brabanter), Falzar (François D'Hondt) and Zidrou (Benoît Drousie). The series, initially titled *Margot & Oscar Pluche*, then *Sac à Puces*, focuses on an eight-year-old girl called Margot and the stray dog she adopts clandestinely, without her parents' consent. A child from a large lower-middle-class family, the central character plays the roles of daughter, sister and friend. This chapter will analyse the representation of Margot through the evolution of her relationship with the dog she calls initially Oscar Pluche, then Sac à Puces [Fleabag]. The first section will describe the publication context of the comics series. Before being released in albums by Casterman and then by Dupuis publishing houses, the comics were pre-published in two Belgian periodicals, targeting a mixed youth audience, and which had French and Dutch editions: *Dauphin / Zonnestraal* and *Spirou / Robbedoes*. Focusing on the French-speaking albums, the second section will link them to a genre, family comics, that is rooted in Flemish comic strip (such as *Jommeke*;

see Chapter 9 for an interview about girls in this comics series). The next two parts will describe Margot's social interactions, first with her large family, then through her exclusive relationship with her dog. The conclusion will show how this comics series combines graphic reproduction with social reproduction.

Between Children's Press and Comics Publishing

This series is symptomatic of the evolution of the representation of girlhood in French-language comics for children, and was published in a context that favoured this evolution. And yet, if the production of albums experienced a strong growth in the French-speaking book market in the 1980s, a journalist wrote in 1985 that "the stories aimed at teenagers and adults are mainly those that are favoured today by most publishers"[1] (Rouyet 9). He explained that "this is somewhat normal, insofar as comics have had to fight for a long time against the tendency to confine them to the role of a consumer object for the youngest. So, it takes its revenge [...] and forgets the children". He continued by mentioning the intergenerational comics series of *Spirou* magazine's publisher, but he conceded that "Dupuis does not address the very young comics lovers". For this audience of children, the comics critic could only recommend the *Yakari* albums published by Casterman.

This was to ignore the creativity of the youth press. Admittedly, many magazines that traditionally pre-published comics disappeared – such as *Pilote* in 1989, as well as *Pif Gadget* and *Hello BD* (formerly *Tintin*) in 1993 – although *Spirou* managed to maintain itself by targeting readers aged eleven to fifteen, leaving the younger children's market to the timeless *Mickey*. Beside comics weeklies, other youth magazines published innovative comics that had several points in common. First, created for magazines, they did not necessarily undergo editorial development, and when they did, they maintained the link with their magazines of origin. For instance, the short comics stories of *Tom-Tom & Nana*, a series created by Jacqueline Cohen and Bernadette Després for the first issue of *J'aime lire* in 1977, which the publishing house Bayard issued a number of collections from 1985 onwards, but which remained attached to the literary magazine. It is worth noting, second, that these magazines for young readers welcomed works by comics authors, including female authors – shortly before Cohen and Després in *J'aime lire*, Nicole Claveloux had opened the way in *Okapi* – at a time when the profession was far from reaching parity. Third, these works stand out for the range of topics they allowed themselves to deal with. As they were independent from the publishing houses specialised in comics, these graphic narratives were freer to follow the innovations of children's literature. A fourth common feature of these comics is that they did not exclusively feature male heroes.

Conversely, the Belgian scriptwriter Denis Lapière (quoted in Daele and Glesener 9–10) deplored, in a 1993 interview, the difficulty of publishing an ambitious work for young readers with a comics publisher: "we are condemned to do third-rate 'tout public' [suitable for all audiences] comics and say they are aimed at children". He continued:

> When we see what exists as topics and as stories told in children's books, what one dares to write in these books, we say to ourselves that comics have a long way to go! Except for comics like *Jojo*, *Jimmy Boy*, *Margot & Oscar Pluche*, *Docteur Poche*, *Billy the Cat*.[2]

However, by mentioning only series centred on male heroes – with the exception of *Margot & Oscar Pluche* – Denis Lapière neglected the feminisation of the characters of the new comics for children. This is precisely why Carine De Brabanter (quoted in Gavo and Dutailly 16) decided to embrace a career as a cartoonist:

> In fact, when I was a child, as soon as I could read, I read comics. [...] What made me want to create comics was that I couldn't relate to them. Because boys could identify with anything they wanted, but not girls. [...] Natacha, for example, is an inflatable doll [...] Yoko Tsuno has no flesh, she's a paper woman [...] In short, I could only identify with Mouche, in *La Patrouille des Castors*. He is a little boy and I thought: "He can do the job, in a pinch". [...] I didn't want to be either Bianca Castafiore or Tante Sidonia [in *Tintin* and *Suske en Wiske*].

The editorial trajectory of *Margot & Oscar Pluche / Sac à Puces* is an example of the renewal of comics for young readers that took place outside the specialised editorial field. The two heroes were the star characters in the weekly magazines *Dauphin / Zonnestraal*, which were (and still are today) broadcast in primary schools, respectively in the French-speaking and Dutch-speaking parts of Belgium. In the 1990s the editions in two languages were designed by a bilingual editorial staff (Ghesquière 37). This educational magazine, part of the catalogue of the Catholic publishing house Averbode, was aimed at pupils in the third and fourth grades of primary education, aged eight to ten. If we take (at random) the no. 29 of *Dauphin* in 1996, we find on the twenty-four pages, two pages of a to-be-continued comic strip (an episode of *Yakari*, from Casterman publishing house), and two pages presenting the contents of the issue, animated by Margot and Oscar Pluche, written by Zidrou and Falzar, with original illustrations by De Brab and Godi. The latter cartoonist was authoring with Zidrou the bestselling series *Ducobu* in another weekly of Averbode, *Tremplin / Zonneland*. In addition to these comics, he drew a new flea of Oscar Pluche in *Dauphin* every week. There is also a double-page spread contributed by the readers, entitled "The good ideas of the week" ("Les bonnes idées de la semaine" 16–17). Children were invited to send their announcements, riddles, jokes, poems and drawings to Margot and Oscar Pluche, to the address of the Averbode publishing house. Several readers' productions (**fig. 1**), including a "flea" in the manner of Godi, make direct reference to the comics heroes.

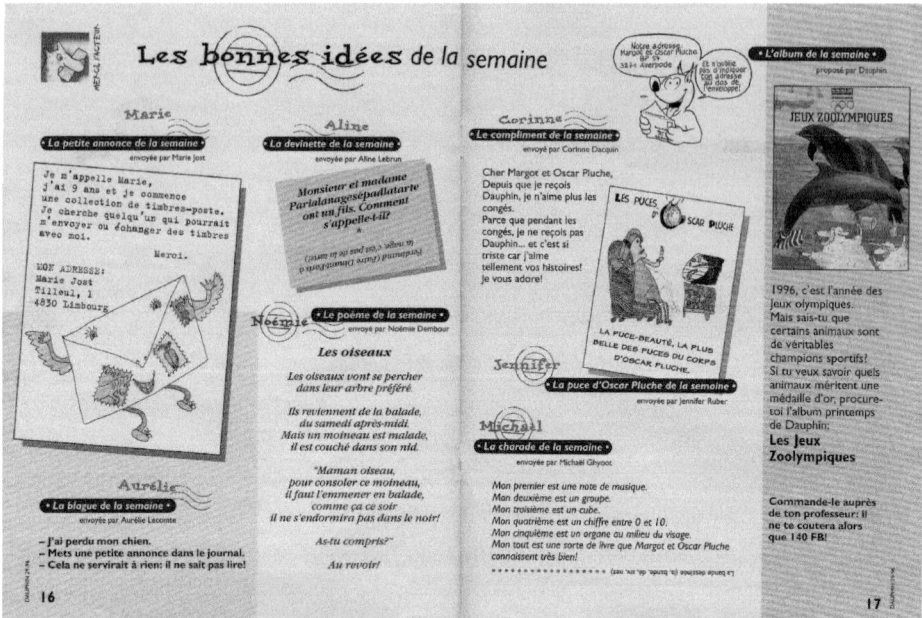

Figure 1 "Les bonnes idées de la semaine", *Dauphin* 29, 1996, pp. 16–17. Reproduced with kind permission from Éditions Averbode.

Along with the pre-publication in *Dauphin / Zonnestraal*, six albums were published by Casterman, a Belgian publishing house unrelated to Averbode. Although it was best known, at the time, for the adult graphic novels that it drew from the magazine *(À Suivre)*, Casterman had a long history with children's books. Paradoxically, it did not realise the innovative potential of some of its series (such as *Yakari* and *Margot & Oscar Pluche*) for young readers. Among other grievances (see Gavo and Dutailly 17), the limited sales of the latter series of albums in the 1990s prompted the authors to continue it with a competing publishing house.

Under a title refocused on the dog, renamed *Sac à Puces / Vlooienbaal*,[3] the series continued into the 2000s in Dupuis's widely broadcasted weekly comics magazine *Spirou / Robbedoes*. According to Carine De Brabanter (quoted in Gavo and Dutailly 17), the change of editor allowed for the renewal of contact with the readers, thanks to the pre-publication of the comics in *Spirou*, since they were no longer published in *Dauphin*. When it serialised the first comics story, *Super maman* [Super Mom], which relates, from Margot's point of view, the arrival of a newborn in her already large family, the magazine hailed the event by inviting its readers to choose the baby's sex and first name. The editorial staff received nearly four hundred ballots and proclaimed "It's a girl! She's going to be called Marine!" ("C'est une fille!" 17) The first albums were published in the "Tout public" [For all audiences] series, intended for family readership. A few years later, Dupuis tried to segment its range of publications for young readers by targeting age groups. Two comic book series were created in the first decade of 2000, under the co-direction of Denis Lapière and Laurence Van Tricht: "the Puceron [Aphid] series, to be read alone from 3 years old" and "the Punaise [Shield bug] series, to be read alone from 6 years old", in which the *Sac à Puces* albums were reintegrated. According to Denis Lapière (quoted in Mixhel 52),

> the Punaise comics are made for children from six or seven years old, who are not yet great readers. It is very important that the story is embodied by the drawing and not only by the text. In Punaise, all the themes are tackled [...], all that makes Life.

Even if the publisher has now abandoned its children's comics series, others remain elsewhere, such as "Mille bulles" [One thousand bubbles] from L'École des loisirs, fed by the catalogues of Casterman, Dargaud, Delcourt, Dupuis and Le Lombard. Significantly, it has reissued the first two episodes of *Sac à Puces* (vol. II1 and II2).[4] It was a return to the roots of the series, since it imports themes from the children's picture books of which L'École des loisirs constituted a prestigious catalogue.

A Franco-Belgian Family Comics

One could be tempted to classify the *Margot & Oscar Pluche / Sac à Puces* series, featuring a large family, in the family strip genre. A French-speaking model of the genre is the still ongoing series *Boule & Bill* (see Capart; Delisle), created in 1959 by the Belgian comics artist Roba. Centred on a fusional boy-and-his-dog duo, it has featured, through hundreds of one-page gags, a limited number of secondary characters gravitating around a stereotypical middle-class family, composed of a housewife, an office-worker father, a seven-year-old boy (Boule) and their English cocker spaniel (Bill). Repeating the same eventless ordinary situation over and over again, the micro-stories are entirely devoted to a humorous objective, without generating any evolution of the characters. The success of this series and its successors – especially in the magazine *Spirou* where it appeared, like *Cédric*, *Le Petit Spirou*, *Kid Paddle* and many others, all centred on the family life of a little boy – has never wavered. Although these series have not been successful on the English-speaking book market, they belong to a comic strip genre that is not local. This is the family strip, developing short-length gags pre-published in the press before being collected in volumes, focusing on daily family life.

In contrast to this transnational genre, the *Margot & Oscar Pluche / Sac à Puces* series presents a family model that is unusual in French-language comics. The Duchêne are a large family from the lower middle class, with a father who is a teacher and later a nursery director, involved in the education of his seven children, even though the mother assumes the traditional role of housewife.[5] They are the owners of a modest terraced house in a small town that could be Belgian or French, but they cannot afford to replace their old estate car, which is perpetually broken down. At the centre of the comics series is a tandem of an eight-year-old girl and a street dog who have everyday adventures, almost always in the neighbourhood where the family home is located. Most of the stories are about forty pages long, the length of a standard album in the Franco-Belgian comic book industry, but two[6] of the fifteen volumes contain shorter stories. Although the pitch of the series – a little girl hiding a dog in her bedroom – generates burlesque situations, the adventure plots are told in a serious, rather than comic, mode.

This French-speaking series is less related to the American tradition of the family strip than to a model that is popular in the Dutch-speaking part of Belgium, but whose translations are poorly exported, except for a few series (such as *Suske en Wiske*, *Jommeke* or *De Kiekeboes*) broadcast in French, especially in the French-speaking part of the country. According to Michel De Dobbeleer (35), "the present-day comics market in Flanders remains dominated by mainstream long-running series commonly known as *familiestrips* [...] that have been widely read from soon after the Second World War". The Belgian comics scholar defines these comics series by their high productivity, since they grow by about two hundred comics pages a year, in the hands of small studios, even if the name of one founding artist still dominates the creations. As they were historically pre-published in the press, the stories still bear traces of the serial storytelling, even if they are now associated with the Franco-Belgian album format (44 comics pages, A4 format, full colour). This is why Michel De Dobbeleer proposes to call those series "family comics" (38) – as opposed to gag-based and press-related "family strips" (39–40) – whose albums contain one long narrative per book, "involving a central (surrogate) family, or at least departing from a family-life situation" (40), and combining "quick-superficial humour and an overarching adventure plot" (41). If the French-speaking series *Margot & Oscar Pluche / Sac à Puces* belongs to the family comics genre, it differs from the *familiestrips* by several features: a lower productivity (about forty-four pages per year), a different relationship to seriality, the children of the Duchêne family growing up (the youngest, Émile, learns to speak; the eldest, Julot, meets a girlfriend, etc.), and an unusual thematic ambition. Although the series tells of everyday adventures, it deals with topics such as the social life of older people (I3 and II8), the balance between family life and professional success for a woman (I4), the arrival of a new child among brothers and sisters (II1), the citizen mobilisation of the youngest (II2), the hospitalisation of a child (II4), the separation of a couple (II7), or the death of a close relative (II8), which had not been dealt with before, or only to a limited extent, in children's comics published in Belgium, both in the French and Dutch languages.

Yet this is a classic girl-and-her-dog narrative, like many others in children's literature,[7] linked to the vast tradition of boy-and-his-dog fictions. The very first short story, relating the meeting of Margot and Oscar Pluche, had been pre-published in 1990 in *Jet*, a bench test for young authors;[8] it was redrawn and shortened from five to four pages, for the album. This short narrative presents a final scene, which was to become recurrent in the series, where the dog, having entered the house secretly, joins Margot in her bedroom, after which they talk and laugh while falling asleep together in the girl's bed. In this first story, the dog is not yet anthropomorphised: it moves only on all fours, and it barks and growls, except in the denouement of the narrative. In a panel of the original version that was deleted in the album, Margot wonders, "You... You talk?", and Oscar answers, "Of course... But not to anyone!" (Boulet and De Brab 11) This dog illustrates the ambivalence of anthropomorphisation in Franco-Belgian comics, which was already complex in the *Boule & Bill* comics series (see Delisle about this complexity), in which the dog Bill cannot speak. From one album to another, Oscar Pluche / Sac à Puces wavers between two of the categories of anthropomorphisation distinguished by the animation scholar Stéphane Collignon (47), as a "cartoony" pet living in a human environment, though "endowed with a human psyche" and "the ability of speech", and as an nonhuman character who is "fully anthropomorphised" (52). Indeed, its morphology can, at times, be distorted to the point of making it look like a human child, when it walks on two paws and uses its forelimbs as hands, or even when (in vol. II6) it wears clothes.

In the first short story, before the girl knows that the dog talks, she gives it a name, Oscar Pluche, as if it were a human child. The name also links it to toys. French-speaking Belgian children use the word *pluche* (in this pronunciation) to refer to a *peluche* [cuddly toy], which is an animal made of plush, such as an *ours en peluche* [teddy bear].[9] The dog is therefore introduced as a playmate for Margot, who immediately develops a special relationship with it. By adopting the dog, without being able to expect any help from her family, since she disobeys her parents by making this choice, Margot feels invested with a responsibility towards her friend. She develops a protective relationship with the dog, evident in their role playing, for example, when she plays the prehistoric mother watching over her "baby mammoth" (vol. I1, p. 26). On the title page of the album *Super maman* (vol. II1), Margot is carrying Sac à Puces, who is sucking on a pacifier, in her arms, echoing a scene from the episode where she is babying the dog, saying "Don't cry, baby. Here's your pacifier! Sleep well, my big baby love!" (vol. II1, p. 27) Margot not only mothers the dog in their role playing but also in their daily life, for example when she organises the clandestine convalescence of the dog, which has a broken leg, in the house of the Duchêne family (in vol. I2). Of course, Oscar Pluche brings something to her in exchange for her care: unfailing friendship. Nevertheless, the relationship between the girl and her male canine companion is indicative of the relationship between women and men in this series.

A Daughter and Sister in a Large Family

The staging of a large family was rarer in French-language comics in the 1990s than in children's literature and on the small screen. De Brab, Falzar and Zidrou's series appeared in a decade when television series, even if they were still far from achieving gender parity among their characters, began to show mostly collective mixed protagonists, whereas they had been dominated, since the 1950s, by solitary male heroes (Sepulchre 94). For a first approach to the gendered characterisation of the characters in *Margot & Oscar Pluche / Sac à Puces*, I borrow a traditional method of analysis from television studies, which has been tested and criticised by the narratologist Sarah Sepulchre, and which is based on a dichotomous classification, predefining "rather male" and "rather female" character traits.

Let us observe a page of presentation of the Duchêne family[10] (**fig. 2**), published in *Spirou* magazine in 2000, reproduced in most of the albums of the *Sac à Puces* series (vol. II2–7), then transcribed and completed in the introduction of the chidren's novel *Pique-nique panique* [Picnic panic] (Falzar 5–7), a novelisation of the comics series published in 2004. The title of the page published in *Spirou*, "Viens chez moi, j'habite chez une copine..." [Come home, I live at a friend's place...], echoes that of a song by Renaud Séchan, evoking an idle young man who spends his life seducing women while bunking temporarily at friends' houses. We find some of these traits in Sac à Puces, who is greedy, dirty, fugitive and kept (by Margot). The introduction to the novel, as well as the comments in the (pseudo-)photographic portrait of the family, are uttered by the dog. He attributes a variable number of qualities to each member of the family. Three of them have at least four character traits: Margot is loyal in friendship, committed, secretive and indifferent to her dog's hygiene, while her parents are (in the dog's view) authoritarian, united, house-proud and dull, but considerate of their children nonetheless. Then there are three siblings with three qualities: the baby, Marine, "has the pleasant odours of soap, milk and poo"; the youngest, Émile, is grumpy and stubborn and does not express affection (except to Marine); and finally, the oldest sister, Sandra, is a mediator, a peacemaker and a know-it-all. The three remaining children are the least qualified: Josette is cheerful and boisterous, the eldest, Julot, is greedy and driven by an exclusive passion (video games), as is his brother Lucien (role playing).

If we compare the portraits of the children of the Duchêne family with the list of supposedly masculine or feminine traits of fictional characters on television (Sepulchre 96), we realise that the three brothers, Lucien, Julot and Émile, are defined by qualities associated with the televisual representation of the male gender (respectively, strength denoted by appetite, passion for fighting games and unawareness of others' feelings), while Sandra, tactful, and Josette, childish, are defined by qualities associated with the representation of the female gender in television fiction. Margot has as many qualities assigned to the two genders (altruism supposedly feminine and toughness supposedly masculine)

Figure 2 De Brab, Falzar, Zidrou and Veerle Swinnen. "Viens chez moi, j'habite chez une copine…" *Spirou*, no. 3225, 2000, p. 10. *Sac à Puces* by De Brab, Zidrou and Falzar, reproduced with the authors' permission.

as character traits not assigned to a specific gender (secretive, faithful in friendship), just as Sac à Puces has qualities supposedly feminine (passivity, weakness, dependence) and others, supposedly masculine (appetite, no fear of getting his paws dirty). We can conclude that the portraits of Margot's brothers and sisters are more polarised than those of the hero tandem, that the latter are more finely characterised than the former and that Margot avoids the polarisation of fictional gender representations. As far as the dog is concerned, beyond the assimilation of male and female stereotypes, the essential issue is anthropomorphisation. His problem is less to be male or female than to be dog or human.

This cursory approach to the system of characters in *Margot & Oscar Pluche / Sac à Puces* is not satisfactory, on the one hand, because the use of a dichotomous model contributes "to an essentialization of [so-called] male and female characteristics" (Sepulchre 104), and on the other hand, because the study of a (pseudo-)family photo taken in 2000 does not account for the evolution of the characters over the whole existence of the series (1990–2010). The remainder of this study will take an alternative route, focusing on the relationships between characters, that is, on their functional characterisation – the role of characters in the narrative, particularly through their verbal interactions – even though individual properties such as age and gender will be taken into account.

To describe the fifteen albums as a whole, I calculated the average number of speech units issued or received by each member of the Duchêne family[11] in the first four comics pages of the fifteen albums of *Margot & Oscar Pluche / Sac à Puces* (**fig. 3**). I take the speech bubble as the unit of measurement for the speakers' utterances. I assume that the first four comics pages of each album, which average forty-four pages, set up the main characters, especially for readers who may begin reading the series with any album. For most of them, which contain a single long story, these initial pages constitute a narrative incipit,

Character	Gender	Age	Nb of incipits where the character is present	Avg nb of monologues	Avg nb of issued communications	Avg nb of communications to everyone present	Avg nb of conversation partners individually contacted	Avg nb of received communications	Avg nb of conversation partners who have contacted the character	Nb of incipits where the character produces bubble(s)
Marine	F	baby	9	0.0	0.4	0.1	0.3	2.8	0.4	4
Emile	M	2	12	0.0	1.0	0.0	0.6	0.8	0.4	6
Josette	F	4	13	0.6	1.6	0.3	0.8	1.7	1.0	8
Lucien	M	6	13	0.1	0.9	0.1	0.6	0.6	0.6	6
Margot	F	8.5	15	0.1	7.6	1.3	1.9	6.2	2.2	14
Sandra	F	12	13	0.0	2.6	0.5	1.4	1.3	0.8	9
Julot	M	13	14	0.0	1.2	0.1	0.9	1.4	0.9	8
Mother	F	adult	14	0.4	3.4	0.2	1.8	3.5	1.9	14
Father	M	adult	14	0.6	6.4	0.9	2.2	4.5	2.0	13
Oscar	M	dog	15	1.4	3.0	0.1	0.7	3.9	1.2	13

Figure 3 Average numbers of speech units issued or received by each member of the Duchêne family, in the first four comics pages of the fifteen albums of *Margot & Oscar Pluche / Sac à Puces*.

setting out the initial situation, but for two albums (vol. I1 and II5), the first four pages cover most of a short story. In all the cases, the main characters enter the scene in these pages and receive an enunciative qualification, which I will study from a quantitative point of view.

The table (**fig. 3**) shows the average numbers of bubbles issued or received by each member of the Duchêne family, including the dog, in the fifteen albums' incipits of *Margot & Oscar Pluche / Sac à Puces*. Quantitatively, I distinguish a main group of speakers composed of Margot, her dog and her parents, and a secondary group formed by the other children. The irregular presence of the brothers and sisters is amplified by their greater tendency to be mute: the baby, Marine, and the boys, Émile, Lucien and Julot, remain mute in one episode out of two where they appear, but the girls Josette and Sandra are less often mute than they are. All these secondary speakers have a stereotypical enunciative portrait. For example, the little Émile starts to speak from the seventh album (vol. II1) to address almost exclusively his parents, to whom he complains in the third person (saying, for instance, "Nân! Mimile veut pas bébé!" [Nah! Mimie no want no baby!]). A more obvious example is the little Josette, who, of all the siblings except Margot, receives on average the most communications and from the most different interlocutors, but it is often the same reproving injunction: "Arrête, Josette!" [Stop, Josette!]. The same separation between primary and secondary speakers is found in the attribution of inner speech. The sixty pages analysed contain only one thought bubble, but some characters speak for themselves in two different ways: on the one hand, Josette and Lucien develop a solitary speech by living centred on their own childish world (they play aloud alone or sing solo at the top of their voices); on the other hand, Margot, her dog and her two parents tend to say out loud what they think, which gives them an intellectual activity that the secondary characters seem to lack.

Regarding communications – in other words, speech bubbles addressed to an addressee – the parents naturally play important receiver roles: they receive many communications from various interlocutors. However, the mother has a weaker enunciator profile than her husband and their daughter Margot. The latter two characters stand out strongly from the others in terms of the amount of communication they send out, particularly the amount of talk they deliver to everyone present – which makes them the main leaders of groups (i.e. the family, in the case of the father, but the siblings or the group of friends, in the case of Margot). Moreover, of all the Duchêne family, Margot is the champion of reception: she receives the most communication and is contacted by the greatest number of different interlocutors. This can be explained by several reasons: she is the one who expresses herself the most, and she therefore provokes more verbal interactions; moreover, she is the only one to discuss with a group of friends outside the family, and finally she is the only human to whom Oscar / Sac à Puces speaks. Quantitatively, the enunciative portrait of the dog is different from all the others: he soliloquises more than everyone else and emits less verbal communication than he receives. Many characters address him, as is the case with the baby Marine, without expecting a verbal response.

Compared to my first approach of the system of characters, this one confirms the separation of the enunciative portraits, between (1) the dog, (2) Margot and her parents and (3) her brothers and sisters. The latter have more stereotypical verbal interactions and are devoid of inner speech (except Josette and Lucien). The sisters Sandra and Josette are less often silent than their brothers. Without being talkative (except with her canine confidant), Margot has an enunciative profile as complete as that of her father: they are verbal leaders who have an inner life, who speak a lot and to whom everyone else speaks. Although the mother also has many conversational partners, she speaks less than her daughter Margot and her husband, and she is also less spoken to. From an enunciative point of view, the patriarch occupies the position of the head of household, even if this modern father is involved in the education of the children.

The Girl-and-Her-Dog Relationship

I move on to an analysis of the evolution of the two main characters, the girl Margot and her dog Oscar Pluche / Sac à Puces, through the relationship they have. Is it a girl-and-her-dog series with a couple of inseparable heroes, or is it the adventures of a little girl accompanied by a nonhuman sidekick, or is it a funny animal comic strip centred on a dog? As announced by the title of the very first album, *Sac à puces*, and as confirmed by the change of name of the dog, linked to the change of title of the series, from *Margot & Oscar*

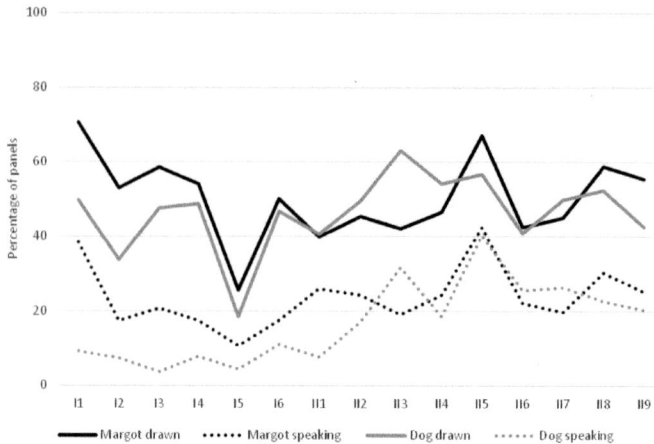

Figure 4 Proportion of panels where Margot and her dog are drawn, and of those where they speak, in each of the fifteen albums of *Margot & Oscar Pluche / Sac à Puces*.

Pluche to *Sac à Puces*, this character acquired, little by little, a prominent heroic stature. For all that, the narration does not refocus on the animal.[12] For an overall view (**fig. 4**), I have counted in each of the fifteen albums the proportion of panels where the girl is drawn (at least partially) and the percentage of those where she speaks (i.e. where handwritten words can be attributed to her). I have proceeded in the same way for the dog.

In the first version of the series, entitled *Margot & Oscar Pluche*, the girl was more represented than the dog, but later, when the series was retitled *Sac à Puces*, the characters were neck and neck, with even a slight advantage for the animal. In terms of speech the pattern confirms that neither character is particularly talkative. In the fifteen albums, the proportion of panels in which Margot appears is twice as high as the proportion of those in which she speaks; the same can be said of Sac à Puces if we consider only the last eight volumes (II2 to II9). In contrast, in the first seven volumes, on average, the dog appears six times more often in the panels (46 per cent) than he speaks – to be precise: he speaks in only 7 per cent of the panels in volumes I1 to II1. Indeed, the dog speaks much more in volumes II2 to II9 than he did in the seven previous ones (**fig. 4**) – even exceeding Margot in some albums (vol. II3, II6 and II7).

This quantitative survey shows that the couple of heroes are increasingly close, but a qualitative study would show that their relationship is not equal. Although the girl-and-her-dog relationship takes the form of a very strong friendship, it is asymmetrical. Margot protects, accommodates and feeds a dog, who could do without this care, but in return gives her his loyalty and affection. This friendship can become a burden for the child. Since she does not have the autonomy of an adult, she does not have the means to assume responsibility for a pet, which often puts her in two difficult situations: separation and punishment. Regularly, the father (or less often the mother) catches the dog in the house and throws it out, accusing it of being a parasite. Inevitably, this separation makes

Margot cry, because she suffers from seeing the dog on the street. In another repetitive scene (vol. I1, II1, II2, II4), the girl is punished by her parents – generally, she is deprived of an outing with the family – because of the dog's mischief in which she did not participate. She herself has no regret or shame, and she never has a guilty conscience about disobeying the adults when she believes she is doing it for the good of her dog. Margot even confronts authorities outside the family. When she cannot find any more meat or chocolate spread – her dog's favourite food – in the family fridge, and she has used up her pocket money, she sometimes steals to feed him (vols. I2, II5, II9), but she is always caught by adults. In addition, when she cannot stand the frustration of her parents, she tends to run away, which does not last more than a day (vol. I3, I4, I6, II8), but worries the adults. Margot explains her first time running away as follows:

> My parents have nothing more to say to me. [...] My parents are mean. Because of them, Oscar Pluche has to sleep in the street [...] He will be cold. He will be sick. And I love him. And they don't care. (vol. I3, p. 24)

In sum, separations and punishments exacerbate Margot's empathetic and protective concern for her dog. The cyclical experience of attachment and loss causes her great frustration, which is not without risk for a child, as psychiatrist John Bowlby studied in his "attachment theory" (synthesised by Tribunella 154–155):

> Since the interaction between attachment figure and child determines the internal working models of the self and the other, the lost figure and the inability to regain it will alter how a child represents itself to itself and how he perceived any subsequent attachment figures.

The half-maternal, half-friendly relationship that Margot weaves with her dog tends to isolate her, as much as is possible in a large family, or at least to reduce her social relations. We have already studied the family roles of daughter and sister that define the character through her dominant enunciative place in the Duchêne family, without her being particularly talkative. She is also the only member of the siblings who develops an extra-familial sociability (apart from Julot with his girlfriend, from vol. II5 onwards). In the first three albums, and again in volume II2, we see her leading her group of friends and convincing her class – including her teachers – to help her take care of her dog. However, as the albums of the first phase (vol. I1–I6) of the series progress (**fig. 4**), she is increasingly less often represented and she speaks less and less. This can be explained by the exclusive friendship she develops with her dog, which grows in the second part of the series. The heroes define themselves as "clandestine lovers" (vol. I4, p. 37). The climax of their love affair is reached in the short story "Vive la mariée" [Long live the bride] in the album *Les*

Lundis au soleil (vol. II5), where Margot and her dog organise, in play, their wedding ceremony and their honeymoon. At the beginning of the story, the Duchêne siblings discuss who they dream of marrying. Margot declares that she dreams of "a handsome Prince Charming". Once alone with her dog, who has been listening to the conversation and is consumed with jealousy, the girl reassures him: "Come on, Sac à Puces! You know very well that I'll marry you when I grow up!" (vol. II5: 35) Her response to her siblings is indicative of the social roles she knows she can and must play. At the beginning of *Gare à ta truffe* (vol. II3), Margot announces to her parents that she wants to join a football club, a ploy she has devised to see the dog in secret, instead of sports training. The father, who played soccer in his youth, supports her, but the mother is surprised[13]: "it is a boy's sport", "our Margot always has to do things differently than the rest!" (vol. II3, pp. 3 and 4)

To understand this last sentence, we can bring Margot closer to an adult who, like her, does not do what others do. In *À l'abordage!* (vol. I4), she gets to know her godmother, who lives in Boulogne-sur-Mer. This young, single, militant woman has great professional responsibilities, which lead her to neglect her family, as well as to keep a romantic relationship with one of her employees secret. Researchers in television studies (quoted in Sepulchre 97) have expressed concern about "the masculinization of women who have men's jobs", worrying that heroines in television dramas might lose their "mothering side" as they climb the career ladder. Without debating these questionable statements,[14] it is clear that Margot's godmother does not fit the model of motherhood that the girl finds in her mother and reproduces towards her dog. The denouement of *À l'abordage!* allows the young woman to reconnect with her family and to publicly reveal her love for her employee, without having to "feminise" herself. The parallel with the secret couple formed by Margot and Oscar Pluche shows that, in the case of the girl too, the balance between the success of her sentimental life and the fulfilment of her roles as daughter and sister requires clandestinity. The solution that the comics series suggests, as most girl-and-her-dog or boy-and-his-dog stories do, is a definitive separation that would allow each of the heroes to live a "proper developmental trajectory" (Tribunella 161) that leads them (separately) towards heterosexuality and reproduction.

Indeed, the last volume of *Margot & Oscar Pluche* (vol. I6) puts the sentimental couple to the test, since Margot falls in love with a boy of her age who gives the album its title: *Balthazar*. He lives clandestinely in a department store, fending for himself, since his mother abandoned him there. Margot cannot tolerate the dog's jealousy of the boy: "Balthazar has been on his own for six years. I know others who couldn't say the same! [...] Parasite!"; "And first of all, what can you possibly understand about all this? You're just a dog!" (vol. I6, pp. 21 and 28) However, the character of Balthazar disappears after this album, which allows for the restoration of the exclusive relationship between Margot and the dog, renamed Sac à Puces. Another album, *De l'orage dans l'air* (vol. II7), starts from an argument between the parents and develops into a quarrel between the couple of Margot and Sac à Puces. When the father reproaches the mother for wanting to practise a sport in the evening, she answers "I remind you that you, you have your work at the nursery. I'm at home all day long. I need to go out, you know?" (vol. 16, p. 7) In a scene modelled on the previous one, the dog absurdly complains to Margot: "I remind you that YOU have your work at the school. MYSELF, I'm out on the street all day long. I need to go out, you know?" (vol. 16, p. 17) Their argument goes much further than that of the adults: Margot pushes the dog to the limit, he bites her, she breaks off their relationship and he takes revenge by vandalising her room, after drinking some beers. This time again, the couple of heroes reconciles. The last volume of the series, *Miss Wif Wif* (vol. 119), reverses the plot of *Balthazar* (vol. 16): this time, Sac à Puces falls in love with a bitch, and they start a family with their first litter of seven puppies. Contrary to Oscar's first reaction to Balthazar, Margot shows no jealousy towards Miss Wif Wif; Margot protects the bitch until the end of her gestation, saying "As for me, I'm not in love!" (vol. 119: 9) In the very last comics short story of the series, the girl proposes to the dogs and to her parents, the two couples being overwhelmed by their seven respective offspring, to babysit while they spend a romantic evening together (De Brab and Falzar 25–26).

Graphic Reproduction and Social Reproduction

To conclude, let us look at two scenes that summarise how the comics series combines graphic reproduction[15] with social reproduction. In the episode *La Gratouille du pedzouille* (vol. 15), the children of the Duchêne family take in abandoned dogs and hide them to prevent them from being thrown in the dog pound. At first jealous, Oscar Pluche is touched by a puppy that Margot puts in his arms (**fig. 5**). The elder sister, Sandra, then becomes the voice of practical reason, asking: "All that is well and good, but how are we going to feed

Figure 5 De Brab, Falzar, Zidrou and Veerle Swinnen. *La Gratouille du pedzouille: Margot et Oscar Pluche 5*. Casterman, 1996, p. 30, panels 3–5. *Sac à Puces* by De Brab, Zidrou and Falzar, reproduced with authors' permission.

our little protégés?", to which the elder brother, Julot, answers: "Great timing: Mom has just filled the freezer!" (vol. I5: 30) This scene synthesises the nurturing, not to say maternal, relationship that the female characters (Margot, Sandra, the mother) in this comics series play towards the male characters, including the dog Oscar Pluche / Sac à Puces. Even if Margot discovers the model of emancipation of her godmother, she knows above all the sentimental and parental model of her parents, an ordinary couple of the 1990s and early 2000s that does not completely break with the conventional roles of patriarch and housewife. In a way, she reproduces this in her relationship with Sac à Puces.

Throughout the series, the girl is constantly worried about her pet, waiting for his return, caring for and feeding him, while the dog remains carefree. In the 2004 children's novel, *Pique-nique panique*, the dog-narrator summarises his passive posture in relation to his mistress:

> Every night, she secretly hosts me in her bedroom and feeds me with bread and chocolate. [...] Margot wants me to live with her, to be together all the time. It would save me the trouble of slipping away every day at 7 a.m. before her parents wake up. (Falzar 6)

The album *Super maman* (vol. II1), relating a pregnancy of Margot's mother, goes even further in the symbolic assimilation of the relationship between the girl and her dog as a maternal one. The pregnant woman catches her children playing out a childbirth scene in the attic of the house: Sandra is the midwife, Margot is the mother, the dog is the newborn. The mother catches the unwanted pet and says, "Say goodbye to your baby" (vol. I1: 21), then she cuts with a pair of scissors the rope, acting as an umbilical cord, that the dog wears tied around his waist. Thanks to her privileged relationship with her dog, Margot is able to experience emotional life with a canine companion, and even motherhood, without breaking the social taboo of premature sexuality. The albums concluding the two parts of the series (vol. I6 and II9) ensure that the "properly gendered children achieve heterosexual adulthood", as girl-and-her-dog stories do (Tribunella 153). These types of stories logically end with the loss of the child-and-his/her-dog exclusive relationship, replaced by multiple human attachments.

Notes

1. All citations from French-language works included in the bibliography have been translated for the purposes of this chapter.
2. To temper this harsh judgement, I must point out that all of the series mentioned have been published in the mainstream weekly *Spirou*.
3. Casterman and Dupuis published albums in French and in Dutch, respectively under the series titles *Margot et Oscar Pluche / Margo en Oscar Pluis* and *Sac à Puces / Vlooienbaal*.
4. From now on, I will refer to the albums, listed in the bibliography at the end of the chapter, by the number of the corresponding series (in Roman numeral, I: *Margot & Oscar Pluche*, II: *Sac à Puces*), followed by the order of publication of the album (in Arabic numeral, thus from I1 to I6 and from II1 to II9).
5. In the last volume (vol. II9), she takes care of the bookkeeping of a butcher shop, without ceasing to ensure the daily management of the household. She does not manage to fulfil herself in both tasks. Her family life does not leave her enough time for a job that is anything but enviable (her boss harasses her even at her home).
6. These are volumes I1 and II5. At first glance, volume I2 also appears to be a collection of short stories, but it actually contains a single narrative divided into chapters.
7. For a study of a contemporary example of our corpus, see Eric Tribunella's analysis (162–163) of Kate DiCamillo's girl-and-her-dog novel *Because of Winn-Dixie* (2000).
8. Even if Carine De Brabanter had already had the experience of drawing a series in *Spirou* (1988–1989), after her artistic training at the Institut Saint-Luc in Brussels. The editorial board of the magazine *Jet*, published by Le Lombard, was composed of in-house editors and authors: Jean-Luc Vernal, André-Paul Duchâteau, Bob De Moor and Georges Pernin.
9. Although the word *pluche* also refers to a teddy bear in Dutch, the translation of the series published by Casterman was entitled *Margo en Oscar Pluis*, which emphasises the meaning of clingy pet. The Dutch *pluis*, like *peluche* in French, refers to a fluff that comes off a plush fabric and remains temporarily stuck to it.
10. Translation of **fig. 2**: Margot. Age 8 1/2. My best friend. Every evening, she shelters me in secret and feeds me with chocolate spread on bread.
    The competent authorities. They don't want me at home on the pretext that the family is already big enough and that I am full of fleas. Nonsense!
    Sandra. Age 12. Know-it-all. Very useful in case of conflict with the authorities.
    Julot. Age 13. Big fan of fries and mayo, as well as video games.
    Marine. The star of the family. She is 4 months old and has the pleasant odours of soap, milk and poo.
    Lucien. Age 6. Alias *Carbine Joe, Sitting Lucien, Barbarouf-the-Terrible-Pirate*, the list goes on and on!

Mérule. Lazy, sluggish and slacker parasite. A cat, you know!

Émile. Age 2 1/2. A stubborn child. He only loosen up to smile at his little sister.

Mischiefs, somersaults and blunders, beware of Josette (age 4)!

This is me, Sac à Puces. Margot's parents cannot stand the sight of me, let alone in a photo!

11. Of all the characters, the dog and the family members, including the newborn, are those who speak in the most incipits. Only a handful of secondary characters speak at the beginning of more than one album: one of Margot's classmates, Lorenzo (II2, II6), her friends Clara and Mousse (I1, I3) and especially Zoé (I1, I3, II6, also present, but without speaking, in the incipit of episode II2), her teacher Ms Nadine (II2, II6) and the newsagent in the Duchêne family's neighbourhood, Mr Bourru (I3, II6).

12. Except in the literary prose that has been derived from it. For instance, the novel *Pique-nique panique* (2004), mentioned above, uses the plot and title of a literary short story that appeared ten years earlier in *Dauphin*. Both versions, told in the first person – the short story, by Margot, and the novel, by her dog – adopt fixed internal focalisations. By contrast, the overwhelming majority of the comics' panels are presented in external focalisation.

13. The initial scene is replayed by the parents, with similar dialogue, when they organise a family table-football match, pitting the girls against the boys (vol. II3, p. 9).

14. The godmother develops another motherhood, in the context of her work, which recalls the relationship between Margot and her street dog. As the director of a revalidation centre for marine animals, she has to take in and care for wild animals, in a sense mothering them, assisted in this task by the employee with whom she is in love.

15. Jenell Johnson (4) coined the concept of "graphic reproduction" to gather comics that address human reproduction.

Bibliography

Capart, Philippe. "Boule & Bill: Unwrapped". *Strong Bonds: Child-animal Relationships in Comics*, edited by Maaheen Ahmed. Presses universitaires de Liège, 2020, pp. 279–285.

"C'est une fille! Elle s'appellera Marine!" *Spirou*, no. 3181, 1999, p. 17.

Collignon, Stéphane. "They talk! They walk! A Study of Anthropomorphisation of Nonhuman Characters in Animated Films". *Animatrix* no. 16, 2008, pp. 45–54.

Daele, Amaury, and Thomas Glesener. "Rencontre avec Denis Lapière". *Rêve-en-Bulles*, no. 7, 1994, pp. 6–11.

De Brabanter, Carine, and Philippe Boulet. "Margot et Oscar Peluche". *Jet*, no. 2, 1990, pp. 7–11.

De Brab, Falzar, and Veerle Swinnen. "Sur la piste des bichons. Sac à Puces". *Spirou*, no. 3774, 2010, pp. 25–28.

De Brab, Falzar, Zidrou, and Bruno Wesel. *Sac à Puces: Margot et Oscar Pluche 1*. Casterman, 1992.

—. *Cache-Cache: Margot et Oscar Pluche 2*. Casterman, 1993.

De Brab, Falzar, Zidrou, and Veerle Swinnen. *La Bande à Rigobert: Margot et Oscar Pluche 3*. Casterman, 1994.

—. "Pique-nique panique". *Dauphin*, no. 48/51, 1994, pp. 4–7.

—. *À l'abordage! Margot et Oscar Pluche 4*. Casterman, 1995.

—. *La Gratouille du pedzouille: Margot et Oscar Pluche 5*. Casterman, 1996.

—. *Balthazar: Margot et Oscar Pluche 6*. Casterman, 1997.

—. *Super maman: Sac à Puces 1*. Dupuis, 1999.

—. *Chauds les marrons! Sac à Puces 2*. Dupuis, 2000.

—. *Gare à ta truffe! Sac à Puces 3*. Dupuis, 2001.

—. *Docteur Pupuces: Sac à Puces 4*. Dupuis, 2002.

—. *Le Lundi au soleil: Sac à Puces 5*. Dupuis, 2003.

—. *Ça déménage! Sac à Puces 6*. Dupuis, 2004.

—. *De l'orage dans l'air: Sac à Puces 7*. Dupuis, 2005.

—. *Mamy galettes: Sac à Puces 8*. Dupuis, 2008.

—. *Miss Wif Wif: Sac à Puces 9*. Dupuis, 2009.

De Dobbeleer, Michel. "Can Stereotypical Housewives in Flemish Family Comics Divorce? The Cases of Jommeke and De Kiekeboes". *Studies in Comics*, vol. 12, no. 1, 2022, pp. 33–56.

Delisle, Philippe. "Bill, second enfant de la famille?" *Milou, Idéfix et Cie: Le chien en BD*, edited by Éric Baratay and Philippe Delisle. Karthala, 2012, pp. 113–132.

Falzar. *Pique-nique panique: D'après la bande dessinée Sac à Puces: De Brab, Falzar, Zidrou*. Mango, 2004.

Gavo, and Thierry Dutailly. "De Brab est une femme, trop rare dans la B.D.", *Poil à gratter*, no. 7, 2000, pp. 16–17.

Ghesquière, Rita. "La maison d'édition Averbode". *Les Presses enfantines chrétiennes au xxe siècle*, edited by Thierry Crépin and Françoise Hache-Bissette. Artois Presses Université, 2008, pp. 29–40.

Johnson, Jenell. *Graphic Reproduction: A Comics Anthology*. Penn State University Press, 2018.

"Les bonnes idées de la semaine". *Dauphin*, no. 29, 1996, pp. 16–17.

Mixhel, Florence. "Les éditions Dupuis à Angoulême". *Spirou*, no. 3640, 2008, p. 52.

Rouyet, Robert "La bande dessinée a bien décollé et file vers des sommets toujours plus hauts". *Le Soir: Temps libre*, no. 121, 1985, p. 9.

Sepulchre, Sarah. "Policier/scientifique, féminin/masculin dans les séries télévisées: Dépolarisation des caractérisations et réflexion sur les outils d'analyse". *L'Assignation de genre dans les médias: Attentes, perturbations, reconfigurations*, edited by Béatrice Damian-Gaillard, Sandy Montañola and Aurélie Olivesi. Presses universitaires de Rennes, 2014, pp. 93–107.

Tribunella, Eric. "A Boy and His Dog: Canine Companions and the Proto-Erotics of Youth". *Children's Literature Association Quarterly*, vol. 29, no. 3, 2004, pp. 152–171.

Chapter 7
Modernity, Aesthetics and the Active Female Body in *Mirabelle* (1960–1967)

Joan Ormrod

The 1950s and '60s were eras in which teenagers made their mark in British culture in music, fashion and subcultural style. From tentative beginnings in the mid-1950s when British teenagers were inspired by American and Continental youth culture, the 1960s saw British youth culture become a globalised phenomenon through pop music and fashion. British culture was revitalised and enriched by youth culture after the difficult times of WWII, and in the 1960s London became the epicentre of cool culture. Teenage girls' bodies were an integral part of these major shifts in British culture when expectations of girls and women coalesced around changing notions of the female body into a more active and modern body, and this was reflected in media representations aimed at teenage girls. This chapter is a historical analysis of movement and the female body in Arthur Pearson's *Mirabelle* (1960–1967), drawing connections between the mediated and cultural body of girls.

Movement of the female body in *Mirabelle* is physical, spatial and psychological. Together, these elements reflect the cultural revolution of the later 1960s and how the influences of counterculture and teenage culture changed societal expectations of teenage girls. In these stories somatic movement is in the physical movement of the body and how this is facilitated by fashion of the 1960s. Psychological and symbolic movement is connected with consumerism in fantasy or daydreams. This type of movement can be described as the sojourn, or the "self-departure" (Rosengren). The sojourn is often connected with imagining the perfect holiday, the perfect date or wearing the perfect fashion item. Fantasies can be seen in holiday brochures, catalogues and advertising. As stated above, the sojourn and consumerism are connected: one buys into fantasies through the seduction of promotion. Spatial movement is the fulfilment of the fantasy or daydream in travelling on holiday or into the city for work, and romance.

The active female body in the 1960s represented a shift in the ways society viewed the potential for girls beyond the roles of wives and mothers. From the early 1960s teen girl comics increasingly featured in stories and articles in which girls were shown holidaying, moving into cities and apartments for employment and becoming more bodily active through leisure activities such as pop music and fashion. The girls who read these comics were in their early to late teens and could be classified as young earners – early school leavers but not yet married with disposable income for consumer goods (Abrams). They, therefore, represented an attractive market for advertisers and manufacturers of teen goods in this era. These representations developed as the 1960s progressed but they were expedited by underpinning cultural and countercultural discourses in leisure and employment. However, they also represented a threat to girls, who were perceived as vulnerable to predatory men, pregnancy and social condemnation if they transgressed sexually when outside the domestic environment.

"Girlhood", like "teenager", was a fluid concept from the mid-1950s when *Mirabelle* was first published, and this is evident in the content of the comic. Early issues of *Mirabelle* were aimed at older teens and women, possibly on the verge of marriage or married; they featured advertisements for Bird's Custard, catalogues and jewellery. The stories, adventure, action and melodramas were often reprints from the Italian women's magazine *Grand Hotel* (1946–present). The stories featured inflated emotions, murders, family feuds, imperilled heroines, brides or fiancées threatened by evil spouses or love rivals. Other teen girl comics in the mid-1950s – such as *Marilyn* (Amalgamated Press Ltd 1955–1965), *Valentine* (Amalgamated Press Ltd 1957–1974), *Roxy* (Amalgamated Press Ltd 1958–1963) and *Romeo* (DC Thomson 1957–1974) – featured similar advertisements and melodramatic stories.

In the 1960s there was a change in the style and aesthetics of the picture stories from scrupulous cross-hatching and realistic representation by British artists towards highly stylised, energetic artwork using linear pen or flowing brushwork from young artists in Spain or Italy. The art was commissioned from two or three studios such as Selecciones Illustradas (SI Artists) or Cosmopolitan (Roach 11). The Spanish and Italian studios' output seemed to epitomise the 1960s zeitgeist of modernity and cool. Roach maintains this artwork had a great impact on British pop culture of the 1960s. They reproduced a simulated cool Britannia based on imagery collected from magazines, sent to the comics artists by the editors of the International Publishing Company (later IPC Magazines Ltd.). As Roach perceptively states:

> this style anticipated the fashion of the '60s. SI's girls with their big lips, elaborately rendered hair and large, heavily mascaraed eyes looked nothing like the

typical British girls of the early '60s, but within a few years a whole generation of girls were trying to look this way. (16)

It may be that the change in concept from older teen to younger teen was in acknowledgement of this changing notion of puberty at that time (Marwick). It was noted by Mark Abrams (1959), in his report on teenage spending, that children reached puberty earlier and were heavier than the preceding generations, thanks to better nutrition. Therefore, I define "girls" in this context as between the ages of twelve and twenty to identify the fluid age range of potential readers of *Mirabelle*.

Teen girl comics featured similar content: picture and text stories in addition to serials (stories told over many weeks), articles about pop music and fashion, advice on relationships, pin-ups of stars and beauty products. Girl's comics differed from girl's magazines in two main ways: they included picture and text stories, and they were published weekly, not monthly. Girl's comics could be published in magazine or comics format (Gibson 2015, 51–53). The magazine format was larger and printed on high-quality paper with more colour and tonal images, whereas girl's comics were printed on cheap newsprint, featured fewer tonal and colour pages and were cheaper than the magazines. Weekly publication of the girl's comics meant that they responded rapidly to the ever-changing fashions and fads of the youth market.

Despite the fluidity of girlhood as a concept in the 1950s, girl's comics were classed as part of the women's magazine market by publishers (Braithwaite and Barrell). However, as Brian Braithwaite and Joan Barrell note, the women's magazine market was the most precarious in publishing; magazines and comics frequently folded within a few years (92). In 1956 *Mirabelle* sales were 547,700 units per week, falling to 272,100 units per week in 1964 and to 175,100 units per week in 1968 (White). Often this waning readership was countered by mergers between publications. *Mirabelle*, for instance, merged with *Glamour* (6 October 1958), *Marty* (23 February 1963) and *Valentine* (9 November 1974) before it was subsumed into *Pink* (22 October 1977). These mergers changed the profile of *Mirabelle*, with the publisher attempting to keep their regular readership whilst encouraging their new readers to stay.

The fall in sales could also be attributed to the popularity of other teen publications in a saturated market. In comics, DC Thomson's *Jackie* (11 January 1964–3 July 1993) was a fresh concept. It was published in magazine format and featured sophisticated picture stories. Gibson (2014) states that "it blurred the boundaries between magazine and comic, as well as between child and adult" (53). Its sales figures rose from 350,000 in 1964 to 451,400 in 1968 (White Appendix IV). As *Jackie* was the nearest equivalent of all the teen girl magazines to *Mirabelle*, in format and content, it is likely many readers switched their allegiance. In addition to *Jackie*, other teen magazines such as *Honey* (1960–1986) and *Rave* (1964–1971) also emerged, aimed at fashion and pop music interests respectively. Fan Carter argues that *Honey* magazine, launched in April 1960, set the tone for fashion and a pop aesthetic with "witty layouts and use of graphics integrated into thematic fashion spreads [...] [connoting] fun and central to the making of a particular feminine self" (204). *Honey* promoted the notion of girls experiencing more freedoms and ambitions than their mother's generation when its cover tagline became "Young, gay and get-ahead" in 1962, "get-ahead" suggesting a more active and aspirational female. In her argument for the importance of *Honey* in the development of an autonomous female identity, Carter is one of several contemporary researchers in women's magazines and comics who challenge earlier criticisms of these publications.

The active female body was a significant indicator in a shift of values from the rigid social hierarchies and culture of the 1950s towards the youth-oriented counterculture of the late 1960s. Teen girl comics were consumer driven, and the connection between girlhood and consumerism is a key factor in criticism of these comics. Teen girl comics attracted criticisms from feminist and sociological researchers, mainly on their alignment with the romance genre, which was often mistakenly regarded as a central feature of these comics. Early research into romance comics claims that they make cultural dupes of their readers. Such criticisms argued that the images and stories were constructed through patriarchal values meant to fool women into thinking the comics were women centred (McCracken). In her study of *Jackie*, the DC Thomson comic Angela McRobbie agrees with the notion of female readership as passive: the aim of the *Jackie* comic is "to win and shape the consent of the readers to a particular set of values" (82). Like McCracken, she claims they treat girls as media dupes. Connie Alderson's (1968) early study of comics such as *Jackie*, *Valentine* and *Trend* regards them as low culture. Alderson sees the solution as encouraging girls to read literature, such as *Jane Eyre*, which will improve their minds; however, she was writing in an era when it was assumed comics were frivolous, childish and could impede reading progress. Later studies examined the historical (Gibson, 2015), production (Round) and reader-centred elements of comics (Barker; Gibson, 2015). Martin Barker argues that comics critics, such as Angela McRobbie, show a disrespect for comics, as they cannot even be bothered to reference correctly the materials they cite. According to Barker, *Jackie*'s stories are retold to fit into the critic's argument, thus we are "dependent on the manner of retellings" (135). Barker further critiques McRobbie's analysis of *Jackie* comics as unchanging and homogenous, because, as I also noted above, the comics change over a thirty-year period. In addition, the often differing content in a single issue can articulate diverse ideological messages.

Criticisms of teen comics also assume they would be read according to dominant ideologies encoded in the texts (Hall). This negates the polysemic qualities of the texts and reader's differing reading positions. Stuart Hall argues that there are many responses to the ideological messages encoded in the text including a response that agrees with the dominant encoding to a negotiated or oppositional position. Mel Gibson's (2015) empirical study of female readers of girls comics shows that women's memories of reading girls comics enabled them to construct their identities as girls, but comics also constituted "a rebellion against 'proper' girlhood" (183). The images and narratives in these stories might promote conformity, but as Gibson points out, they offered a resistance to the restrictions of girlhood.

My analysis is informed by Penny Tinkler's proposal that magazine and comics analysis should be contextual and examine the ideas through the content and format of the comics. Tinkler argues in favour of a holistic approach, taking into account magazine production and layout and "engaging with different types of content within a magazine and how they are presented, particularly the relationship between text, images and design features" (43). For this chapter I used a quantitative analysis of *Mirabelle* so that I could compare how the imagery and rhetoric developed in the eleven years of its publication up to 1967. I classified female bodies in advertisements, stories and articles into the discursive categories based on movement: somatic (bodily and affect), psychological (movement in the head in day-dreams, desires and ambitions) or spatial (from the domestic to the public, from the town to the city, from home to tourist destinations). I mapped the themes through case studies to show how British culture affected and reflected the ideas in the stories.

The polysemic nature of *Mirabelle* could promote and challenge female agency over several issues but sometimes in the same issue. Underpinning the promotion but also the challenge to female agency were the publisher's identification and appeal to more youthful audiences, the necessity of protecting young girls and the need to reinforce patriarchal norms. The potentially conflicting messages presented to readers could be encapsulated in the two categories that underlie many of the images and much of the rhetoric – zany and cute. Sianne Ngai argues that aesthetic categories of the eighteenth century such as the sublime and the beautiful were connected with religiosity and greater myths. Contemporary aesthetic categories, like zany and cute, trivialise representations in postmodern culture and "evoke subjects under subjection to a number of demands (including [...] the division of labor)" (Ngai 12). The use of cute and zany as aesthetic categories presents a conflict in the potential for female agency in 1960s *Mirabelle*. Zany and cute began to appear in *Mirabelle* in the early 1960s, which described girls, fashion and pop as "new", "madcap" and "zany". There was an increased use of exclamation marks in editorials and articles. A free "Charm Club" pull-out booklet, presented in the 13 October 1962 issue, emphasised individualism, youthfulness and energy:

> Y Young…Y is also for You…Be an individual – not just one of the crowd! Z is for Zany
> – the look you can get away with!…also for Zest one of the most important beauty
> ingredients…Be alive…take an interest in everyone and everything! (Harrison)

Zany, as a category, "calls up the character of a worker whose particularity lies paradoxically in the increasingly dedifferentiated nature of his or her labor" (Ngai 9). In her analysis of the ramifications of using aesthetic categories, Ngai argues that zany is connected with the blurring of lines between work and leisure: "zaniness is as much about desperate labouring as playful fun" (23). Work becomes pleasure and emphasises the pleasure in performing and labour output. It is also characteristic of countercultural values in its notions of work as play (Brake). An example of this zany ethic is *Mirabelle*'s editorial staff who, by 1967, were coded as youthful and zany in their work. For example, "Jumping Julie, *Mirabelle's Girl on the Go! Go! Go!*" reported on pop music from April 1967. She was joined by Jumping Jim (written by Keith Altham) on 6 May 1967. Julie was shown hopping like a kangaroo and Jim sliding down a fireman's pole. As Ngai suggests, this is a type of desperate labouring where the pleasure is almost painful in its striving for output.

The zany girl, enjoying her work lifestyle, was juxtaposed with the cute girl, who became more prevalent, mainly through fashion, in later 1960s *Mirabelle*. As a category cute simplifies, infantilises and diminishes. It is powerlessness and weakness, the futility of attempting to succeed in a task, a quality Ngai also aligns with the zany. Cuteness is signalled in descriptions of girls as "dollies", which developed from the mid-1960s and was represented in dolly girl fashion. Dolly girl fashion emphasised the prepubescent female body and its associations with a child's toy connoted girls dressing in this style as cute. This categorisation of childishness was connected with a change in the idealised female body from the curvaceous 1950s body to the androgynous, boyish figure of the 1960s. The next section examines the development of shifts in British culture that can be identified in the stories and the impact of the cultural revolution on the active female body of the 1960s.

British Culture, the Teenage Market and Mass Media, 1958–1967

The political and cultural discourses of the 1950s provided the fertile soil necessary for the burst of creativity and the cultural revolution of the 1960s. The keywords that apply to much of British society from the early 1960s were modernity, utility, aesthetics, technology and movement. Many of these concepts apply to the arts, architecture, fashion and popular culture, but they were also aligned with youth. Youth seemed to epitomise future developments in technology, design, aesthetics and were regarded as the keys to energising British culture (Marwick 1998). The cultural revolution of the 1960s was driven by youth culture, but the elements integral to this cultural revolution were already present in British culture and popular culture from the late 1950s (Marwick 12). They included a focus on technology and consumerism, criticism or questioning of the status quo and "new modes of self-presentation, involving emancipation from the old canons of fashion, and a rejoicing in the natural attributes of the human body" (Marwick 18). Thus, as Marwick argues, the fashions of the 1960s were perceived as freeing the human body from the constraints of the 1950s. However, the cultural revolution was not a "unified, integrated counterculture, totally and consistently in opposition to mainstream culture" (Marwick 12), but here countercultural values increasingly "*permeated* and *transformed* [society]" (13). The radical shifts in art, culture and youth of the 1960s were already set in place by post-WWII political and social movements, art, design, music and technology, and this contributed to the development of the countercultural revolution in the late 1960s.

Political and cultural upheavals in Britain in the early 1960s included infrastructure building, aesthetics and education from the mid-1950s. The devastation of bombing to Britain's inner cities after WWII prompted a huge building programme from the mid-1950s. New builds used prefabricated buildings based on Le Corbusier's brutalist principles and new building materials. In 1964 a Labour government was voted into power, and they won a second general election in 1966 – the latter with a majority of ninety-six seats. The Labour government embraced the changes deemed necessary to modernise Britain: they embarked on rebuilding transport and housing infrastructures and attempted to erase class inequalities. The New Towns Act (1965) designated the development of new towns and high-rise tower blocks in inner cities. Construction on the infrastructure was also developed with motorways, dual carriageways and city bypasses built from 1959. These enabled better transport links between the cities and the regions, although the emphasis was still on London as the epicentre of UK culture and creativity. However, there was also a rise in interests in regional culture, for instance, in Liverpool music, which instigated the beat music of the British invasion led by the Beatles. Kitchen sink drama fetishised predominantly northern working-class people in films such as *Saturday Night and Sunday Morning* (Reisz) or *A Kind of Loving* (Schlesinger). Many of these stories featured "angry young men" revolting against the stifling class system, the social pressures to settle down into family life and the oppression of the older generation. Although these kitchen sink dramas articulated masculine alienation and anomie, female roles seemed to consist of getting pregnant and causing problems for the protagonists. The British Board of Film Censors often classified the films as suitable for adults, making them inaccessible to comics readers.

Despite the restrictions on working-class men shown in the kitchen sink dramas, the late 1950s offered opportunities for young working-class boys and girls to enter higher education. The diffusion of new ideas and ideologies based on existentialism or class often led to a vibrant culture in coffee bars or folk and jazz clubs surrounding universities and art colleges (Marwick 57). This also encouraged a notion of the classlessness of youth culture through the mixing of different sectors and ethnicities of the community.

In addition to the stifling influences of class and the older generation, Britain in the late 1950s was regarded as an "empty vessel", heavily influenced by American and European cultures (Marwick 36). There was a worship of American popular culture, particularly pop music, fashions and consumer goods. Style and fashion were imported from France and Italy. In response to these global influences British culture presented its own versions of pop stars and styles for the profitable teen market. The spending habits of teenagers and the youth market were identified in Mark Abrams (1959) and the Albemarle Report (1960), which was informed by Abrams's study. Young people, especially girls, were responsible for changing patterns of consumption and taste. In general, girls took low-skilled and low-paid jobs but had regular, disposable incomes with which they shopped to get "the look" mainly "with respect to fashion, cosmetics, and magazines" (Abrams 44). Teen girl comics were a significant part of the marketing machine, as they promoted fantasies to their readers – from meeting pop idols and going on holiday to buying fashion and beauty items (Ormrod 2016).

From the mid-1950s UK teen comics were a part of a cross-media promotion network that produced a vortex of publicity promoting pop music fashion and consumer products to teenagers (Doherty; Ormrod). *Mirabelle*, for instance, sponsored a music show from the late 1950s and featured articles purportedly written by pop stars and teen stars or about the latest films. From the late 1950s into the 1960s there were more films produced in America but also the UK to exploit the teenage market. Pop music television programmes were rare in the 1950s, but from the early 1960s programmes such as *Ready Steady Go!* (1963) introduced the latest music, dances and fashions to teenagers. Commercial radio stations such as Radio Luxembourg and Radio Caroline broadcast pop music and gossip regularly from 1964. As the 1960s progressed there was competing competition from other media platforms such as television, pirate radio and teen films. Television increasingly featured pop music and fashion, and BBC radio featured more pop music. However, teenagers increasingly turned to narrow casting pirate radio stations like Radio Caroline, which broadcast pop music daily. In addition, pirate radio was considered more hip and youthful than the BBC, as their DJs were nearer the ages of their listeners.

Britain was becoming more aware of itself in a global context in this era through travel and the expansion of pop culture. The Holidays Pay Act (1938) provided paid holidays for working-class people. The post-WWII affluence enabled by full employment meant that people could go to holiday in Butlins or Pontins holiday camps around Britain. Working-class people might also travel abroad with cheaper package holidays (Barton). Popular destinations were the Spanish Costa Brava, Palma and Corsica.

Travel featured in many of the popular films of the 1960s, particularly in the pop music and spy films of this era. In 1963 the two top popular films in the UK were *Summer Holiday* (Yates) and *From Russia with Love* (Young). *Summer Holiday* was a teen musical in which teen heartthrob Cliff Richard and his friends toured Europe in a London bus. Along the way they picked up a group of girls, also on a tour of Europe, and together had fun and romance. In the film girls were shown dancing and leaping in the public sphere. There was no overseeing parental control as with many teen films of the early 1960s (Doherty). The main parent, whose daughter was a pop singer who had sneaked aboard the bus, was an antagonist attempting to prevent her daughter's agency.

Female autonomy and independence were shown in *Smashing Time* (Davis), in which Brenda (Rita Tushingham) and Yvonne (Lynn Redgrave) arrived in London from the north for the dream of being in the in-crowd. Despite the setbacks of having their money stolen, being mocked by a photographer and conned by a workman, both "make it". They exhibit agency in somatic and spatial movement. In *Smashing Time*, London is signified by speed, the superficial and consumerism. Fashions are based on the future, the avant-garde, and they are fleeting. To be revealed as unfashionable opens one up to mockery. To become the rage is to be exploited and commercialised. Within a few days both girls become famous, but they reject the superficial consumer-led London lifestyles to return north.

I chose these films to show how representations of female agency were not just restricted to comics but featured in other media representations in this era. Both films were produced in Britain and introduced female protagonists who moved from their drab lives at home to potentially exciting new lives. Both films show the problems with the generation gap. *Smashing Time* shows the growing impact of London in British culture, and the alignment of fashion and the avant-garde.

The following sections explore the themes of movement discussed above, manifest in *Mirabelle* through its stories, artwork and articles. I focus on fashion and pop culture (there are other stories and genres dealing with movement such as the spy craze that this paper has no room to cover). First, I map the differing classifications of the female moving body through fashion. Then I examine psychological and spatial movement through travel or migrations. Finally, I analyse the active female body in a picture series, "Marina Square" (8 April 1967–7 October 1967), which incorporates all of these elements but simultaneously challenges the positive elements of the agentic female body with warnings or cautionary tales.

Physical Movement: Fashion, Modernity, Aesthetics

It is difficult to determine whether fashion moulds the shape of the body or vice versa. As proposed above, 1960s fashion connoted modernity, agency and the freer female body. Joanne Entwistle claims the dressed body is a "situated object" in the social world:

> Dress and the body exist in dialectical relationship to one another. Dress operates on the phenomenal body; it is a very crucial aspect of our everyday experience of embodiment, while the body is a dynamic field, which gives life and fullness to the dress.

Thus, the body moves and feels in accordance with the clothing worn. The cut of 1960s clothing was aimed at the youth market. Skirts were shorter, and stockings were replaced by more functional tights. The new types of clothing and materials used in fashion were aligned with modernity, aestheticism and youth culture.

The 1960s saw a democratisation of fashion with a move towards cheap, ready-to-wear clothes which "brought the *haute couture* look within the reach of every girl or woman who had the fashion sense to make the best of her appearance" (White 162). The look, as Mark Abrams noted, was avant-garde and based on clean lines, geometric patterns and bright colours and cut in basic shapes. According to Mike Brake mod style popular in the mid-1960s exemplified the superficial for it, "not only embraced but amplified the neuroses of late twentieth-century capitalist life – its obsession with surfaces and commodity fetishism" (159). Modernity was connoted through the futuristic, with prints often modelled on the visual acrobatics of pop art or the asceticism of the Mondrian look popularised by Yves St. Laurent. Go-go boots were also a futuristic addition to the wardrobe and completed a dolly girl look. The futuristic was furthermore connoted in the utility of modern synthetic fabrics, such as plastic, or that looked like silk, such as Orlon and bri-nylon. These materials were marketed as crease free and easy to maintain.

Fashion and shopping were signs of self-expression, informality and the entrepreneurial spirit, and these were epitomised in the boutique. Boutiques "gave voice, form, and location to the youthful desire for independence and personal freedom, and in turn led to an unprecedented awareness of fashion as a vibrant medium of self-expression" (Fogg). Boutiques introduced an informality to the shopping experience. They tended to cluster on the outskirts of the city, and, as they sold goods on a small scale rather than mass production, they connoted individuality and small-scale production. Many designers, such as Jean Varon and Mary Quant, were further validated because they were working-class children who could not enter college, and they started out designing with small-scale productions.

Fashions produced for boutiques were designed for a youthful female body that connoted classlessness, youth, naturalness and energy. Shift dresses and miniskirts were promoted as enabling female equality, described by James Laver as "the final word in the emancipation of women – in proving her economic independence [...] [short skirts] scream: 'I am stepping out'" (Laver 8). The arenas for the display of these youthful styles were incorporated in British popular and consumer culture and the cross-media promotion of fashion and teen music was already well developed by the mid-1960s. Film, television and pop stars were used to endorse fashion and pop music in comics and magazines (Ormrod). Fashion was promoted in magazines and comics by television stars like Cathy McGowan and Samantha Juste or pop stars like Lulu, Cilla Black, Sandy Shaw, who all produced their own clothing ranges. Many of these stars were of a similar or slightly older age than the readership of *Mirabelle*, and their star profile could be compared with that of the older sister to the reader. Inside the issue, Lulu, who was particularly associated with vitality because of her energetic performances and brash star image, was featured in

Figure 1 Active youthful pop star bodies,
Mirabelle, 1 October 1966, p. 13.

Figure 2 Lulu as zany and fashionable star,
Mirabelle, 1 October 1966, p. 11.

a four-page fashion feature "What's it all about" (**fig. 1**) (Usden, 1966). In this feature she and several pop stars are shown "getting a kick out of life!" (13) The same issue featured a cross-media promotion between Pond's Fresh-Start cleansing gel and "The super stripy Lulu-skirt" (**fig. 2**).

The face and body of the 1960s was that of Twiggy. She became famous aged seventeen, a similar age to many *Mirabelle* readers, and her androgynous body with a boyish haircut and large eyes replicated the look of many of the ingénue heroines in the comic. Twiggy is also a good example of the speed with which comics responded to new trends. She first broke in the press in February 1966, and she was named face of the year in 1966 by *The Daily Express*. Within a few weeks of her first appearance, there were images of Twiggy-like drawings by Alan Parry. Alan Parry also illustrated an article in *Mirabelle* on 8 April 1966: "!!! Prints! The Powerful Prints!" (Lane) (**fig. 3**) The swirls of the dress prints reflected pop art imagery and provided a simulation of body movement. This movement was emphasised by the diagonal poses of the bodies.

Fashions in the 1960s inferred symbolic agency but also denied it in the control it demanded on girls and women. Cute and zany can be applied to the active female bodies in these examples. Twiggy and Lulu were cute, characterised by their youthfulness, their childish bodies and their short height. Lulu could also be described as zany; she

Figure 3 The pop art aesthetic in fashion prints, *Mirabelle*, 8 April 1967, p. 15.

is described as a bombshell, the "liveliest girl on Britain's pop scene" (Usden, 1967). In the four-page fashion pull-out she describes corduroy fabric as "Tough enough to jump around in!" (Usden, 1967), emphasising her tomboy qualities.

The lean female body of the 1960s was presented as natural, needing no artifice in its construction. Despite the freedoms the new fashions and fabrics of the 1960s promoted, the cut of the clothing restricted the female body. Where, in the 1950s, corsets controlled the curves and excess of female bodies, Twiggy's ideal prepubescent body meant that the only way an older woman or curvier girl could wear miniskirts was by dieting. Dieting articles appeared at this time, and dieting became an invisible corset on the female body. As Naomi Wolf and Susan Bordo argued several years later, the emphasis on dieting and achieving a beautiful body distracted women from attempting to achieve equality.

Sally Tuffin and Marion Foale, founders of Youthquake fashion, designed jackets with trousers instead of skirts for girls and noted how, "We suddenly didn't want to be chic; we just wanted to

Figure 4 The trouser suit – note the multiple connotations of "pop", *Mirabelle*, 1 October 1966, cover.

be ridiculous" (Bernard 19). Trouser suits became more acceptable to wear in the mid-1960s and, like the miniskirt, they were promoted as enabling female equality. *Mirabelle*, on 1 October 1966, featured a jumping girl in a trouser suit on the cover and an inset panel promising to "pop 'n' around" to visit the Walker Brothers. "Pop" not only connoted pop music but the pop of bubbles in fizzy drinks and the immediacy of popping in on pop stars. The trouser suit copy inferred female empowerment: "Who wears the trousers in your house? It should be you!" (**fig. 4**) The trouser suit was regarded as masculine attire and so deemed unprofessional to wear in the work environment. Despite the promotion of the trouser suit on the cover and in an article on the fashion pages, the editor was careful to issue a warning against wearing trouser suits to the office, "I think it's O.K. when [Julie is] out interviewing, but not when she's bashing away at her typewriter!" and grudgingly, "Still maybe I'm old fashioned!" (2)

Psychological and Spatial Movement: Fantasising Travel and the City

The second type of movement was in the psychological or spiritual. As noted above, the psychological, exemplified by the sojourn, concerns daydreams and fantasies in travel magazines, films and television. Idealistic images of travel or the good life were often shown in travel television and films which gave girls a "window on the world" (White 162). The fantasy which is based on consumerism and ambition always leads to disappointment when the reality fails to achieve the romance of the dream. Inevitably, reality, in the shape of a boy, usually provides a recompense for disappointment.

In "Faraway Places" (Goodall and Romero), Ann illustrates stories of exotic locations for a magazine. She dreams of a romantic gondola ride in Venice with a handsome gondolier, ignoring Bill, the boy-next-door accounts clerk. Roger Brent, a writer, compliments her on her illustrations of his stories, and she is attracted to his glamorous, well-travelled lifestyle. However, he tells her he has never been to any of the places mentioned in his stories, and her dreams are dashed. Bill comes to the rescue and helps her to realise that love is right under her window. In the last panel she muses "It isn't the time or place that matters...it's the right boy. When you've found him, every little thing you do is romantic!" (28)

A similar story but this time where the heroine achieves her dream happens in "I lived for a dream" (Goodall et al.). This story is from the true-life series, which purports to be based on real examples. A heroine (never named) dreams of a better life in America, but her dreams are based on glamour, modelling and television work – in all of which she has no experience. Despite her boyfriend Dave's protests, she leaves England for America. When she arrives she discovers her dreams do not account for a lack of experience in modelling. She ends up working in a grocery store: "Life was harder than I'd expected, but I still had my dreams" (27). Like Ann, her dreams are shown to be baseless. Her date with self-proclaimed television executive, Greg, soon puts her right. He claims he can introduce her to television contacts, but he wants sex in return, something she is not willing to give. Then she remembers the boy she left back home, and the last panel shows her writing to Dave.

The last story, "The Touch of Gold" (Art and Carlos) is humorous and tells of Tracy, a lift attendant, who dreams of travel and being rich. In her dreamy state she keeps bumping into the store manager, the dishy Mr James. Mr James tells her she is a menace and an incompetent lift girl. The humour in this story comes from the notion of Tracy as a girl on the move – but it's only up and down. However, her dreams show she has a creative mind and potential. Like the other two girls in these stories, travel and exotic boys are often eschewed in favour of the boy next door. In all of these stories, the heroine shows imagination and vision. She has ambitions for a better life, but she discards her dreams for romance and, presumably marriage and reality, with the boy next to her.

In these stories and articles girls' bodies move spatially on holiday, through employment, from the provincial or northern town to the city (often London). Better travel links and the growing focus on big cities, in particular London as a place of creativity, glamour and better prospects for young girls reflected in stories from the early to late 1960s. The girls in these stories are shown as optimistic about the future, but where the city is often shown as a place of promises and potential, it is also cold and friendless. An example of this type of story is "It's Written in the Stars: Miss Taurus" (Copp and Romero), part of an ongoing series about girls based on their astrological star signs. Penny leaves her hometown because everyone expects her to marry Bill. It is a classic fish-out-of-water narrative. The big city is bewildering, and Penny muses "all these people [...] and no one ever stops to talk" (Copp and Romero). The story ends with her looking to an optimistic future when the boy upstairs invites her to his party: "Yes, tonight, I can feel it starting! The new chapter in my life!"

In "Is He the One?" (Douglas and Romero), set in London, Judy knows nothing of real-life romance until she meets Eddy, an old-time chum from school. They date regularly, and then he tells her he has to leave for South America. Again, there is an optimistic ending in which Judy is left hoping to meet someone like Eddie who can give her a genuine lasting love. There is a bittersweet flavour in both stories, as London is depicted as a cold city where people don't talk to each other. The third story purports to be advice from "Letters to Lesley", a regular problem page. Jane, a northern girl, despairs as she does not fit in because of her accent. Lesley advises her that she should not show her real feeling for fear of being labelled touchy: "After all your accent does make you special" (Gorman and Clapera). All of these stories feature the fantasy of travel or movement and the disillusion when that fantasy is not fulfilled. They serve as warnings to girls not to place too much faith in their dreams and to accept reality.

"Marina Square", 1967: Fashion, Modernity, Aesthetics

To show how these ideas came together, the final part of this chapter analyses the moving body in "Marina Square". There were three pages per episode, and it usually ended on a cliffhanger. The scripts were by staff writer Douglas Sampson; the artwork, which tended to be decorative and textured over the page surface, was by Spanish artist Enrique Monserrat. "Marina Square" initially ran over thirty weeks (8 April 1967–28 October 1967). The story features the protagonist, Carol, a fashion designer who arrives in Bursea, a seaside town on the south coast. She is employed initially by Gear Girl, a boutique in Marina Square, and the first series concentrates on her relationships and love life with boys and her ambitions. The story was developed in two further series (10 May 1969–26 July 1969). In these series she takes over ownership of Gear Girl but doubly fails in her ambitions; she gives up her ambition of moving to London in order to stay in Marina Square and marry her friend Hugo. Unlike *Smashing Time*, where Brenda and Sandra make it in London, turn their backs on romance and return north, Carol turns her back on London and her northern roots, for romance and marriage.

I concentrate on the first series, as it incorporates the issues discussed above. Many of these issues are encapsulated in the town of Bursea that can be read as a metaphor for Britain in the late 1960s – with tensions between the old and young, tradition and progress, the conventional and non-conventional, responsibility and irresponsibility. Although the stories seemed to be weighted in favour of youth, they often show how the old and new should coexist. The protagonist, Carol Jones, must balance her ambition, associated with youth, with her sense of duty as a daughter, employee and girlfriend. Carol, a would-be fashion designer from the north, arrives in the southern seaside town of Bursea to take up employment in what she believes is a modern boutique. She is dismayed to discover that it is old fashioned and not ready for her modern, youthful designs. However, the opportunities on offer in Bursea are much like those in *Smashing Time*, and on exploring Bursea she discovers it is a town of two halves: the old, traditional town and the youthful, modern, get-ahead Marina Square, a newly built shopping arcade. She is immediately offered a job in Gear Girl, a boutique in Marina Square run by Katherine, an older woman.

The first image we have of Carol is where she strikes a pose declaring, "Watch out Bursea! I've arrived!" The scene is set in Bursea railway station and is a reminder of Fan Carter's notion of individuality, the girl on the move "striding out, striking a pose and going far" (Carter) (**fig. 5**). Carol epitomises what Hilary Radner describes as the '60s single girl who represents "culture in transition" (Luckett). However, Carol and Bursea exist in the liminal space between several clashing discourses, the past and the north, the future and the south, youth and modernity versus age and tradition, new towns versus old towns, the sojourn and reality. It is described in the first episode as a place where everyone, including Carol, is making a new start.

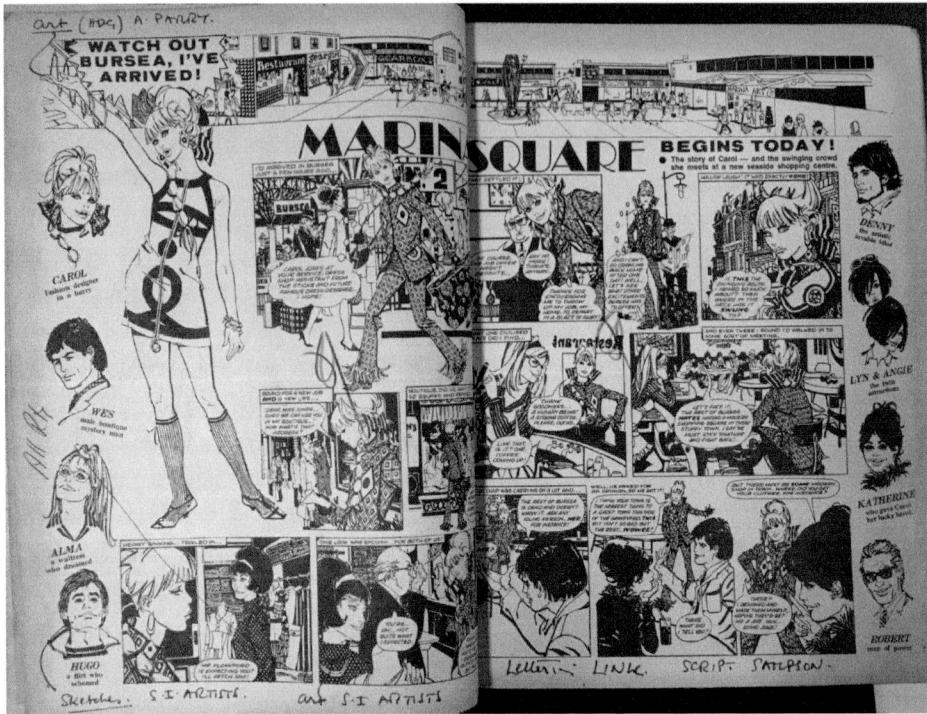

Figure 5 Carol strikes a pose in her Mondrian-inspired dress, *Marina Square* (writer Dave Sampson, artist Enrique Montserrat), Episode 1, 8 April 1967, pp. 6–7.

In Marina Square avant-garde fashion, youth and modernity are brought together. Carol is shown wearing a trouser suit when she arrives in Bursea. The trouser suit is over elaborate in its design and tassels and epitomises Sally Tuffin and Marion Foale's assertion that they did not want to be chic and would rather be ridiculous. Marina Square is modern and clean – remarked on by Carol on her first encounter with the square, "It's such a nice square...so new and clean!" (Sampson and Montserrat, 8 Apr. 1967). In episode two, Carol shows Mr Kenner, chair of the Marina Square Development Corporation around the square. Kenner thinks the square is too noisy and she tells him, "Look young people [...] We set the pace nowadays. Get us young people to Marina Square and the world will follow" (Sampson and Montserrat, 15 Apr. 1967, 10). This statement aligns Marina Square with modernity and youth.

The importance of Marina Square as a youthful place of innovation is emphasised in the banner that crosses the first two pages of every episode, with a facade view of the square (**fig. 5 top**). The two front pages are encompassed by a character list around the edges to reflect the cast list in television soaps. Marina Square is a modern shopping arcade, which would be similar to many new build shopping centres across Britain in the 1960s. The architecture is based on Le Corbusier brutalism, with cuboid shopping units and a modernist sculpture of Neptune in the centre. The shops reflect the bohemian public spaces of the Chelsea set from the early 1960s. There are two boutiques, Gear Box and Gear Girl, an art gallery and a restaurant where Carol encounters the characters in the story. The continuous repetition of this image in every episode provides continuity over the series and the page, because symbolically they bring together the story within the space of Marina Square.

Carol's attitude to life epitomises the notion of work as play. Although not in the frenetic energy of the zany, she is willing to try any job, including shop assistant. Her friends, however, do display zany characters as with the Spinner twins, Lynn and Angie, who work in the record store and model Carol's "miniminimum", a pair of hot pants that are considered by Katherine, and even many of her friends, as too ridiculous to sell in Gear Girl.

The continuing theme of the series is in the conflict of old and new, traditional, modern age and youth, a questioning of "stuffy convention", usually in the form of the older generation. Change and innovation is the province of the younger generation and within the specific space of Marina Square, but Marina Square is a place with the potential to renew and heal the problems of the older generation. The potential for female agency is continuously challenged by the requirements of familial responsibility and care of the older generation. Often Carol is called upon to step in and heal the problems of the older generation, and this is often a challenge for her ambitions. In episode 8 (Sampson and Montserrat, 27 May 1967) Gear Girl owner, Katherine Kenner, and her relationship with her husband, Robert, flounders, and the boutique is threatened with closure. Carol helps them to heal their marriage – "I do love you even though I'm a pig-headed bully", "And I love you Robert...Even though I am too independent for my own good!" (24) – and is made manager of Gear Girl. The inference in the confessions of Katherine and Robert suggest the negative characteristics of men and women: stubbornness in men, independence in women. Women's independence and ambitions often clash with their responsibilities towards their families and relationships, and in episode 6 (Sampson and Montserrat, 13 May 1967) Carol has to return to her northern home to care for her sick mother. On her return Carol finds life in the north is dull and repetitive. When she meets her friends, she says, "it was the same talk as I'd heard so often before" (7). She concludes: "they're not my crowd anymore [...] just as this isn't my town. I've outgrown them both" (8). Her mother's loneliness and isolation after the death of her husband are healed in Marina Square when she travels there in episode 30 (Sampson and Montserrat, 28 Oct. 1967). She finds solace in a meeting with an old friend. Carol muses: "she shouldn't be lonely [...] nobody should be lonely" (12). This sentiment, of course, reflects her own loneliness, which at the end of this series, is healed by the reappearance of her boyfriend, Wes. All of these stories attempt to reconcile the past with the future, which are often brought together in Marina Square.

Intergenerational tensions are represented in episode 23 (Sampson and Montserrat, 9 Sept. 1967), which features "a clash between the old and the new" (22) at the summer festival. The episode depicts an annual carnival during which each business decorates a carnival float based around a theme. This year the older people, led by Alderman Black, "the stuffiest stuffed-shirt in Bursea!" (22), want to make the theme Bursea's glorious past whereas the young people look to the future with a rocket to the moon. Black continuously criticises the young people, including his daughter, Jill, who models the futuristic clothing: "I thought I forbade you to wear that [...] shocking costume [...] or appear in the parade?" However, when his float breaks down, Wes, the owner of Gear Box, offers to give him a tow, as Carol reflects, "so the future pulled the past through Bursea that day [...] the future and the past can learn to live with each other" (24).

Modernity continuously either remakes history in its own modern consumerist image or drags tradition into modernity. A further example of the clash between the modern and the old can be found in episode 25 (Sampson and Montserrat, 23 Sept. 1967). Carol cannot work because of the noise made by an archaeological dig in Marina Square. Again she learns to reconcile the future with the past when she is inspired to design her fashion collection around the Roman finds. Unveiling the collection at her fashion show, the emcee comments: "the clothes you'll see today are in the style of those worn on this very spot nearly two thousand years ago! History repeats itself!" (28) Carol muses: "a Roman look! Two thousand years old but as modern as tomorrow!" (27) As noted above, the old is hijacked by consumerism; this is a Roman garment styled by fashion, modernity and consumerism as a Roman gimmick. In this instance, the future saves the past. The series suggests Carol could achieve her ambitions. She becomes manager of Gear Girl, but the first series ends with Carol's ambitions frustrated. She does not get to London as she is not ready for it. Nor does she achieve her ambitions at the end of series 3. Instead, she settles for romance and marriage with boyfriend Hugo in Marina Square.

Conclusion

Fan Carter argues that *Honey* magazine reflected the freedom that young women experienced in Britain from the early 1960s but this was expressed through mass consumption, leisure and fashion. Comics such as *Mirabelle* represented them, in some cases, as infantilised. Hence, female bodies may have seemed freer and more energetic in this era, yet they remained restricted in more ideologically coded ways through the tensions between the aspirational versus the expectations of female looks, style and behaviour. In this chapter, I used Sianne Ngai's notion of aesthetic categories "zany" and "cute" to show how, in the representation of the active female body, female agency is continuously challenged. The potential for the advancement of female agency offered by consumerism, leisure and fashion is stymied by the fantasy of romance.

In "Marina Square" Carol is the model of the new woman continuously moving and innovating her designs and style. She epitomises the innovation of youth in Britain in the 1960s, which enriched and modernised British culture and the economy. She moves spatially from the north to Bursea. Physically, her body often overlaps the panels, and her movements are expansive. She waves her arms and strides out of panels. Her fantasies also prompt her moving body. She aims to move to London to "make it".

This chapter, like the other chapters in this volume on comics history, deals with the mediated cultural experience of girls in their historical context to reflect on cultural limitations and mediated limitations placed on teenage girls. Carol's movement and her active body might connote ambition and success, but she settles for conformity, and this reflects the lives of many girls in this era. Carol has to balance her responsibility as a daughter like many girls who were expected to take care of ageing parent or younger siblings. Forward-looking modernity often clashes with British traditions of the older generation and the necessity of attempting to reconcile the past with the present and future. The stories show that daydreams and fantasies of a better life are often confounded by cultural pressures on girlhood and finding the right boy, who is often the nearest boy.

Despite the ultimate conformity of girls in many of the stories and articles, *Mirabelle's* content represented female movement, modernity, independence, agency and youthfulness. It provided girls with the opportunity to dream about possibilities. Readers did not have to conform as the heroines in the stories. As Mel Gibson shows, girls often read different meanings in the content. Above all, the active female body in *Mirabelle* of the later 1960s offered an alternative for psychological movement, fantasies of careers, travel and independence that became a major expression of 1970s feminism.

Bibliography

Abrams, Mark. *The Teenage Consumer*. London Press Exchange, 1959.

Ang, Ien. *Watching Dallas: Soap Opera and the Melodramatic Imagination*. Methuen, 1985.

Art, Lewis, and Jose Carlos. "The Touch of Gold". *Mirabelle*, 28 Mar. 1964, pp. 12, 17–18.

Barker, Martin. *Comics: Ideology, Power, and the Critics*. Manchester University Press, 1989.

Barton, Susan. *The Working Class and the Development of Popular Tourism*. Manchester University Press, 2005.

Bernard, Barbara. *Fashion in the Sixties*. Academy Editions, 1978.

Braithwaite, Brian, and Joan Barrell. *The Business of Women's Magazines*. Kogan Page Ltd., 1987.

Brake, Mike. *Comparative Youth Culture: The Sociology of Youth Cultures and Youth Subcultures in America, Britain, and Canada*. Routledge and Kegan Paul, 1985.

Carter, Fan. "A Taste of Honey: Get-Ahead Femininity in 1960s Britain". *Women in Magazines: Research, Representation, Production and Consumption*, edited by Sue Hawkins et al. Routledge, 2016, pp. 195–209.

Copp, P., and Jordi Badia Romero. "Written in the Stars: Miss Taurus". *Mirabelle*, 23 Feb. 1963, pp. 3–5.

Davis, Desmond. *Smashing Time*. Paramount Pictures, 1967.

Doherty, Thomas. *Teenagers and Teenpics: The Juvenilization of American Movies in the 1950s*. Unwin Hyman, 1988.

Douglas, Phillip, and Jordi Badia Romero. "Is He the One?" *Mirabelle*, 3 Mar. 1964.

Entwistle, Joanne. *The Fashioned Body: Fashion, Dress and Modern Social Theory*. Polity Press, 2000.

Fogg, Marnie. *Boutique: A '60s Cultural Phenomenon*. Mitchell Beazley, 2003.

Gibson, Mel. "Comics and Gender". *The Routledge Companion to Comics*. Routledge, 2016.

—. *Remembered Reading: Memory, Comics and Post-War Constructions of British Girlhood*. Leuven University Press, 2015.

Goodall, Scott et al. "I Lived for a Dream". *Mirabelle*, 1 Dec. 1962, pp. 25–27.

Goodall, Scott, and Enrique Badia Romero. "Faraway Places". *Mirabelle*, 14 Sept. 1963, pp. 26–28.

Gorman, Ann, and Josep Clapera. "Letters to Lesley". *Mirabelle*, 4 Feb. 1967, pp. 30–31.

Hall, Stuart. "Encoding/Decoding". *Culture, Media, Language: Working Papers in Cultural Studies, 1972–1979*, edited by Stuart Hall et al. Taylor & Francis, 2005, pp. 128–138.

Harrison, S. "Diane Carr Tells You How to... Wise Up on Your Beauty ABC". *Mirabelle*, 13 Oct. 1962, p. 8.

Lane, Trilby. "Powerful Prints". *Mirabelle*, 6 Mar. 1966, pp. 14–15.

Laver, James. "Mini Skirts". *Women's Wear Daily*, 22 Mar. 1968, p.8.

Luckett, Moya. "Sensuous Women and Single Girls: Reclaiming the Female Body on 1960S Television". *Swinging Single: Representing Sexuality in The Sixties*. University of Minnesota Press, 1999, pp. 277–298.

Marwick, Arthur. *The Sixties: Cultural Revolution in Britain, France, Italy and the United States, c. 1958 – c. 1974*. Oxford University Press, 1998.

McCracken, Ellen. *Decoding Women's Magazines: From Mademoiselle to Ms*. Macmillan, 1993.

McRobbie, Angela. *Feminism and Youth Culture: From Jackie to Just Seventeen*. Macmillan, 1991.

Ngai, Sianne. *Our Aesthetic Categories: Zany. Cute, Interesting*. Harvard University Press, 2012.

Ormrod, Joan. "Reading Production and Culture UK Teen Girl Comics from 1955 to 1960". *Girlhood Studies: An Interdisciplinary Journal*, vol. 11, no. 3, 2018, pp. 18–33.

Reisz, Karel. *Saturday Night and Sunday Morning*. Bryanston Films, 1960.

Roach, David. *Masters of Spanish Comic Book Art*. Dynamite Entertainment, 2017.

Rosengren, W. B. "The Rhetoric of Sojourning". *Journal of Popular Culture*, vol. 5, 1971, pp. 298–314.

Sampson, Dave, and Enrique Montserrat. "Marina Square: Episode 1". *Mirabelle*, 8 Apr. 1967, pp. 6–8.

—. "Marina Square: Episode 2". *Mirabelle*, 15 Apr. 1967, pp. 6–8.

—. "Marina Square: Episode 6". *Mirabelle*, 13 May 1967, pp. 6–8.

—. "Marina Square: Episode 8". *Mirabelle*, 27 May 1967, pp. 22–24.

—. "Marina Square: Episode 23". *Mirabelle*, 9 Sept. 1967, pp. 22–24.

—. "Marina Square: Episode 25". *Mirabelle*, 23 Sept. 1967, pp. 26–28.

—. "Marina Square: Episode 30". *Mirabelle*, 28 Oct. 1967, pp. 10–12.

Schlesinger, John. *A Kind of Loving*. Anglo-Amalgamated, 1962.

Tinkler, Penny. "Fragmentation and Inclusivity: Methods for Working with Girl's and Women's Magazines". *Women in Magazines: Research, Representation, Production and Consumption*, edited by Sue Hawkins et al. Routledge, 2016, pp. 37–52.

Usden, Arline. "Special 4-Page Fashion Pull-Out!!" *Mirabelle*, 2 Dec. 1967, pp. 14–17.

—. "What It's All About". *Mirabelle*, 1 Oct. 1966, pp. 13–15.

White, Cynthia L. *Women's Magazines 1693–1968*. Michael Joseph Ltd., 1970.

Yates, Peter. *Summer Holiday*. Warner-Pathe Distributors (UK), 1963.

Young, Terence. *From Russia with Love*. United Artists, 1963.

Chapter 8

The Demon Girl of Malayali Comic Strips: The (Im)possibilities of Comic Imagination

Aswathy Senan

"All children, except one, grow up"
—J. M. Barrie, *Peter Pan*

Estha and Rahel, the twin protagonists of *The God of Small Things* (1998), introduced to international readers the life and landscape of Malayalis through the eyes of children. The Syrian Christian[1] boy-girl twins have become emblems of the Kerala childhood to the worldwide readership, thanks to the Booker Prize and the subsequent popularity of its author, Arundhati Roy. While these twins grow from their traumatic childhood experiences to deal with the adult world, Boban and Molly, the twins of the comic strip *Bobanum Moliyum*[2] that this paper elaborates upon, remain stuck in an eternal childhood and are forced to make sense of the adult world from their limited perspective. Analysing various episodes of the series and tracing the spaces and actions the twins engage in and juxtaposing them with other comic strips which have similar twin characters, this paper examines the recurrent trope of childhood in the genre of comic strip. This paper argues that rooted in the adult reality of the artist and the readers, these children, rather their childhood, feature as a vantage point that offers space and distance for the artist to critique and comment on several aspects of the adult everyday. The site of childhood thereby features as a fluid space that allows transcending the boundaries of the child and the adult space of action, and this has facilitated its journey through various publications and a varied set of readers for over six decades. Taking this fluidity as the point of departure, this paper presents how the comic strip reorients itself to appeal to the childhood of the readers, who may not necessarily be children most of the time, using the girl child as the device to do so.

Children's Literature: By Adults, for Adults?

Peter Hunt, in his edited volume of *International Companion Encyclopedia of Children's Literature* (1996) and *Understanding Children's Literature* (1999), studies the history, genealogy and practice of children's literature in different countries and languages, highlighting its porous nature. Stating that the words "literature" and "child" are "equally slippery", Hunt points out the inherent flaw in "making judgments on behalf of present or past children" by pointing out the difference in orientation, skills, reading habits and perception between the adult and the child reader (1999, 3–4). He goes on to say that "if we judge children's books (even if we do it unconsciously) by the same value systems as we use for adult books—where they are *bound by definition* to emerge as *lesser*—then we give ourselves unnecessary problems" (Hunt, 1999, 4). The tendency to consider childhood as this pristine, innocent phase in one's life and the pressure to ensure that children are provided with unadulterated literature to ensure emotional nurturing makes such scrutiny mandatory for them. But it is invariably the adult writer/critic or the parent reader/buyer who makes that choice on their behalf.

For cartoons and comic strips, the question of authorship and readership is a fundamental concern, as the reception of the genre and its positioning within the framework of children's literature itself has been blurry, since comics for a long time were considered to be part of pop culture. In their study on Donald Duck's[3] influence on American culture, Ariel Dorfman and Armand Mattelart state that the child in the Disney comics is a manifestation of the adult anxieties and conceptions about childhood, as there is a "virtually biologically captive, predetermined audience" (30). They add:

> Children's comics are devised by adults, whose work is determined and justified by their idea of what a child is or should be [...] The comics show the child as a miniature adult, enjoying an idealized, gilded infancy which is really nothing but the adult projection of some magic era beyond the reach of the harsh discord of daily life [...] Juvenile literature, embodying purity, spontaneity, and natural virtue, while lacking sex and violence, represents earthly paradise. (30)

Studies on children's literature imply that it is conceived, read, theorised and chosen for children by adults. This attempts to project the adult's own "angelical aspirations" onto childhood as if it is separated from the reality of the everyday: as a "special domain where these values can be projected uncritically" (Dorfman and Mattelart 30). This is reflected in most of the books listed under that category of children's literature, as the texts contain elements of magic, adventure, fantasy, anthropomorphism and so on. These unusual and unreal experiences that the children experience in these narratives could be an extension of what the artists remember of their own childhood dreams and lived experiences.

By including his article on the *Peanuts* comic strip in *The Oxford Handbook of Children's Literature* (2011), Charles Hatfield draws attention to how comic strips constitute "an ever-present but underexamined part of the larger cultural scripting of childhood" (168). Hatfield states how comic studies itself underplays the link between comics and childhood to "boost the art form to a higher seriousness" (168). His allegation regarding comics practitioners and critics struggling to make comics seem part of the "higher arts" proves true when Henry Jenkins, in his introductionto *Critical Approaches to Comics: Theories and Methods* (2012), while mapping the history of comic studies, states how comics were initially read "in relation to a larger category of lively arts, which included jazz, slapstick film comedy, the Broadway musical, the night club, revue performance and the comic newspaper column" (2). Jenkins then proceeds to identify the technicalities of the form of comics, and finally focusing on its most serious and recent manifestation: graphic novels.[4] This tendency to juxtapose comic strips or graphic literature vis-à-vis high art is visible in Malayalam comic strips as well: the only comic strip that the Malayali readership considers as serious graphic literature is Aravindan's *Cheriya Manushyarum Valiya Lokavum* (henceforth *CMVL*).[5] In the case of *Bobanum Moliyum*, the series was initially published in *Malayala Manorama*, again a "popular" weekly, with children as main characters, juvenile in nature, with hardly any discussion on the profound or serious matters of life – although the theme and space of action expanded from the juvenile to the more "political" space, towards its later phase and with its publication in *Kalakaumudi*. Even with the shifts in thematic and stylistic changes that the characters and the series have itself undergone, there is a sense of retention of a "model", which is purely illusionary. The following section will detail the manner in which the spatial and thematic transition the children as protagonists of the series have undergone in the two periodicals: *Malayala Manorama* and *Kalakaumudi*.

The Journey of the Twins: Spaces and Characters

The twins in *Bobanum Moliyum* are stuck at age eleven, the "mischief age", which Toms sees as a flexible and poignant vehicle for laughter, thought and criticism. Toms attributes Boban and Molly's arrested development over the years to the time that a cartoonist needs to make his characters familiar and acceptable to his readers. In his autobiography

Figure 1 *Bobanum Moliyum. Malayala Manorama.* 2 November 1957.

Ente Bobanum Moliyum [My Boban and Molly], Toms mentions that it is by retaining stagnancy of the characters and surroundings that he was able to establish a familiar and comfortable space of action which has allowed the series to stay in the memory of the readers for such a long duration (*Ente* 56). It is the familiarity that the strip and its characters have been able to develop over the years that have given it a unique character, or rather evoked a singular response from the readers as being a funny, witty piece of graphic literature. To understand the series within the framework of children's literature, an examination of the spaces and themes depicted in the series becomes essential. A survey of the comic strips published in Malayalam magazines during the second half of twentieth century illustrate that the topics chosen, the characterisation, the spaces depicted and the kind of humour that the comic strips illustrate reflect and complement the contents, political orientation and readership of the magazine in which they were placed. Mapping this chronologically helps to understand the evolution of the form that is considered as essentially funny or even juvenile.

In the first year of its inception, the series presented the space of action as the familial space that the twins inhabited with their parents, neighbours and house guests. The stories revolved around children and how they tackled their everyday life and outsmarted those who tried to make them work or study. Many of these strips were silent ones, and hence heavily action oriented, and used facial expressions and action strokes. The pleasure it evoked can be attributed to the visual depiction of incidents and the manner in which the twins dealt with them (**fig. 1**). They had no speech bubbles, and the meaning of the story evolved as the panels progressed through the acts and mannerisms of the characters.

A close examination of the contents of the magazine indicates that the readership of *Malayala Manorama* was not children; however, the comic strip seems to be something that could be appealing to the child reader as well. Most of these comic strips are similar to the material that one might find in a children's magazine or a picture storybook. Once Toms started his own publishing house, he reprinted several such comic strips: the contents of

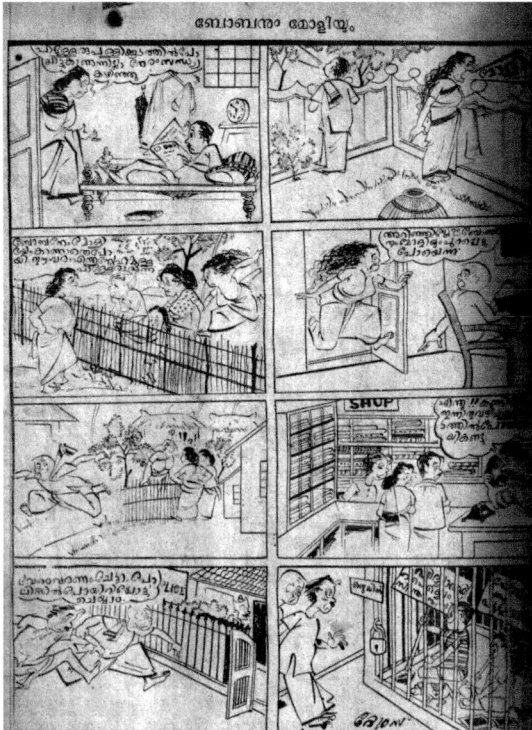

Figure 2 *Bobanum Moliyum. Malayala Manorama.* 2 August 1958.

various productions of Toms Publications highlight this aspect of lucidity and familiarity of the readers with visual literature, thereby appealing to the child reader by reprinting most of these earlier comics and also creating similar ones that range between juvenile and adult literature.

In less than a year after its launch in *Malayala Manorama*, *Bobanum Moliyum* expands the area of the twins' action, and they start being part of socially and politically charged issues. The twins in these episodes become part of the larger and more vibrant issues of the surrounding society, talk about freedom, flood, try to fool the film theatre authorities when they refuse them movie tickets, play pranks on the seniors and so on. One wonders whether these are acts that "normal" eleven-year-old children would engage in or acts that the artist pushes them into in order to negate those boundaries between the adult and the child. It is an example of cross-writing, which, as defined by Mitzi Myers and U. C. Knoepflmacher, entails "a dialogic mix of older and younger voices [that] occurs in texts too often read as univocal" and features "interplay" between adult and child perspectives, one that implies a mixed readership and an author who respects adult and child readers equally (vii). The comics page in newspapers or magazines is, in fact, a space that practically encourages such cross-writing, a space that could belong to and engage both children and adults alike. Visually, although the format is neatly divided into eight panels with equal gutter space, the relationship between images and text are not neatly arranged (**fig. 2**). There seems to be a struggle in placing the text and images in an organic fashion in this format.

We have seen that the kids, consciously or unconsciously, negate any kind of hierarchy and fixed norms by being equal partners in crime, thereby transgressing demarcated spaces together. For example, consider the comic strip from 15 August 1959, which has the twins organising a rally for women's rights. They campaign in the village, asking women to join the programme, but everyone refuses to join them on various pretexts. Finally, the boys decide

Figure 3 *Bobanum Moliyum*. *Malayala Manorama*. 15 September 1973.

to dress like women in sarees and cover their heads. With Molly leading the march they hold placards which read "Long Live Women's rights", "Fight until death", "See the Women's Unity", and the like. This kind of cross-dressing is quite common in child play, but to use it for a protest was unusual.

By the mid-1960s *Bobanum Moliyum* had become a space to showcase the public-private concerns of the common public. Although the action is centred on protesting, rallies and cries for justice, the participants are all students, schoolchildren to be precise. This capturing of the vibrant children's life beyond playground, schools and houses was an important feature of this comic strip. By then, the artist had mastered the logic of the form as there is an organic merging which one can see regarding the text and images in the series. The late sixties cartoons focused on the everyday of the villagers and their interactions with parents. The episodes in this period lack uniformity and feature unpredictability of how each issue is dealt with – something peculiar to this series and which also contributes to its sustainability as a seemingly formulaic narrative. This is the period when the twins become more of a unit rather than two entities, and they are even referred to as "kids" or "twins" rather than by their individual names.

In the seventies, with the advent of Appie Hippie, the twins are exposed to or are made party to several romantic liaisons of the young Romeo figure. They tag along with Appie during his courting sessions, listening to tales of his love-struck heart and the Hippie movement he wants to dedicate his life to (**fig. 3**). Juxtaposing such instances with the juvenile spaces and conversations are modes through which the artist expanded its scope and readership. The inclusion of a character like Appie Hippie in the series makes it evident that the series repositioned, redesigned and reoriented itself, possibly drawing on newer conventions of comic culture from the West. Here again, visually, the artist uses various graphic devices like dream clouds, bold text for shouting and inscriptions on things to indicate what they are.

By the mid-1970s the series becomes text oriented, animated, crowded with visuals and props, and the themes they deal with also shifts to grimmer and darker ones. The 18 May 1974 episode (**fig. 4**), on the series' twentieth anniversary, comes across as a peculiar

Figure 4 *Bobanum Moliyum*. *Malayala Manorama*. 18 May 1974.

episode of the initial years, as the artist uses heavy actions and sound effects in narrating the story. Although this mode of criticism of political action and governmental policies are features of newspaper cartoons, and not necessarily of comic strips, *Bobanum Moliyum* was also used as a site for the same. The series was fluid in making use of the characters and the space to tell tales and make comments on anything and everything that the artist deemed fit. In this twelve-panelled comic strip, the twins speak once, and they are hardly seen. This is the time around which the children lose their prominence in the comic strip, and the series began to deal with the more serious issues and discuss political developments in the state. In comparison with the rest of the content of *Malayala Manorama*, the comic strip by then had become starkly different stylistically and thematically.

The eighties, however, witnessed a major transition, as the artist made his shift from *Malayala Manorama* to *Kalakaumudi*, and simultaneously started Toms Publication, which led to the copyright case.[6] In most of the comic strips during this time, the children hardly talk. The comic strips centre on politicians and the workings of the various political parties and trade unions. Even the stock characters like Appie Hippie, Chettan and Chettathi vanish from the familiar, humorous domestic spaces and move on to the more serious, politically vibrant space of streets, police stations and protest venues. Toms's shift to *Kalakaumudi* (in 1987) made the artist experiment with the format and style of the political cartoon mode by imitating the seriousness of his predecessors O. V. Vijayan and G. Aravindan, major literary figures of that period. This tendency managed to affect the comic strip in *Kalakaumudi* in addition to its readership, which made it far removed from, and less accessible to, child readers. One can infer that the artist was attempting to reformulate the series in a format that would make it appealing to the readership of *Kalakaumudi*, which was starkly different from *Malayala Manorama*.

Mapping the thematic evolution of the series using the twin children as the main characters of the series, and the orientation of the magazine in which it was published, was to understand how the comic strip locates itself within the large pool of readers stretched over such a long span of time. There is a sense of fluidity and uncertainty with regard to the target audience of the series and in none of the interviews or write-ups does the author-artist or publishers mention who they are addressed to. The comic strip has always retained a mode of flexibility to design itself and be presented to any kind of audience: children, adolescents or adults. The comic strip dissolves the binaries in terms of theme, narration and readership, which are insisted upon by knowledge systems with regard to adults and children. But one can infer that the children and childhood are kept alive or brought back within a few episodes of the series discussing the adult issues. To understand this evolution of the series concentrating on the trope of childhood, it becomes imperative to also examine the various imitations or independent versions of the comic strip. This also helps to understand *Bobanum Moliyum* as an important influence within the genre of Malayalam comic strips.

Twin Children: The Site of the Comic Everyday

Bobanum Moliyum gave the Malayali reading public a familiar space in the comic format – the village in which the twins live, the familiar characters placed in familiar situations – the everyday in comics. However, the twins did not remain the same visually or themati-cally over the years. The twins were stick-thin figures in the initial years of the comic strip, they became healthier in the seventies and by the eighties were plump kids. Although their attire remains more or less the same, their facial expression changes drastically. The faces in the initial strips are cruder and less clear; the later ones gain more character and sharpness. The caricatures of the children gain naughtiness and childishness by the eighties, though the children themselves started losing significance and prominence in the series. The panels are often action filled, featuring the characters running or jumping or moving around. The twins are often featured to be in a "jumping in the air" position, with heads held high. Molly's skirt always flies up in the air, which could probably refer to the free-spirited, overenthusiastic and impulsive nature of the girl child. She conforms to the characterised "*demon* child", "socially marginal, ambiguously positioned type of character who could reach young and old readers alike" (Hatfield 170) and who "so often upended or poked fun at the idea of childhood innocence" (171). Although the series has the twins as inseparable characters, there are points at which the girl child and her gender specificity is brought out humorously. She is almost always referred to as *shalyam* (a nui-sance) or *pani* (work, colloquially meaning "troubles") because of the two, she is expected to be docile compared to the male child.

The everyday of the twins is demonstrated through their interaction with the adult world, highlighting its hypocrisies, hierarchies and norms. Although the children had become mute observers towards the end of his term in *Malayala Manorama*, Toms made the children more prominent and active once he started *Tomsinte Bobanum Moliyum* [Toms' Bobanum Moliyum] in *Kalakaumudi*. Compared to the *Malayala Manorama* version, created by unknown artists, which reduced the size of the panels (and hence increased the number of panels) and filled the panels with props, numerous characters and several dialogues, Toms made the children and familiar characters prominent again, like in his initial days. A close comparison of the comic strips would show that Toms was cleverly trying to assert that the comic strip in *Kalakaumudi* was by the real artist, while another parallel series in *Malayala Manorama* was by a "ghost artist". He did this by reinforcing the twins: their faces became bigger, their witty nature became prominent again and their presence over the panels increased, especially that of the girl child Molly. However, this didn't last for long, owing to the fact that the readership of *Kalakaumdi* was different, and Toms reoriented the strips to include more politically charged topics and characters. The title of the series remained *Tomsinte Bobanum Moliyum*, even in the episodes in which the twins were absent, making them much more than just about the twins: it became the title of the series that encompassed the stories of all the characters that were created through the series and even the imaginary village in which they were placed. This trope of the twin children is something that was imitated by several other artists and cartoonists of the time in several other magazines as well. Though none of those imitations (except, *Mayavi*) has sustained for more than a few years, listing and examining them thematically is imperative to understand the reason behind so many cartoonists using the trope of the children and several of the type characters produced through the *Bobanum Moliyum* series.

The first imitation of the *Bobanum Moliyum* series in Malayalam could be *Laluvum Leelayum* [Lalu and Leela] by K. S. Rajan in *Manorajyam* weekly. The comic strip ran from 11 July 1973 to 23 December 1981 and had twins, a boy and a girl Christian around ten years of age. The strip featured their life amongst friends, parents and neighbours. From the dressing style of the children and their mother, they could be from a more affluent family than Boban and Molly. But their mannerisms and engagement with the world outside is similar to those of Boban and Molly. The series also had several characters whose names, looks and characteristics were exactly the same. Take, for instance, the episode from 11 July 1973 of *Manorajyam* weekly: it has the Christian children praying but getting disturbed by the chant "Hare Rama Hare Krishna". They rush outside to find Hippichayan chanting the song in pursuit of a young woman, an exact replication of Appie Hippie's tendencies in *Bobanum Moliyum*. The last panel has the children covering themselves in a saree, one on top of the other, to give a sense of a grown woman to fool Hippichaayan. This is an exact replica of the *Bobanum Moliyum* series from the 10 July 1971 *Malayala Manorama* (**fig. 5a and 5b**). This depicts that *Bobanum Moliyum* was a reference point or even a

Figure 5a *Lauluvum Leelayum.* 11 July 1973.   **Figure 5b** *Bobanum Moliyum.* 10 July 1971.

model for imitation for subsequent artists. The twin children and the type of characters the series created had engrossed the Kerala literary public to such an extent that it even led to a series with panel-to-panel imitation.

Chandrika Weekly published a series called *Samuvum Seemayum* [Samu and Seema] from 15 May 1982 to 20 August 1983, created by Majeed Nanmanda. The main characters, Samu and Seema, possibly twins, move around the village, school and domestic spaces, commenting on and involving themselves in other people's issues. However, the artist seems to grapple both with the technicality of merging the texts and images in a coherent and smooth fashion, which also shows that the form in itself was still one that was developing. The division of the panels and the design of the speech balloons are done in a systematic fashion, but the figures are cruder and lack the charm or smoothness that other similar popular series had. The two children were almost always stuck together – similar to Boban and Molly.

Mayavi of *Balarama*, a popular children's digest of Manorama publication, also has a boy-girl pair – Raju and Radha – as its lead. Started in August 1984 (**fig. 6**), *Mayavi* was sketched in colour and still continues to be a favourite among children. One cannot trace any resemblance between these children and the twins, as the series was mostly located in the forest, with witches and thieves as main characters. The parents or house of the children never becomes a part of the narrative, and they are never shown as partaking

Figure 6 *Mayavi. Balarama.* August 1984.

in any routine activity like going to school or eating or playing. It is never mentioned whether the two children are siblings or twins, but they are always placed as a team in opposition to the evil forces that confront them or in trying to capture Mayavi. None of the earlier mentioned comic strip series gained as much popularity as the original naughty twins; however, Raju and Radha from the *Mayavi* series managed to yield strong readership among children. Toms Publications also published series such as *Little Chattan* [Little Spirit], *Lallu-Lalli*, *Babu-Sally* and *Tara-Soni* – all of which had children displaying similar features. Toms used the same style that he had used in *Bobanum Moliyum* to create new characters with similar characteristics to the twin children caught in the intellectual property rights debate. Through these imitations, he could have been conveying that he is capable of creating several similar characters while regaining their popularity, even if he loses the copyright case, or even developing them as an alternative option to continue telling the story. In all these comic strips, one feature that is common is the age of the children. It could be inferred that they all are in similar age group, probably between nine and thirteen, neither children nor young adults. It also highlights that there was a lot of imitation and replication of character, settings and even situations.

Toms states that he had made the twin kids stuck at the age of eleven, as he finds it to be the right age for them to enter any domain – social or familial – and provoke conflict or trigger laughter. This trend to use children to portray or discuss serious issues or merchandise products has been prevalent in the history of comics from the time of the emergence of the genre.[7] But, in none of these, including *Bobanum Moliyum*, are the children portrayed as innocent, guarded or protected entities. They are on their own, out in the world interacting with elders and children, though there is no clarity on how they would react or behave in each episode. This sense of ambiguity prevents a reader from anticipating what is in store for the reader in an episode; it could be smart twins, scary twins, silent twins, foolish twins, revolting twins, helpful twins or even invisible twins.

But in one of the anniversary productions, the cover page of the series highlights the difference between the girl and boy child, where Toms features one of the characters who is asked why the children are stuck at childhood. His response to this is that he cannot afford to get Molly married off, as that would mean raising a huge dowry, which would fall heavily upon him financially. This instance starkly marks the difference between the two children and makes the characters heavily gendered, which cannot be seen in any of the subsequent episodes. But this tendency to portray the female characters as a burden or pain persists throughout the series, though not primarily through Molly.

The comic strip had always been of a fluid nature, in terms of theme, narrative and humour. Though the twins were the main characters, the series did not always have them as the central characters, nor did they always evoke laughter. In fact, the series was not always humorous, but still it managed to retain people's attention and appreciation for six decades. However, when other magazines and artists came up with the same or similar pattern of boy-girl twins in that medium to articulate similar stories, they did not have the same effect on the readers, which brings us to the question of the particularity of this comic strip in relation to the pleasure it evokes.

Pleasures of Reading: The Comic Imagination

Though children's periodicals had started circulating in Kerala by the mid-1970s, *Bobanum Moliyum* played a particular role in shaping the genre of comic strips or picture stories for subsequent graphic literature in Malayalam. Compared to political cartoons and other graphic narratives, the comic strips in magazines or popular weeklies reach the reader "unbidden" (Duncan 7) due to their placement and thematic unpredictability. The spatiality and temporality of comic strip that appears in a weekly or daily newspaper is a factor that aesthetically and commercially deprives them of "the possibility of narrative development" (Eco 16). For the film *Bobanum Moliyum* (1971), the majority of the readership was women and children, men were predominantly involved only in the creation, production and circulation process. This lack of clarity regarding the intended audience of the series is something that still exists for *Bobanum Moliyum*. In spite of these ambiguities and differences, there is a certain manner in which it has appealed to readers over the generations and two reasons could be identified for this.

The series often defies the norms of what the children do and fearlessly intervenes into all walks of life – from politics and romance to monetary issues and governmental policies. This method of the adults using children to achieve their desired goals is a recurrent theme in the series. Their childishness is often featured as naive jokes, and their seemingly childish actions and their "naivety" become the radical tools through which the regressive and violent acts in history get exposed. The visuals in the panels, such as the descriptive banner and sign for the operation theatre, denote the spaces that are featured in the series. It is not always the case that the comic strips are necessarily condemning or trivialising the situation; readers are encouraged to laugh at the uninhibited actions and words of the children, at their unassuming unpredictability. Though cartooning as an art form is not self-consciously didactic or pedantic, nor does it hope to transforming society, the mark it leaves on those who are the objects of ridicule might not be trivial. But the children in this series are not the kind who blurt out sentences or words unconsciously or do things stupidly. They are featured as sharp, conniving, though at times silly beings that provoke laughter and thought aimed at themselves or other characters of the series or the readers themselves. The twins are always placed together, as a team, in contrast to everything else – family, friends and the villagers. There were instances where the artist did try to separate them but immediately brought them back together, which implies their separation is almost impossible. They defy the forces together; even visually they are most of the times stuck to each other, like conjoined twins. They get involved in everything, or are silently present on some occasions, and nothing limits their intervention as far as spaces or issues are concerned, which brings us to the second point about their scope of action.

There is an element of surprise regarding what each episode offers through the series. It is not formulaic in nature, and this lack of pattern is what could be considered as characteristic of the *Bobanum Moliyum* comic strip. Though the comic strip had managed to create a familiarity among the readers with arrested development, placed in unchanged conditions, interacting with the same set of people, that reaches the readers at a regular interval of a week on the last page of a periodical, there is something unexpected or unfamiliar about how the narrative progresses. The lack of a solid plot prevents the reader from the usual process that they follow in comic book reading, in other words, skipping through the panels without actually reading all the text or closely viewing all the images in order to find out what happens next. The comic strip offers a space of relief, recurrence and comfort with a set of characters who are placed in the same setting dealing with similar situations, making the readers think and laugh. In the *Bobanum Moliyum* strips, since a page rarely tells a story and an episode is more of an event than a narrative, the content of every panel becomes important. All this was done within the constraints of having not more than a single page for the comic. This restricted space, with the frequency of being published only once a week, might have made the artist crowd each panel with maximum images and text.

When the author started Toms Publications, it is evident that he was trying to market it to the child reader and the parent buyer. There is nothing static or concrete about the manner in which the humour operates in the series. It is a fluid site in which, by using a set of characters, the artist has managed to sustain an impression of humour. By evoking a certain feeling that the name generates, the comic strip has managed to sustain itself

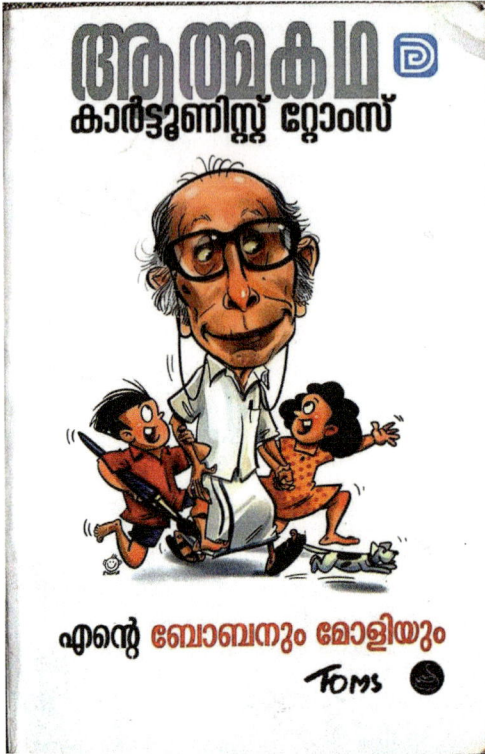

Figure 7 Toms. *Ente Bobanum Moliyum.*
Don Books, 2015, cover page.

for more than six decades, and still continues to, considering that the publication is continuing even after Toms's demise.

The anthology of the series, which came out in its fiftieth year of publication, was titled *Tomsinte Bobanum Moliyum*, with the image of the children and all the main characters on its cover page. The choice of the title of the book, which was same as the name of the comic series in *Kalakaumudi*, is clearly a dig at *Malayala Manorama*. Toms's serialised memoir in *Madhyamam* weekly, titled *Ormakalude Rekhachithram*[8] [Sketches of Memories] also had the image of the twins on the cover page on the 11 October 2010 issue announcing the series. Even the title of his autobiography, *Ente Bobanum Moliyum* [My Boban and Molly], with the possessive pronoun, is a statement to denote his sole ownership of the twin children and the series. The cover page of this book (**fig. 7**) has the artist Toms holding hands with the twins – with Boban holding his paintbrush and Molly showing him the way – and the dog, Tippu, running ahead. In all this, the focus is the twin children and the animated image of the twins in a jumping position, which intend to appeal to the child reader and the child in the adult reader. This becomes even more apparent in the latest issues of Toms Publications, titled *Bobanum Moliyum*, which comes with a subtitle on its cover that reads *Malayalaalikalude Baalyam*, meaning "The Childhood of Malayalis". The juxtaposition of the words "Malayalis" and "Childhood" is a sharp, calculated marketing strategy that Toms, the artist-publisher, has devised for understanding the various trends that the series has undergone and its everlasting appeal among those readers who have grown up reading them and the shifting reading practices.

Since the first decade of the 2000s, there has been a proliferation of children's magazines, English and Malayalam picture books for children, the advent of satellite television channels which led to the mushrooming of cartoon channels, cartoons dubbed in Malayalam aired by most of the Malayalam satellite channels, and animation production houses. All this could have contributed to the fall in popularity of the series and triggered the series to be brought out in an animation format. For the ever-nostalgic Malayali adult reader, in their late thirties to sixties, apart from *Amar Chitra Katha* and a couple of children's magazines, *Bobanum Moliyum* was the main form of graphic literature. Such nostalgia has been a factor in sustaining the appeal of the artist and publisher. This is apparent even from the fact that letters to the editor, published in Toms in 2014 are similar to the ones published in 1984. The sense of reliving the past by recollecting the experience of reading the cartoon series – waiting for the weekly to arrive, fighting over it with friends, reading the weekly from the last page and laughing at and enjoying the one-page comic strip – is narrated with a strong sense of nostalgia. The whole set of actions regarding the reading practice of the series is something that the artist and the series attempt to market and even recreate. The point of departure for categorisation of the *Bobanum Moliyum* comic strip within the critical paradigm of children's literature would be this sense of nostalgia, that it evokes or tries to evoke – as it is this yearning of what one has lost through the years, a phase of life that one cherishes – and wants to design beautifully for the coming generation which in turn is the base of most of children's literature.

In her study on the classic children's fiction *Peter Pan*, Jacqueline Rose observes that children's fiction "rests on the idea that there is a child who is simply there to be addressed and that speaking to it might be simple" (1) and adds that it hangs on an impossibility: "the impossible relation between adult and child" (1). She draws upon the complexity of children's literature and how it builds "a world in which the adult comes first (author, maker, giver) and the child comes after (reader, product, receiver), but where neither of them enter the space in between" (Rose 2). She brings our attention to the trap of misreading the image of a child inside a book as more than the author's projected intention. She identifies *Peter Pan* as a book which conceals the nonidentity of the child audience and reader, which, instead of asking "what children want, or need, from literature", has asked "what it is that adults, through literature, want or demand of the child" (Rose 137). *Bobanum Moliyum* has done something similar for Malayalis. The series did not start as a cartoon strip published in a magazine meant for children, nor was it specifically aimed at a child audience, but it has over the years chosen to project itself as something catering to the child audience, or appealing to the child in the adult reader. The question of the shift between adult and child reader effectively disrupts the notion of the adult/child dualisms, which becomes central in understanding this comic strip. This comic strip shifts between who the main characters are, which spaces they occupy, what their concerns are and even who the readership is. If we are to use the factors of children's literature to analyse *Bobanum Moliyum*, it satisfies and defies them at the same time and hence refuses to be part of any such category. Having been written, sold, consumed and marketed primarily by adults, such literature can be considered as being part of cross-writing or crossover literature, which crosses "age boundaries, the boundaries (for example, young child, nine to fourteen, young adult, adult) [...] [and] subject[ed] to constant redefinition" (Falconer

557). Projecting itself as the childhood of Malayalis, through the icons that Toms has created over almost six decades, the series transcends the desire to appeal exclusively to the child reader, and instead appeals to the child within each reader. This emotion that the children or one's childhood evokes was also central in the copyright case that the comic strip was party to, the discourses around which were mostly about the rightful "parent" of the twins.

Notes

1. St Thomas Christian or Syrian Christians are an indigenous religious group known for their use of the Syriac language in their Mass, though most of their practices are taken from the Hindu customs.

2. My PhD project "The Comic Strip of the Kerala Everyday: *Bobanum Moliyum*, 1957–2014" details the relevance of the popular comic strip *Bobanum Moliyum* as the only continuous, artistic expression of the fifty-seven years of Kerala's life by a single artist. *Bobanum Moliyum* [Boban and Molly] is the longest-running comic strip in Kerala, created by the artist Toms (VT Thomas); it started in *Malayala Manorama* (14 May 1957) and later continued in *Kalakaumudi* (from 22 November 1987 to 19 April 1992) and is now continuing through various issues of Toms Publications. My dissertation intends to understand the Kerala everyday as constructed in the comic form, which takes the most banal and most phenomenal implications of the sociopolitical changes that the state has gone through since its inception in 1957.

3. A cartoon character created by Walt Disney Productions in 1934, Donald Duck is an anthromorphic white duck that is famous for its animated cartoons.

4. Recently, many graphic novels offer first-person accounts of intimate relationships, cultural displacement, historical memory and shifting identities: *Maus* (1980), *Persepolis* (2000) and *Bhimayana* (2011) are a few examples. What constitutes a graphic novel and the scope of themes that the genre can deal with has undergone drastic changes. In addition, the establishment of comic studies departments and academic conferences on the same have contributed to the genre being considered as part of "serious" literature.

5. While a huge pool of cartoons and comics, mostly published in Malayalam periodicals, has been left unexplored, studied or even anthologised for that matter, this piece of graphic literature by one of the most reputed film-makers in Malayalam became the epitome of intellectual and artistic creativity. We cannot ignore that one of the reasons for this prejudice stems from the fact that most of the graphic pieces have been part of "popular" reading material or children's magazines.

6. The *Bobanum Moliyum* comic series was the centre of a major litigation on copyright during 1987–1992 between *Malayala Manorama* vs. the artist Toms and *Kalakaumudi* to own the exclusive right to the title *Bobanum Moliyum* and to sketch and publish the comic strip with the twins as main characters in their publication. The cover page of the fiftieth anniversary anthology edition of *Bobanum Moliyum* states: "The cartoon that created a Comic War in the Supreme Court of India".

7. The *Yellow Kid* and "Amul girl" are two important examples. *Yellow Kid* was an American comic strip, conceived and illustrated by Richard F. Outcault, that featured a young boy who lived in an alley with other kids, was bald, with buck teeth and jug ears and wore an oversized yellow robe (which also served as a space for the word balloons). It was the first example of the "potential of comic characters to capture the public's imagination and boost newspaper circulation" (Gordon 32). The closest comparison to this phenomenon in the Indian imagination would be "Amul girl", the mascot of Indian dairy products. Featured in the advertisements of Amul, she is a young girl in a polka-dotted frock with blue hair and a grin on her face. She comments on contemporary issues using a tag line that would be a word pun vis-à-vis some contemporary incident. Over the years, she has emerged as a political commentator too.

8. *Ormakalude Rekhachithram* was serialised in *Madhyamam Weekly*, another prominent weekly magazine in Kerala. It started on 11 October 2010 and ended abruptly on 22 August 2011.

Bibliography

Aravindan, G. *Cheriya Manushyarum Valiya Lokavum* [Small Men and the Big World]. Bees Book, 1978.

Aries, Philippe. *Centuries of Childhood: A Social History of the Family*, translated by Robert Baldick. Vintage Books, 1962.

Barrie, J. M. *Peter Pan*. Harper Collins, 2013.

Bobanum Moliyum. Directed by Sasikumar. Performance by Madhu, Kaviyoor Ponnamma and Adoor Bhasi. RA Productions, 1971.

Chandrika Weekly. Muslim Printing and Publishing Company Limited, 1982–1983.

Dorfman, Ariel, and Armand Mattelart. *How to Read Donald Duck: Imperialist Ideology in the Disney Comic*. International General Editions, 1975.

Duncan, Randy, and Matthew J. Smith, editors. "Introduction". *Critical Approaches to Comics: Theories and Methods*. Routledge, 2012, pp. 1–23.

Eco, Umberto. "Seriality". *The Limits of Interpretation*. First Midland, 1990.

Gordon, Ian. *Comic Strips and Consumer Culture*. Smithsonian Institution, 1998.

Hatfield, Charles. "Redrawing the Comic-Strip Child: Charles M. Schulz's Peanuts as Cross Writing". *The Oxford Handbook of Children's Literature.*, edited by Julia Mickenberg and Lynne Vallone. Oxford University Press, 2011, pp. 167–188.

Hunt, Peter. "Introduction: The World of Children's Literature Studies". *Understanding Children's Literature*, edited by Peter Hunt. Routledge, 1999, pp. 1–14.

—. editor. *International Companion Encyclopedia of Children's Literature*. Routledge, 1996.

Jenkins, Henry. "Should We Discipline the Reading of Comics". *Critical Approaches to Comics: Theories and Methods*, edited by Matthew J. Smith and Randy Duncan. Routledge, 2012, pp. 1–23.

Knoepflmacher, U. C., and Mitzi Myers. "From the Editors: 'Cross Writing' and the Reconceptualising of Children's Literary Studies". *Children's Literature*, vol. 25. Yale University Press, 1997, pp. vii–xvii.

Kalakaumudi Weekly. Kalakaumudi, 1987–1992.

Lesnik-Oberstein, Karin. "Essentials: What is Children's Literature? What is Childhood?" *Understanding Children's Literature*, edited by Peter Hunt. Routledge, 1999, pp. 15–30.

Manorajyam. Manorajyam Publications,, 1973–1981.

Malayala Manorama Weekly. Manorama Press, 1957–1987.

"Mayavi". *Balarama*. MM Publications, August 1984.

Myers, Mitzi. "Reading Children and Homeopathic Romanticism: Paradigm Lost, Revisionary Gleam, or 'Plus Ça Change, Plus C'est la Même Chose'?" *Literature and the Child: Romantic Continuations, Postmodern Contestations*, edited by James Holt McGavran. University of Iowa Press, 1999, pp. 44–84.

Nanmanda, Majeed. "Samuvum Seemayum". *Chandrika Weekly*. Muslim Printing and Publishing Company Limited, 1982–1983.

Rajan, K. S. "Laluvum Leelayum". *Manorajyam*. Manorajyam Publications, 1973–1981.

Rose, Jacqueline. *The Case of Peter Pan or: The Impossibility of Children's Fiction*. Macmillan, 1984.

Roy, Arundhati. *The God of Small Things*. Penguin Books, 1997.

Toms. *Ente Bobanum Moliyum* [My Boban and Molly]. National Book Stall, 2015.

—. "Babu-Sally". *Toms Comics*. Toms Publications, n.d.

—. *Tomsinte Bobanum Moliyum: 50th Anniversary Collection*. Toms Publications, 2007.

—. "Little Chattan". *Toms Comics*. Toms Publications, n.d.

—. "Lalu-Lalli". *Toms Comics*. Toms Publications, n.d.

—. "Ormakalude Rekhachithram" [The Sketches of Memories]. *Madhyamam,*Ideal Publications Trust, 11 Oct. 2010–22 Aug. 2011.

—. "Tomsinte Bobanum Moliyum". *Kalakaumudi Weekly*. Kalakaumudi, 1987–1992.

Chapter 9

Reading Girl- and Womanhood in the Classic Flemish Family Comics Series *Jommeke*: A Conversation with Katrien De Graeve and Sara De Vuyst

Michel De Dobbeleer

Soon after the Second World War, the comics landscape in Flanders – the northern, Dutch-speaking part of Belgium[1] – started to be dominated by the "family comics" (*familiestrip*) genre.[2] Even today the sales of comics in Flanders remain led by some four or five family comics series, all of which feature at least one hundred albums. Whereas the readers of these series often consist of adults and children alike, this contribution deals with the series that has always addressed specifically the *youngest* reading public (around seven to ten years old): Jef Nys's *Jommeke* (for its protagonists, see **fig. 1**).

It is no exaggeration to say that in Flanders there are few fictional characters better known than Jommeke. One of the best known Flemish comics journalists, Gert Meesters (2005), has calculated that all Flemings, from infancy to old age, must have an average of ten *Jommeke* albums on their bookshelf. Notwithstanding this success, the blond hero's fame hardly extends beyond Flanders' borders: translations of *Jommeke* albums have generally not been successful,[3] and in the Netherlands, where people can read the albums in

Figure 1 The protagonists of Jef Nys's *Jommeke* (original title, until 2013: *De belevenissen van Jommeke* [The Adventures of Jommeke]), 1955–present: pre-published in newspapers (1955–present) before appearing in albums (1957–present); continued by, among others, Philippe Delzenne and Gerd Van Loock. From left to right: the very playful Filiberke, Jommeke's best friend, accompanying him in almost all his adventures – the twin sisters Annemieke and Rozemieke, usually less prominent and more passive and/or frightened than the boys – the bright title hero, Jommeke, an only child (just like Filiberke) – the three pets: Flip, Jommeke's parrot (who thinks, talks and makes stereotypical remarks like an adult man), the twins' monkey Choco and Filiberke's black poodle, Pekkie. The four children are all eleven years old. Each Jommeke adventure (album) consists of about forty-six pages. Image source: www.hln. be/showbizz/gezocht-extra-tekenaar-voor-jommeke~a7545da0/, © 2022 Standaard Uitgeverij.

the original language, *Jommeke* is little known or denounced, often for being too Flemish (especially with respect to Jef Nys's language; Meesters 2012).

In the past, *Jommeke*, just like most other Flemish family comics series, has been increasingly criticised for its stereotypical portrayal of certain population groups, especially foreigners, but also women.[4] To find out whether there is an evolution between the old and the recent albums with respect to the representation of girls and women, I had a long conversation with two gender studies scholars who grew up in Flanders – associate professor Katrien De Graeve and postdoctoral researcher Sara De Vuyst[5] – about their reading experiences with three particular *Jommeke* albums. We discussed the performance of the series' female characters through a selected corpus (**fig. 2**), consisting of "Het Hemelhuis" [The Heaven House] (1960, no. 6), "De supervrouw" [The Superwoman]

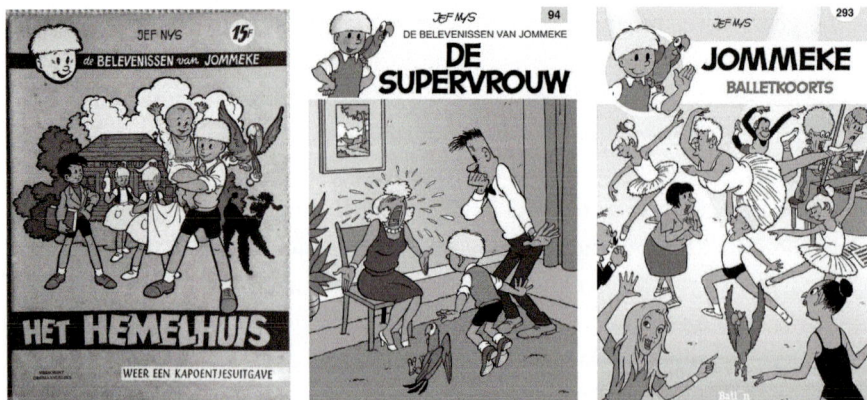

Figure 2 The three selected *Jommeke* album covers. © 2022 Standaard Uitgeverij.

(1979, no. 94) and "Balletkoorts" [Ballet Fever] (2019, no. 293), the first two by Jommeke's spiritual father Jef Nys (1927–2009), the latter by one of his successors, Gerd Van Loock.[6] I chose these three – out of more than three hundred – *Jommeke* albums because they explicitly deal with gender-related themes. At the same time, I tried to pick out albums which represent the early ("Het Hemelhuis") and the contemporary *Jommeke* ("Balletkoorts"), as well as the album which most explicitly addresses the feminist theme ("De supervrouw").

Girls' and Children's Comics in Flanders

Michel De Dobbeleer (MDD): As a child, did you often read comics, and in particular *Jommeke*?

Sara De Vuyst (SDV): I did – and from a very young age. So young in fact that I couldn't yet read the text (very well),[7] but only looked at the pictures. I mainly read *Jommeke*, *Suske en Wiske*[8] and *Pitch*:[9] the last one was my favourite series, and I really collected those albums. Then came a break of many years, and now, as an adult, I have found my way again in the medium, thanks to graphic novels.

Katrien De Graeve (KDG): No, I've never been much of a comic book reader, but I have read *Jommeke*. I come from a working-class family where books were not highly rated. We actually had very few books at home, and no comics at all. I don't remember there being a library in our village at the time either. So I only started reading books from secondary school onwards. But we did have the newspaper *Het Volk* at home, and that's how I knew about *Jommeke*.[10] My father always drew little Jommeke heads. I loved that and I often asked him to draw those little heads for me.

MDD: For me *Jommeke* was one of the first comics series I read, and surely the first which I wanted to read systematically. When I started reading it, the series already comprised some 130 albums. In fact *Jommeke* was my first introduction to choosing and reading books all by myself. I probably owe it to the series that I learned to read autonomously. Is that recognisable, in a way?

SDV: I think that *Jommeke* and the other children's comics indeed did help me learn to read. On the one hand, you can always skip the difficult things in those speech bubbles. But on the other hand, it certainly wasn't encouraged; when we went to the library in elementary school, we would always hear things like "you can only take a limited number of comic books" and "you have to take real books too".

MDD: Yes, that sounds familiar. Comics were "too easy", and the language was considered to be bad.

Mel Gibson, a pioneer in the field of comics reader history, found that many British women to a certain degree have repressed their childhood experiences with comics [as discussed in Chapter 1]; does this apply to you?

Figure 3 Cover of Gijs Haag and Marcel Marlier's children's book *Tiny leert paardrijden* [Tiny Learns to Ride Horses] (1969).

KDG: (laughs) Well, it turned out that I *did* read "De supervrouw" already, whereas I strongly doubted this when you brought me the albums a few weeks ago.

MDD: Yes, perhaps it does apply to Flemish women, too, then, since now you also come up with this story about your father drawing Jommeke heads for you. You didn't seem to remember that a few weeks ago. Maybe it is ingrained in our culture that comics are something for boys?

KDG: Well, I certainly didn't see *Jommeke* as a boy's comics series. I felt just as much addressed as a girl. And the same goes for *Nero* or even *De Rode Ridder*.[11]

MDD: In spite of the fact that all these series have male protagonists?

KDG: Apparently, as a young reader I could just as easily identify with a male protagonist like Jommeke. I also read *Tiny* [**fig. 3**],[12] but that was such an upper-class thing and so far away from my own world, whereas *Jommeke* was much closer to it; it clearly didn't matter that the main hero was a boy.

SDV: *Tiny* didn't appeal to me either. I remember that I received such a book as a present once, but I postponed reading it because I didn't like the drawings.

MDD: My oldest daughter also got a *Tiny* book as a present, but she really liked it and asked me to borrow other *Tiny* adventures from the library. My youngest daughter, now four, likes it too; my son – together with his elder sister a *Jommeke* fan – rather doesn't. In any case, if one Belgian children's book series was (and – judging by the enthusiasm of my daughters – still *is*) popular and specifically known as "for girls", it must be *Tiny*. But of course that's not a comic book series.

Did you think Flanders lacked (or lacks) a girls' comics series? In the UK and the US there were comics specifically for girls.

KDG: I never thought about that at the time. As for children's books (so maybe not comics), I vaguely realised that there existed certain genres for girls, but I didn't have access to them anyway. I have the impression that the range of books – but also of clothes, toys, etc. – on offer used to be much less gendered when I was a child, that children were less seen as an important commercial target group.

MDD: So you didn't feel the need for specific girls' comics, and overall didn't consider children's comics (with their often male protagonists) as something for boys?

SDV: Yes, just like Katrien, I never thought: "*Jommeke* is a series for boys".

MDD: Neither did I, but when I look back now, and when I read the albums to my children – which they really love – I have my doubts about that.

SDV: It's true, of course, that there are many male characters in *Jommeke*, and in comics overall, especially in the leading roles. Maybe that's why I quit at a certain age.

KDG: I remember the video that was made to promote the book *Good Night Stories for Rebel Girls* (Favilli and Cavallo). In the video a mom and her daughter stand in front of a bookcase and take out every book that actually focuses on men or boys. At the end, there aren't many books left...

MDD: Yes, I think if that bookcase had been full of *Jommeke* albums, very few – if any – would have remained.

SDV: I find this more striking in comics than in other children's books. In adventures and quests, such as in the *Jommeke* albums, everything revolves around *men*. If there is a confrontation or fight, it is between men; women are secondary – or sometimes they cause problems that the men have to solve. In TV series from my childhood, it was less so. *The Teletubbies*, for example, are not really gendered. Or in *De boomhut* it was the female Alida who was central.[13]

MDD: My children – my son too – are fond of Pippi Longstocking, a contemporary of Jommeke, so to say. Such a character *could* have been a comic book protagonist, couldn't it? But maybe just not in Flanders?

SDV: You indeed didn't have such characters in popular Flemish comics.

MDD: A question for you as parents, or hypothetically future parents: did your children read comics, or would you let them read comics? Any comics, or did or would you "guide" them in this regard?

KDG: Comics were rare in our house, instead of picture and other children's books. Though I don't really have a clear view of what my children read when they were young. Maybe they read comics behind my back. (laughs)

SDV: I don't have children, but I don't think that we must overprotect them when navigating media or "panic" in the assumption that they cannot find their way themselves and be critical. When reading aloud as an adult for children, it is good, though, to make comments where needed, for example when things are woman-unfriendly.

MDD: Yes, that is what I do when reading aloud *Jommeke*. I regularly hear myself saying things such as "in those days, women almost always washed the dishes". And my children understand why I'm saying such things, because they often see me doing the dishes, too. Are there any Flemish (Dutch-language/translated) comics that you consider more suitable than *Jommeke* as reading material for young Flemish girls or children in general?

KDG: Well, I never bought *Jommeke* for my children, but I wouldn't have minded if they got those albums into their hands.

SDV: For me the same, I wouldn't buy them either.

MDD: And what about *Suske en Wiske*? Wiske is definitely a strong female protagonist.

SDV: *Suske en Wiske* is certainly preferable to *Jommeke*, because in the former you really have female protagonists. I also have pleasant memories of Aunt Sidonia, although I have now read that her position as a housewife is being criticised. That is not how I saw her at the time. I thought the series featured an intriguing family composition – one that was just different from the traditional composition (as in *Jommeke*).

MDD: Related to this, years of library visits with my children taught me that there are municipal libraries – at least in the province of East Flanders – that do not have *Jommeke* albums or books of the *Tiny* series in their collection, whereas most libraries have many dozens if not hundreds of them. A small-scale inquiry taught me that one library does not buy *Tiny* books because they are considered too sexist, while another one bans *Jommeke* albums because of the "poor" Dutch in it. What is your opinion? Should a comics series such as *Jommeke* or a children's book series such as *Tiny* be banned from our municipal libraries? And if so, why?

SDV: For me *Jommeke* should not be banned, just like you shouldn't forbid children to read it. The most important thing for me is that libraries put enough effort into offering comics that challenge gender stereotypes. So they should also actively look for such comics if they find that their current collection contains mostly comics that confirm stereotypes. Children should be able to choose from a wide range of comics that are not sexist.

KDG: I can only concur with Sara. I'm not an advocate of banning books either. It certainly can't do any harm for children to learn about different views of the world, including conservative views. It can encourage them to think critically about the ideological frameworks that shape everyday life, and whom or what these frameworks exclude. It does become a problem, though, when children's imaginations are only fed with gender-stereotypical, but also heteronormative, neocolonial, etc., representations. For instance, the fact that in Hungary, very recently, the conservative government [under Viktor Orbán; June 2021] only wants to give children access to heteronormative representations of sexuality, relationships and family, shows that this battle has not been fought yet. Indeed, libraries can play an important role here by providing a sufficient counterbalance with stories that are norm-breaking.

MDD: To conclude this long first set of questions, is the Flemish children's comics market still too male-oriented? Are there too few comics for girls available?

KDG: I think the approach, the "angle", of this question is not the right one; comics or books in general shouldn't be "for boys" or "for girls". Obviously, it is also important for boys that they get to see men and women in nontraditional roles. Of course, there is no direct causal link between reading *Jommeke* and becoming misogynous or racist.[14] The harmful thing, however, lies in the repetition of these images. Through this repetition they become fixed in the minds of the children. I'm not a comics specialist, but at least in picture books, such as – in Flanders – those by Hanne Luyten and Noëmi Willemen, I see how artists and narrators are now trying to pay more attention to all of this. In such books girls don't have to wear cute miniskirts (as the twins in *Jommeke* do) and the like.

MDD: Regarding that cliché: in more recent times there have been Flemish children's comics series with less stereotypical female (co-)protagonists, such as Jan Bosschaert and Marc Legendre's *Sam* (1990–2008) or Charel Cambré's *Jump* (2007–2015), but they apparently couldn't compete with the persistent success of the established series, such as *Jommeke* or *Suske en Wiske*.

Gender (and Diversity) Studies Concepts and *Jommeke*

MDD: What concepts from your field of expertise, gender and diversity studies, can be applied to *Jommeke* in general, and to these three individual albums in particular?
SDV: Quite a lot, in fact. First of all, the so-called male gaze[15] – the idea that in fiction, for instance in comics as well as in cinema, we very often look through the eyes of men. The reader/viewer is always asked, as it were, to identify with the male characters. Women or girls, for their part, are mostly passive "objects" of this gaze.
MDD: So you would then relate this concept to the fact that, certainly in the past, and particularly in Flemish family comics, comics creators were almost always men? *Jommeke*, for example, even after Jef Nys's death, has been predominantly created by men. Only the colourist nowadays is a woman: Jef Nys's daughter, Agnes Nys.[16]
SDV: Not necessarily; the burden of that male gaze weighs on female artists too, resulting – for instance – in critical views on women's appearances or in women turned into objects in the works by female creators as well.
MDD: Of the more than three hundred *Jommeke* albums, only one was authored by a woman, namely Jef Nys's granddaughter, Sarina Ahmad(-Nys), who after his death wrote and drew "Het Nianmonster" [The Nian Monster] (no. 278), the last album to appear in the jubilee year 2015, when *Jommeke* turned sixty. Although it features a quite intriguing new character, Rosalieke,[17] one couldn't really say, indeed, that the gaze has become female in that album. Annemieke and Rozemieke, by the way, are not involved in the story.
SDV: Except for the male gaze, one can also apply, more or less, the concept of "symbolic annihilation" to the *Jommeke* stories. This term from the seventies, refined by Gaye Tuchman, points to the symbolic denial, in media coverage, of the existence of certain groups of people, in particular women. In the news, but also in a lot of fiction, women are often invisible. In *Jommeke*, too, women – for example, the twin sisters, Annemieke and Rozemieke, in "Het Hemelhuis" – are clearly secondary, in the background.[18]
Particularly applicable to comics is "oppositional reading".[19] As a reader you can always do something else with the text than what the creator has decided or wanted you to do (assuming we can figure that out). So in comics you have, for example, the freedom to skip certain balloons or panels, or to change the chronology, apart from interpreting the work as you want, of course. In this respect, I think about queer readings of Batman and

Robin, and how their bond has been read as a love relationship. I should reread *Jommeke* more thoroughly, but I think such oppositional reading could probably be done through the character of Filiberke. Isn't he somewhat softer than Jommeke?

MDD: Well, Filiberke is at least known for his unbridled imagination. He can play a kangaroo or a cucumber, often for an entire album [resp. in Nys 1973 and Nys 1988]. However, the hypothesis that he is gay, if that's what you mean, is not very widespread.

SDV: Yes, can't that be read between the lines?

MDD: That some readers might think about it, read it that way is, of course, the fate of many male comics protagonists always hanging out with each other during all those adventures. Think of what is often insinuated about Tintin and Captain Haddock [De Weyer, 2009]. But Filiberke, in any case, now and then really falls in love with girls,[20] and as an adult – which he will evidently never be in Jef Nys's *Jommeke* universe – he will "unquestionably" marry Rozemieke (just like Jommeke will marry Annemieke).

SDV: Sure, but it is of course inherent in oppositional reading that the readers consciously choose to deduce their own story. The point that I would like to make here is that the meaning of comics is not fixed, but that it is shaped as well by the readers and their different perspectives on the text. On another note, one can also approach the *Jommeke* series with the paradigm of "hegemonic masculinity": certain allegedly male traits are idealised, such as cleverness or strength and serve to justify male dominance. I found it remarkable that in "Balletkoorts"[21] Jommeke, while dancing ballet, still has to distinguish himself by being strong. It's not just female characters who come off poorly in this respect. Men who do not live up to ideals of hegemonic masculinity are often mocked. When Jommeke's mother, Marie, in "De supervrouw" becomes a superwoman, his father, Teofiel, in the end feels so unworthy that he leaves his family to become a hermit. And judging from the jokes, Baron Odilon [van Piependale] is seen as clearly too short for a man [in "Balletkoorts"], especially when compared to his wife, the countess [Elodie van Stiepelteen; **fig. 7**], who can be said to represent the "female grotesque" [Russo], to introduce yet another concept to approach the series.

MDD: Yes, because the children, especially the boys and Jommeke in particular, take on the heroic roles,[22] adult men are usually just fumbling around. In a way this even counts for Gobelijn, the professor of the series: of course, he is a genius who can invent anything, but he has the spirit and impetuosity[23] of a child (which is precisely why he invents anything). As for grotesque women, Countess Elodie van Stiepelteen has been rightly connected to *Tintin*'s Bianca Castafiore [e.g. Mennes 24]: at least the physical similarities are striking.

KDG: In response to the question about the concepts from our field of expertise, I focused on "De supervrouw".[24] That album fully plays with the trope of the unhappy housewife, a concept from Betty Friedan's *The Feminine Mystique*, describing the uneasiness of married women regarding their imposed role as housewife. As an American, Friedan concentrated on the US context, but of course it applied to Europe as well, and was highly influential here. Friedan raised the issue of how housewives should take pleasure in caring for others while not being paid to do so. Basically, this boils down to a system of making people work unpaid – and they are expected to be happy about it. It is important to note that Friedan has been criticised for generalising the experience of only a *limited* number of women. The single-earner household was an ideal that the white working class was supposed to pursue, yet was not an option for a vast number of women. These women simply *had* to go to work and do the unpaid housework on top of their poorly paid employment. Nevertheless, those women who could afford living "the ideal", felt frustrated by their work being undervalued and even no longer considered "real" labour. My mother, for instance, became a housewife as soon as my parents could afford it, after she had been forced to quit school at the age of fourteen, and after she had worked in a factory for about ten years. The lifelong undervaluation of her talents and work still makes her angry and frustrated. It is this dissatisfaction that "De supervrouw" addresses, I think.

MDD: If there *is* a nuclear family in Flemish *familiestrips*, like in *Jommeke* and *De Kiekeboes*, the mother is typically a housewife (who is supposed to be happy in this role). In *De Kiekeboes* there is also an album, a bit younger than "De supervrouw", with the same point of departure: the mother being fed up with her role.[25] How then did Jef Nys, in your opinion, play with this trope of the unhappy housewife in "De supervrouw"?

KDG: Well, as I said, the album clearly refers to the whole idea, but it doesn't really criticise it – quite the opposite. The idea behind the album seems to be: let those women see how it is to be on the other, male side of society, and soon they will be happy to take up their role of housewife again. For me, "De supervrouw" is an anti-feminist book. The problem is actually laid at the door of feminism: it seems to imply that it is not the unequal division of labour that makes women unhappy, but feminism. It is feminist ideas that make Marie's head spin at the beginning of the album, and thus it is actually feminism that makes her unhappy. All this reminded me of Sara Ahmed's concept of the feminist killjoy, which points to the feminist who highlights existing injustices as the spoilsport and the

Figure 4 Jef Nys, "De supervrouw" (*Jommeke*, no. 94, 1981 [1979]: 46, strip 176, panel 2)[26] © 2022 Standaard Uitgeverij.

source of trouble and unhappiness. At the end of the album, the author quickly gets rid of the feminist concerns with the message that the husband should help a little in the household.

MDD: Yes, at the end, Teofiel promises to help wash the dishes [**fig. 4**] – so that his wife can be happy again, which she indeed immediately is.

SDV: I also found it remarkable that Marie's demand for more equality is seen as stemming from a problem she is struggling with. That she is overstrained, even hysterical, is also seen as something typical of women.

KDG: Yes, and the cover speaks volumes [**fig. 2**]: she doesn't look like a superwoman at all. (laughs)

SDV: The way Marie sits there on that chair also made me think of the Dutch word *ploetermoeder* [literally: "plodding mother"], a term that, just like "superwoman", is still used today in feminist theory. A *ploetermoeder* is a mother who has to toil hard to combine work outside the home with taking care of the family.

Annemieke and Rozemieke

MDD: Enough about Marie for now. How would you describe the twin sisters Annemieke and Rozemieke, the so-called Miekes, the girls as well as their role in the series?

SDV: What immediately stands out is the girls' stereotypical portrayal by means, also, of their clothes: those cute little skirts and the like [**fig. 1**]. Unlike what we read about other women in the series, I found no negative comments about the Miekes' physical appearance, so that must be pretty much the ideal image for the author. As for their role, the reader quickly understands that they are secondary, as I already said: clearly background characters.

MDD: Yes, and what about the fact that they are identical twins? I never thought about it as a child, but now it doesn't seem like a coincidence to me that *if* there are twins in the series, that they are two *girls*. Perhaps somewhat disrespectfully, one could see it as a kind of convenience solution for Jef Nys. He only had to invent one girl and could immediately draw it twice. As the inseparable sisters which they are since their first appearance,[27] he could always just let them chat with each other in order to have some "girl conversation" in his albums. He could let them behave stereotypically, you could say, not just towards the boys, but easily also towards each other.

SDV: Yes, sometimes there is some competition between the two [**fig. 5**], the kind of competition, jealousy sometimes, where you see the author thinking: that's typically feminine!

MDD: In general, do you think that the twin sisters have evolved throughout the years?

SDV: No, not really. After all those decades one might expect that they would each have gained identity, but in fact they haven't.

Figure 5 Jef Nys, "Het Hemelhuis" (*Jommeke*, no. 6, 1960: [unpaged], strips 55–56)[28] © 2022 Standaard Uitgeverij.

Figure 6 Jef Nys, "Het Hemelhuis" (*Jommeke*, no. 6, 1960: [unpaged], strip 107)[29] © 2022 Standaard Uitgeverij.

MDD: I agree, and it is notable that many other characters, like Countess Elodie van Stiepelteen in the recent "Balletkoorts", almost always address them together. As if after so many albums she still doesn't think it matters who is who.

SDV: They are really replaceable. I remember a scene in "Het Hemelhuis" in which Jommeke's mother literally says that it remains the same if she addresses one sister by the name of the other, since they are twins anyway [**fig. 6**].

MDD: And the fact that they always wear the same clothes does not help, obviously.[30] Sure, Jommeke and the other characters, too, almost always wear the same clothes, that's something you often see in the *familiestrip*,[31] but it's of course a choice you make as an author to let identical twins also be indistinguishable through their clothing.

KDG: All this even more deprives them of their personality. As girls they are already laden with clichés. As twins, you could say this is doubly reinforced, as if "squared".

MDD: Yes, they are not exactly round characters. Sometimes, however, their being twins is vital to the plot. There are albums in which enemies initially only see one of the girls. Later on they are surprised and fooled by the fact that the same girl (that is, actually, her sister) suddenly turns up somewhere else, whereas they thought that they had already, for example, captured this girl.

This is also the right place to talk about Philippe Delzenne's one-shot *De Miekes: Zonnedorp op z'n kop* [*The Miekes: Zonnedorp Upside Down*] (2017), a spin-off album in which not Jommeke, but the twin sisters get the leading part. As the title indicates, the occasional heroes quickly turn Zonnedorp, Jommeke's fictional hometown (somewhere in the neighbour-hood of Antwerp), upside down. I found such a spin-off a very nice initiative, although I didn't like the album's specific adventure (but that may be just me; De Dobbeleer 2019). It would have been better, perhaps, if someone who is *not* one of the regular creators of *Jommeke* had made such an album. In an interview afterwards, Philippe Delzenne said the album sold less well than the regular albums. According to him, this may be because there are probably still more boys than girls reading the series. They may not have been attracted to such a "girl's album" (Stabel 10).

Energetic, Incisive Women are Not Feminist per Definition

MDD: From Annemieke and Rozemieke to another kind of female character. We have already mentioned her quite a few times: Countess Elodie van Stiepelteen. Gert Meesters, himself a fan of *Jommeke* as a child, wrote a positive piece on the series in 2005, on the occasion of the blond hero's fiftieth birthday. Meesters acknowledged that the series could indeed be blamed for a number of reasons. For a long time it was criticised for its bad Dutch (while it was mainly Jef Nys's intention to write in Flemish [Meesters 2012]), and the gender pattern was certainly conservative. This definitely applies to Jommeke's mother, Meesters says, as well as to Annemieke and Rozemieke, who "have a supporting role that consists of a lot of cooking and sewing". But Meesters also wanted to add a note of caution to this woman's image, criticised from feminist angles. In his opinion, "the feminists overlooked incisive women such as Elodie van Stiepelteen, who not just physi-cally dominates her husband, baron Odilon, or Madam Pepermunt, who can easily stand her ground" [Meesters, 2005].[32]
The recurring character of Madam Pepermunt didn't appear in the three albums we discuss here, but do you agree with Gert Meesters concerning the character of Countess Elodie?
KDG: Well, to begin with, I regret the way in which he formulates all of this. Actually, this quote can be considered an example of anti-feminism. It somewhat insinuates that femi-nists only see what they want to see. And as for those energetic, incisive female characters: I find that a problematic, false impression of things, though also very recognisable to me. I often heard it during my childhood: that cliché of the domineering wife. People always made jokes about it, with the husbands invariably being under the thumb, etc., which is just an absurd representation and a reversal of the power relations within a household model that makes women financially dependent on men. (laughs)
SDV: You can see this also in the workplace now: female managers are said to be bossy and so on. If women "stand their ground" (as in Meesters's quote) in those roles, they are crit-

icised for not being "feminine" or "womanlike" enough, and for crossing boundaries of gender-appropriate behaviour. At any rate, I am not a fan of (the idea behind) the expression "women standing their ground"[33] in the sense of being able to cope with, being a match for men.

KDG: It is not because such a woman, like the countess, is a strong character that it is therefore a feminist character.

MDD: That's an important point. I guess, precisely to accentuate this idea of resoluteness, yes, of "standing her ground", the countess has been given such a short husband.

KDG: The fact that she is an upper-class person also plays a role, I think. I assume that it is no coincidence that it is a woman of nobility that is allowed to play another role than that of a housewife. It would be revealing to conduct a class analysis on the series. The families of Jommeke and his young friends are clearly part of the working class, in the sense of people doing wage labour (not merely in the sense of blue-collar workers). While reading the albums, I had the feeling that one of the underlying aims of the *Jommeke* series was or is to discipline this class.

Spirit of the Times?

MDD: Stereotypical women's images, like stereotypical images of other groups, have to do with or are part of the so-called spirit of the times or zeitgeist. At least that is what we often read and hear. What is your point of view on this, related to women's images in *Jommeke*?

KDG: The series' images of women seem to be more in line with the zeitgeist of the 1950s or 1960s than with that of more recent times, but it is important to stress that a zeitgeist is never the zeitgeist of a whole population.[34] Even then, what was drawn upon was the zeitgeist of the more conservative people. The same goes for the stereotypes in a recent album such as "Balletkoorts".

SDV: As for "Het Hemelhuis": if I had been a researcher or, say, a critical reader back then in the sixties, I think I would have had the same reservations as I do now: why do women always have to be mothers – or girls, like the Miekes, always in the mother role? And if you look at the series as a whole, you always encounter the repetition of the same clichés. And that repetition is precisely the essence of stereotyping, in this case, linking certain characteristics to a binary idea of gender and constantly reusing them. Even in the series' early days, this didn't show a lot of creativity, I presume. Perhaps these clichés were also used because the artist could always fall back on them.

MDD: Exactly, the use of clichés was and is in the DNA of this kind of series. You could probably go so far as to say that that kind of repetition has to be in it or you don't have family comics, which is not to say, though, that such repetitions have to be woman-un-friendly, of course.

SDV: Well, I don't know; an alternative that comes to mind – although not for children, I admit – is Alison Bechdel's *Dykes to Watch Out For* [1983–2008]. That's an example of a comic strip that avoids clichés.

MDD: Definitely, but it is more recent and with a different target audience, as you say.

SDV: Younger, yes, but not that young, and in any case: when you read it now, it is still topical, relevant. Here you are less likely to refer to the spirit of the times because everything's so creative.

MDD: Regarding *Jommeke*, referring to the spirit of the times makes sense in my opinion, although I agree that is often all too easy to do so. Besides, I would also like to point to something like the Flemish "comics landscape conditions" at the time. These were obvi-ously related to the conservative Catholic zeitgeist in Flanders, but they in fact made the Flemish creators even more conventional or cautious than the so-called zeitgeist would have dictated without these "comics landscape conditions" – if zeitgeists are able to dictate things... From the late 1940s onwards, making comics in Belgium was seriously hampered by the directives of French publishers. Thus, even before Frederic Wertham's *Seduction of the Innocent* (1954) and the Comics Code Authority in the US, these directives (as from 16 July 1949) boycotted the success of Belgian authors by means of exaggerated, not to say absurd, censorship regulations. Draconian measures regarding the depiction of violence and sex, references to politics and so on were imposed on all Belgian comics – to protect the French youth, but certainly also to protect the French market, since for French comics creators, these "rules" were less strict.[35] Most Belgian comics authors, think about Willy Vandersteen, and especially their publishers, wanted to make it in France, but in order to do this, they had to drastically reduce the sensuality of their female characters. Notorious, in this respect, is the near absence of women in Hergé's *Tintin* universe.[36]

Soon the strict French rules were adopted by the Belgian comics publishers themselves, also for series that did not make it in France. Understandably, comics authors who targeted the general public practised self-censorship. And this also applied to artists in conservative Flanders whose work was *not* translated into French. *Jommeke* has been translated into French, from 1961 onwards, but without achieving any real success in the French-speaking world.[37] All the same, when Jef Nys started *Jommeke*, he was part of a comics landscape in which his examples, the authors he admired, and thus he himself in fact could only afford to depict two kinds of female characters: young girls, like Anne-mieke and Rozemieke, on the one hand, and (older) adult women who were allowed to look anything but sensual. It is a crude way of putting it, I realise, but what both types have in common is that there was no need to depict breasts. Of course, adult women, espe-cially mothers, like Jommeke's, had breasts, but they were to receive as little attention as possible. At any rate, the reader should not be able to distinguish an individual breast.

Hence why adult women, such as Castafiore, but also Marie in the oldest *Jommeke* albums, got what De Weyer (2015) – hesitantly searching for the right word – calls a "facade".[38]

KDG: Yes, I noticed the difference between how Marie was depicted in "Het Hemelhuis" and how she looked in "De supervrouw".

MDD: As a matter of fact, this kind of look, that "facade", best suited bossy women, with whom the husband is under the thumb. Clichés aplenty, I know… That's enough of a long "history lesson". I say all this because *Jommeke*'s old-fashioned and certainly very limited image of women may also be partly due to this medium-specific context. And, as we can see, that "outmoded" world – and women's – view has continued long after those French measures were lifted, at the end of the sixties. Unquestionably, we are dealing here with a conservative comics format and, on top of that, a conservative creator.

KDG: For me that does not justify the women's image in the younger *Jommeke* albums, for instance, "De supervrouw". I also don't see why women should have large (discernible) breasts in order to be able to be more daring, less stereotypical characters.

MDD: You are right. Comments like that about Flemish family comics are actually too rarely heard, I think.

SDV: For me what mattered when reading the albums was not how the girls or women are portrayed physically, but how the other characters react to how they look. What struck me is that there are many jokes and remarks made about women who do not fit traditional Western beauty standards.

KDG: Yes, even still in the most recent album of the three, "Balletkoorts". There's really a kind of obsession with being slim [**fig. 7**]. This obviously reinforces the problematic issues we already dealt with regarding gender in the series.

MDD: Believe it or not, as a child I really never noticed it, but now as an adult, I realise that this obsession is prominent in the series.

SDV: I don't think we should take these remarks about physical appearance lightly. In their personal lives, many young readers must have asked – and still ask – themselves

Figure 7 Gerd Van Loock, "Balletkoorts" (*Jommeke*, no. 293, 2019: 9, strip 26, panel 1)[39] © 2022 Standaard Uitgeverij.

questions about these issues. This is something you can be bullied about at school. And then you are again confronted with such remarks while reading comics. Once more, this endless repetition shows little creativity, in my opinion. Why do these remarks always have to be at the expense of women? Why is their appearance so much more important than that of men?

MDD: Fat men are certainly made fun of too in the series,[40] but you are right that women are too often the target of remarks concerning their physical appearance.

To close this part about the zeitgeist: in general, have you noticed an evolution over the three albums regarding the portrayal of the girls and women in the series?

KDG: Amazingly little evolution, actually.

MDD: That's curious, because, as you know, I have chosen these three albums because they each originate from three different "time periods" in the series' history.

SDV: If you hadn't said it, I might not have even noticed it. Of course, you can tell by the colour edition that "Balletkoorts" is the youngest, but purely in terms of content, I wouldn't have realised it was so recent.

MDD: Well, and I especially chose "Balletkoorts" because that album got some media attention. When the album appeared, you could read how Jommeke was now really becoming a child of his time and things like that.[41] That a male character in this series would take up ballet would indeed have been unthinkable in the first decades of the series.

To Wrap Up...

Can I conclude this conversation by assuming that you can agree, at least partially, with this quote from the call for papers for the Sugar and Spice conference: "As gendered products, comics have constructed feminine role models and identities to which girls have replied with both rebellion and conformity". And if so, how exactly does this apply to the reading of *Jommeke*?

KDG: It applies, according to me, but readers have replied more with conformity, I'm afraid. Evidently, as I already said, there is no direct causal connection between the ideas the series propagates and the behaviour of people who once read (a lot of) *Jommeke* albums. But that doesn't mean that the dissemination of ideas in comics is innocent or harmless. It is the constant and everyday repetition of limited images of women that sediments into people's bodies and minds.

SDV: I don't think either that we should speak of a direct, demonstrable influence. But, indeed, that doesn't prove, of course, that those albums had no influence at all. It is just more nuanced than a direct causal relationship.

KDG: As I said, I identified myself rather with Jommeke than with the Miekes. One could say: as a child you do what you want with the things you read on your own... but, for example, those fatphobic or sexist remarks: as a child you internalise them; it certainly impacts the way you perceive and value yourself. If we now realise how much our society is imbued with woman-unfriendly ideas and images, then we also have to look in the direction of children's comics.

MDD: Yes, and the fact that *Jommeke* and the Flemish family comics series in general have had immense commercial success since the 1960s – and even today are still among the bestselling books according to the figures – makes these concluding comments all the more thought-provoking.

Notes

1. Although some people call the Dutch spoken in Belgium "Flemish", it is a kind of Dutch. The degree of difference between Dutch from Belgium and Dutch from the Netherlands is comparable to that between British and American English. When I use the term "Flemish" here, I mean belonging to the culture of the northern, Dutch-speaking part of Belgium, and thus not to that of the Netherlands. The southern part of Belgium is French-speaking.

2. On the difference between family strips and family comics (both are called *familiestrips* in the Low Countries, but elsewhere I have argued to reserve the term "family strips" for comic books with one gag per page), see De Dobbeleer (2021a). On the particularity of the publication format of the Flemish family comics (first in newspapers – two tiers a day – where the main/first readers were adults, then in albums – approximately four new albums a year – whose main readers were children), see Lefèvre.

3. Only recently do the Chinese (see De Weyer 2018) and German (re)translations (see Hüster) of several albums seem to appeal to new reading publics.

4. See Herten, Malcorps and Tyrions (87–88, 194), Mennes and more recently De Lille.

5. Katrien De Graeve (Ghent University) is an anthropologist whose research has consistently focused on inequalities and exclusions in the personal spheres of life. Sara De Vuyst (Ghent University) studies different aspects of gender, sexuality and media. Her current postdoc focuses on the representation of older (queer) women in comics, zines, art, cinema and other types of media and on the construction of alternative narratives on ageing, gender and sexuality by media producers.

6. Until album 45 (1971), Jef Nys did all the work himself (De Ryck 140). From the following album onwards, a small-scale studio gradually formed around him, but Nys kept meticulous control over each album. After his death in 2009, two studio employees took over most of the work: Philippe Delzenne and Gerd Van Loock.

7. I have put round brackets around words that were effectively said during the interview, e.g. a little later, to clarify something or in places where it might be difficult to

immediately understand the sentence without these round brackets. Square brackets are placed around words that have not been said, but which the reader (unfamiliar with *Jommeke*) requires in order to follow the argument properly.

8. Willy Vandersteen's (1913–1990) *Suske en Wiske* (in the UK known as *Spike and Suzy*, in the US as *Willy and Wanda*), with more than three hundred albums, is the longest-running Flemish family comics series (1945–present).

9. *Pitch* is a Flemish comics series written and drawn by Bart De Neve (1998–2001; 3 albums).

10. The Catholic *Het Volk* [The People] was the Flemish newspaper in which *Jommeke*'s adventures were published from 1958 until 2008. *Het Volk* was also the publisher of the first 175 *Jommeke* albums (until 1994).

11. Marc Sleen's (1922–2016) family comics *Nero* (1947–2002; 216 albums) and Willy Vandersteen's medieval-based sword-and-sorcery series *De Rode Ridder* [The Red Knight] (1959–now; more than 270 albums) are also two of Flanders' best known comics series.

12. *Tiny* is the Dutch name of the popular French-language Belgian children's book series *Martine* (1954–2010), written, until 1998, by Gilbert Delahaye (whose name was changed for the Dutch-language market to the Dutch-sounding "Gijs Haag"; see Brems 122) and illustrated by Marcel Marlier.

13. *De boomhut* [The Tree House] was an award-winning educational children's programme broadcast by the Flemish public television service from 1994 to 2006.

14. Here, De Graeve refers to a statement by Jelle De Beule, the writer of a recent homage/parody *Jommeke* album (De Beule and De Cloedt): "I do not feel that I have become misogynous or racist by reading *Jommeke* albums", although he acknowledges that women's and other images in the albums can be considered questionable (De Dobbeleer, 2021b, 45).

15. This important concept in feminist film theory was coined by Laura Mulvey.

16. Since 2000 Agnes Nys colours all *Jommeke* albums (De Ryck 147).

17. Rosalieke is intriguing because it seldom happens that an everyday young women gets a substantial role in *Jommeke*.

18. In "Het Hemelhuis" Jommeke, Filiberke, Annemieke and Rozemieke – without the knowledge of their parents – take care of an abandoned baby, Polleke. Whereas the girls take on the motherly tasks, the boys build the "Heaven House" from the album title.

19. The idea of oppositional reading, to indicate that readers can oppose the dominant or preferred reading of the text and reject it, was developed by Stuart Hall in 1973 (see Hall).

20. Although we can often read in the albums how in a distant future Jommeke and Filiberke will marry Annemieke and Rozemieke respectively, Filiberke sometimes falls heavily in love with other girls (esp. in Nys 1970, but also in Nys 1994).

21. In this 2019 album, Jommeke helps out the local ballet school (with which Annemieke and Rozemieke are affiliated) by performing dances in Tchaikovsky's *Swan Lake* to celebrate the school's one hundredth anniversary.

22. Actually, also the pets (see **fig. 1**) take on heroic roles, cf. Meesters and Lefèvre (63–64).

23. For this impetuosity, see De Beule in De Dobbeleer (2021b, 44).

24. "De supervrouw" opens with how Marie is overstrained and fed up with her life as a traditional housewife. As is often the case, Professor Gobelijn comes to the rescue. The pills which he prepares to help her get back on her feet are so powerful that Marie transcends herself, whereupon a roller coaster of adventures can start. First, Marie starts doing her husband's office work, far better and more quickly than him, then she easily concludes difficult trade agreements in the US, she plays a decisive role in the World Cup soccer final (i.e. of the men's tournament), she lands an almost crashing plane and so on. Near the end, Marie actually becomes the first president of Europe (thirty years before her fellow countryman Herman Van Rompuy would be the first to hold this position). Throughout, Jommeke watches closely to make sure that his mother always gets Gobelijn's pills on time; without her knowledge, he mixes them into her coffee. However, when the pills have finally run out, Marie – happy after all – takes on her old position in the household.

25. Merho's *De Kiekeboes* [The Kiekeboes; the surname Kiekeboe means "peekaboo"] is one of the somewhat younger popular family comics series in Flanders (1977–present; more than 160 albums). For a comparison between the album in question, "Het lot van Charlotte" (*De Kiekeboes*, no. 30, 1985) and "De supervrouw", see De Dobbeleer (2021a).

26. Marie: "Teofiel! I'd better wash the dishes again ... | Teofiel: "Marie! I will help ..." | Flip (paraphrasing the concluding verses of the late eighteenth-century Dutch children's poem 'Het goede voorbeeld' [The good example] by Hieronymus van Alphen, which have become popular wisdom): "Only there can be love, only there life is sweet, where people quietly and freely do everything for each other!"; "Einde", on the placard in this album's final panel, means "The end".

27. Just like Filiberke, the twins appear for the first time in the second *Jommeke* album, "De zingende aap" [The Singing Monkey] (1959).

28. Annemieke: "Rozemieke, Jommeke has found a little baby, and he asks if I want to be the mother." | Rozemieke: "Hey, Annemieke, I can do that too." – Annemieke: "But if Jommeke asks me! | Rozemieke: "I would like to be the mother!" – Annemieke: "No, I am the mother!" | Rozemieke: "I – I – I – I!" – Annemieke: "I – I – I – I!" | Rozemieke: "Okay, then we are the mother both at the same time." | "Are we twins or not!"

29. Marie: "What do those cloths mean???" | "Annemieke, where did you get those cloths?" | Rozemieke: "I am not Annemieke, madam. I am Rozemieke." | Marie: "That remains the same; you are twins after all!"

30. The fact that their names both end in "-mieke", does not help either. That Jef Nys called them Annemieke and Rozemieke enables the narrator as well as the other characters to just call or address them briefly as *de* ("the") *Miekes* (which was also used in the spin-off album devoted to them).

31. For the "obsession" with having the characters wear the same clothes all the time in Flemish family comics, cf. Horsten (137) and Stabel (9).

32. As can be seen in **fig. 7**, Odilon van Piependale is much shorter than his wife, Elodie. Madam Pepermunt (Dutch for "peppermint") is an enthusiastic and bustling American woman who lives alone on a ranch and shoots with a gun loaded with peppermints, hence her name.

33. In Dutch (also the expression used by Meesters): *zijn mannetje staan*, literally translated: "to stand one's little man".

34. De Graeve refers here to a comparable remark by Jelle De Beule (supra, note 14) in De Dobbeleer (2021b, 45).

35. For this protectionism, see De Weyer (2015, 84–87) and Groensteen (296–297).

36. In Geert De Weyer's history of Belgian comics (85), opera singer Bianca Castafiore, the most famous woman in *Tintin*, is called a mix of the three then-dominating women types: "the witch, the cow and the mannish woman".

37. In the sixties some fifteen *Jommeke* albums appeared in French as *Les aventures de Jojo* [The Adventures of Jojo]. cf. Ed Solie's detailed *Jommeke* website: https://stripheld.hoembeka.be/jommeke/weetjes/jojo.html. In the seventies some twenty-five appeared as *Gil et Jo* [Gil and Jo]; cf. De Ryck (186) and the Belgian comics database *stripINFO*: www.stripinfo.be/reeks/index/24594_Gil_et_Jo.

38. In De Weyer's Dutch: "voorgevel" (2015, 85), indicating the heavy "pack" above the belly, in which no *individual* breast is discernible (which might have been too sensual). Compare **fig. 6** to the cover of "De supervrouw" (**fig. 2**), where Marie no longer has a "facade". In the 1970s the measures had been lifted.

39. Elodie van Stiepelteen: "Unfortunately, I had to stop dancing when the years started to manifest themselves!" – Odilon van Piependale: "She means the kilograms!"

40. The pinnacle is probably the second half of "Het monster in de ruïne" [The Monster in the Ruin] (1980, no. 101), where Jommeke and his friends continuously call a group of Amazonian people Fatsoes or potbellies and the like.

41. See e.g. De Poorter. For more on "Balletkoorts" specifically, as well as on the question whether it would be worthwhile to rewrite the (older) *Jommeke* albums, see De Dobbeleer (forthcoming).

Bibliography

Ahmad-Nys, Sarina. "Het Nianmonster". *Jommeke*, no. 278. Ballon, 2015.

Ahmed, Sara. *The Promise of Happiness*. Duke University Press, 2010.

Brems, Elke. "Brousse, Rimboe, Oerwoud or Jungle? Retranslations as Sites of Negotiations". *Dutch Crossing: Journal of Low Countries Studies*, vol. 45, no. 2, 2021, pp. 121–132.

De Beule, Jelle, and Thijs De Cloedt. *Jommeke in de knel én de penarie*. Standaard Uitgeverij, 2021.

De Dobbeleer, Michel. "De 'spin-offbaarheid' van Zonnedorp: over 'Jomme' en de weifelende escapade van de Miekes". *Stripgids: derde reeks*, vol. 43, no. 5, 2019, pp. 30–34.

—. "Can Stereotypical Housewives in Flemish Family Comics Divorce? The Cases of Jommeke and De Kiekeboes". *Studies in Comics*, vol. 12, no. 1, 2021a, pp. 33–56.

—. "Schatverdamme! Jelle De Beule over zijn Jommeke, vroeger en nu". *Stripgids: derde reeks*, vol. 46, no. 9, 2021b, pp. 42–45.

—. *Jommeke op de Blandijn*. Forthcoming.

De Lille, Bruno. "Is Jommeke een macho van 65? Haal het seksisme uit de strips". *Knack: Opinie*, 26 Oct. 2020, https://weekend.knack.be/lifestyle/maatschappij/is-jommeke-een-macho-van-65-haal-het-seksisme-uit-de-strips/article-opinion-1657913.html. Accessed 1 June 2021.

Delzenne, Philippe. *De Miekes: Zonnedorp op z'n kop. Allemaal helden*, no. 1. Ballon, 2017.

De Poorter, Eva. "Jommeke gaat pirouettes maken: 'Ballet is niet vreemd, ook niet voor jongens'". *Het Nieuwsblad*, 26 Nov. 2018, www.nieuwsblad.be/cnt/dmf20181125_03985956. Accessed 1 June 2021

De Ryck, Luc. *Jef Nys: ongekend veelzijdig*. Mezzanine, 2005.

De Weyer, Geert. "'Kuifje is homo', aldus The Times". *De Standaard*, 8 Jan. 2009, www.standaard.be/cnt/ch24qgb4. Accessed 1 May 2021.

—. *België gestript: het ultieme naslagwerk over de Belgische strip*. Dragonetti, 2015.

—. "Jommeke trekt naar China: 'Met Vlaamse creativiteit veroveren we de wereld'". *De Morgen*, 6 June 2018, www.demorgen.be/nieuws/jommeke-trekt-naar-china-met-vlaamse-creativiteit-veroveren-we-de-wereld~bb73d7ca. Accessed 10 May 2021.

Favilli, Elena, and Francesca Cavallo. *Good Night Stories for Rebel Girls: 100 Tales of Extraordinary Women*. Timbuktu Labs, 2016.

Friedan, Betty. *The Feminine Mystique*. Norton, 1963.

Gibson, Mel. "Professional Identity, Girlhood Comics, Affection, Nostalgia and Embarrassment". Paper presented at the Sugar, Spice, and the Not So Nice: Comics Picturing Girlhood International Symposium, Ghent University (online), 22–23 Apr. 2021.

Groensteen, Thierry. "Femmes (1): représentation de la femme". *Le bouquin de la bande dessinée: dictionnaire esthétique et thématique* (drawings L. Trondheim), edited by Thierry Groensteen. Lafont, 2020, pp. 296–303.

Haag, Gijs, and Marcel Marlier. *Tiny leert paardrijden*. Casterman, 1969.

Hall, Stuart. "Encoding/Decoding". *Culture, Media, Language: Working Papers in Cultural Studies, 1972–79*, edited by Stuart Hall et al. Taylor & Francis, 2005, pp. 128–138.

Herten, Staf. "Een kleine bijdrage tot 25 jaar scheldproza: sfeervol bulshitten met Jef Nys". *Humo*, 24 May 1984, pp. 28–29, 31, 34.

Horsten, Toon. *Merho: zwart op wit*. Manteau, 2013.

Hüster, Michael. "Seit 2011 bei Stainless Art: Jommeke. Ein Interview mit Verleger Mario Wagner". *PPM: Peter Poluda Medienvertrieb*, 23 Apr. 2021, www.ppm-vertrieb.de/news/2877/Ein-Interview-mit-Verleger-Mario-Wagner.html. Accessed 1 June 2021.

Lefèvre, Pascal. "Narration in the Flemish Dual Publication System: The Crossover Genre of the Humoristic Adventure". *From Comic Strips to Graphic Novels: Contributions to the Theory and History of Graphic Narrative*, edited by Daniel Stein and Jan-Noël Thon. De Gruyter, 2013, pp. 255–269.

Malcorps, Johan, and Rik Tyrions. *De papieren droomfabriek*. Infodok, 1984.

Meesters, Gert. "Bekentenissen van een ex-verslaafde: 50 jaar Jommeke". *Knack Focus*, 8 June 2005.

—. "To and Fro Dutch Dutch: Diachronic Language Variation in Flemish Comics". *Linguistics and the Study of Comics*, edited by Frank Bramlett. Palgrave Macmillan, 2012, pp. 163–182.

Meesters, Gert, and Pascal Lefèvre. "Towards an Unexpected Equivalence: Animals, Children and Adults in the Popular Flemish Strip Jommeke". *Strong Bonds: Child-Animal Relationships in Comics*, edited by Maaheen Ahmed. Presses Universitaires de Liège, 2020, pp. 51–70.

Mennes, Paul. "Oedipus in Zonnedorp". *Geheimzinnige sterren: over het Belgische stripverhaal*, edited by Rik Pareit. Dedalus, 1996, pp. 13–44.

Mulvey, Laura. "Visual Pleasure and Narrative Cinema". *Screen*, vol. 16, no. 3, 1975, pp. 6–18.

Nys, Jef. "De zingende aap". *De belevenissen van Jommeke*, no. 2. Het Volk, 1959.

—. "Het Hemelhuis". *De belevenissen van Jommeke*, no. 6. Het Volk, 1960.

—. "Filiberke gaat trouwen". *De belevenissen van Jommeke*, no. 43. Het Volk, 1970.

—. "De hoed van Napoleon". *De belevenissen van Jommeke*, no. 61. Het Volk, 1973.

—. "Het monster in de ruïne". *De belevenissen van Jommeke*, no. 101. Het Volk, 1980.

—. "De supervrouw" [1979]. *De belevenissen van Jommeke*, no. 94. 2nd print, Het Volk, 1981.

—. "Komkommer in 't zuur". *De belevenissen van Jommeke*, no. 146. Het Volk, 1988.

—. "Paniek op de Akropolis". *De belevenissen van Jommeke*, no. 179. De Stripuitgeverij, 1994.

Russo, Mary. *The Female Grotesque: Risk, Excess and Modernity*. Routledge, 1995.

Stabel, Mario. "'De modernisering van Jommeke speelt zich af in de verhalen, niet in de kledij.' Interview Philippe Delzenne". *Stripspeciaalzaak.be*, Oct. 2018. https://stripheld.hoembeka.be/jommeke/upload/Phidel2.pdf. Accessed 1 August 2022.

Tuchman, Gaye. "The Symbolic Annihilation of Women by the Mass Media". *Hearth and Home: Images of Women in the Mass Media*, edited by Gaye Tuchman et al. Oxford University Press, 1978, pp. 3–38.

Van Loock, Gerd. "Balletkoorts". *Jommeke*, no. 293. Ballon, 2019.

Chapter 10

Death and the Maiden: Some Notes Concerning Charlotte Salomon's *Leben? oder Theater?*

Sébastien Conard

In the summer of 2020 I rather unsuspectedly visited an exhibition on the influences of cinema on *Leben? oder Theater?* [Life? or Theatre?] (1941–1943) by Charlotte Salomon (1917–1943).[1] I was acquainted with this peculiar graphic narrative by the young and early disappeared German-Jewish artist but had not read it, nor had I seen any of the original paintings, who were partly on display here since the Joods Historisch Museum (Jewish Museum, Amsterdam) conservates the entirety of *Life? or Theatre?*

The large gouache illustrations – most of them wordless pictures, others full text (often monologue), many a combination of both – are of an intriguing up to compelling quality, even if one tries not think of Salomon's short life and tragic fate. Being persecuted by the Nazis, Salomon fled Berlin for the south of France but would eventually be caught and deported to Auschwitz, where she was murdered in 1943. Charlotte Salomon was twenty-six years old, recently married and pregnant when she was gassed. This terrible outcome is hard not to have constantly in mind when looking at the pictures she made in the years before, even less when reading the whole work, which was meant as her testimony as she felt death closing in – not only via the persecution but also through the burden of a recurrence of suicides on her mother's side of the family. Her mother disappeared when Charlotte was only a young girl, and as a youngster she would have to deal with the depressive tendencies of her grandparents.

Facing death in so many ways, Charlotte chose to continue and finish her semi-autobiographical legacy – a message for humanity, as she described it herself. Maybe she even discarded the possibility she might have had to leave the occupied zone, through the interposition of Ottilie Moore, who had already sheltered Charlotte and her grandparents. One cannot deny the heavily melancholic and even messianically sacrificial hue of *Leben? oder Theater?*. The cruelness of its underlying content only intensifies the necessity of its realisation and the unbelievable brightness and lucidity of the pictorial language. At a time when young Hergé – ten years her elder – was inventively imposing long-lasting fundamentals on Western comics making, working in an editorial context and against a personal background that fostered anti-Semitism, the young, persecuted Charlotte Salomon fled her country and developed a graphic narrative form of her own, including creative applications of transparencies. It would only be made public and authenticated half a century later. Salomon was barely influenced by the codified comic strips of her time, but more so by impressionist, expressionist and "naive" painting, as well as opera, classical music and silent cinema. Out of a sheer urge to survive beyond her own threatened existence and for strong autobiographical reasons, she developed a "form" of its own, which inevitably fits a broader conception of what we call now graphic novel. Since *Life? or Theatre?* almost disappeared and didn't historically emerge within the fields of comics (as a typically published work with a targeted audience, for example), it's not part of the graphic novel canon... yet. But it should be.

The four-page graphic essay I propose here is an associative exploration of themes, names, motifs and verbal quotes and graphic citations from and around Salomon's work. I make transhistorical, tentative links, sometimes paradoxical or at least heterodoxic. In that way I approach some possible nodes, sharing instantaneous insights concerning form and content, allowing a more intuitive interpretation while trying to keep close to what Salomon's gesture might have been. Clearly, my essay only makes more sense when one has read Salomon's "song play". Obviously, doctor, you've never been a thirteen-year-old girl...[2]

Der Todund das Mâdchen

Der Tod und das Mädchen
Der Tod und das Mädchen
Der Tod und das Mädchen in Uniform
Der Tod und die Uniform
Der Tod und
Der Tod

Not a girl any longer; not yet a woman? Yet a mother.
Almost a mother. Already pregnant. With child. Bearing.
A young, married mother. A melancholic maker. Verfasser.
Woe-man. Mother-to-be. Daughter of the professor. Kann.
Salomon. Saloman. Salmon. Saul-man. Souldman. Knarre. K.
Grünwald. Grünewald (Matthias°): Crucifixion. Madonna. M.
M. for Murder. Murderous granddaughter. Draughtsman. D.
Draftsman. Daberlohn. Alfred Wolfsohn. Wolf's son. Ama-
deus. A-dolf Hitler. Metropolis. Jeanne d'Arc. Dreyer.
Carl Theo-dor. Bücher. Kristallnacht. Nebel. Shoah. Holo-
caust.Holocaust. Holocaust.

Girlhood. To be(or not to be) eines Mädchen. Obviously,
doctor, you've never been a 15-year-old girl.Jeffrey K.
Eugenides; Sofia Coppola; The Virgin Suicides. Obviously,
Doctor, you've never been a 13-year-old girl. Wolfsohn/
Daberlohn: Wie die jungen Mädchen wennsie anfangen zu
zeichnen (so erklärte mir ein 16-jäiges mädchen) und sie
sind trüber Stimmung, so kommen aus ihrem Pinsel trübe
Farben heraus. Sind sie jedoch froh, so macht der Pinsel
rote und gelbe punkte. Den Beweis sah ich in zwei Zeich-
nungen die mir ein anderes junges Mädchen schenkte. Ich
fand dabei heraus dassin manchen jungen Mädchen eine ge-
wisse Änlichkeit mit einem unserer grossen Philosophen
(Nietzsche) liegt der in vielen seiner Gedichte eben die-
selbe"gelbpünktliche" Naivität des Berührtseins der Seele
offenbart. Meine Hoffnungen liegen also bei den zukünfti-
gen Jungmädchen Naturen die gewillt sind den Christusweg,
 den Orpheusweg in das Eigene Innere zugehen zur eigenen
Befriedung (etc. etc.)

Leben? oder Theater? Mord? oder Selbstmord?
Das Mädchen (neutral); Die Mädchen (plural)
(das) Mädchen = (die) Mädchen (one = many girls)
Coupes mobiles (Bergson) et immobiles (Deleuze)
Schizofrénie. Découplement (découplement, le couple ment)
Dépeuplement. Die Judenfrage. Multiplication. Simulta-
néisme (see also some images by Frans Masereel)

www.maedchen.de: Alles über Beauty, Fashion-Trends,
Gossip, Aufklärung

Aufklärung?! Gossip Girl, xo-xo - I'm a Brooklyn baby.

"... so macht der Pinsel rote
und gelbe Punkte."

Follow the yellow brick road (The Wizard of Oz)
Adapt her adapter (Dropout Boogie, Captain Beefhaert)
Ya got to support her...
You told her ya love her so figured her mother
Ya love her adapt her
Adapt her adapter
'n' what about after that
(tu-du-du-dum tum-tu)
(ploinky ploinky ploink, ploinky ploinky ploink)
(etc.)

" Hab Tag und Nacht zu Tun -
und keine Zeit mich ausruh'n."
(nehmen sie Platz)

Die Männer (Dr. Klingklang, sic!:
Singsang/ Kurt Singer; Joseph Goebbels,
der Ministа von Propaganda; und also
Amadeus Daberlohn/ Alfred Wolfsohn)

The blue-red living room
(blue-red is not purple, that would be
their logical mischung; blue-red is
a simultaneous, double or schizo-
colour expressing sadness and passion
at the same time, or several moments
at once, coldness and warmth, loss &
love, death and life, mourning and
resurrection etc.)

"Ich möchte gerne auch den Tod und das Mädchen haben.
Das sind wir beide."
" Uns beide wird man später noch einmal ansehen."
" Ich gehöre also zu denen dieda sagen: zwei Seelen
wohnen, ach, in meiner Brust."

Also sprach Amadeus Daberlohn

Several moments at once, several souls in one body,
the dead ones with the living, the deceased within
a young life, burdened with what she could not know
(and had been told already only later on, at the time
of the Apocalypse, the Holocaust, when it was already
too late, by an abusive (?) grandfather), many desperate
existences stacked up, piled up in one, the end of the
line at the End of Times, the Death of Civilization...

No poetry after the Holocaust? But at its treshold?

Not properly 'sequential' (film; comics) nor exactly
'mutational' (Henri Van Lier): Leben? oder Theater?
is not a 'hard cosmogony'. Words and images, yes, words
are images and vice versa. Consecutive words and images
to be perceived simultaneously, then read or absorbed
in varying order (not always from the left to the right
and from top to bottom). (cfr. Kibédi-Varga 1989)
Sometimes the text is integrated as monologue, dialogue
, remark, legend or voice-over within the picture but
always Charlotte is telling us the story, typographical
colours change but the handwriting remains the same:
a cursive, hasty but timeless flow runs through the
book, many voices let themselves being heard through
Charlotte's hand. She shows/sees herself from the back

and we incorporate that ghostly gaze; the viewpoint of
a ghost spectre haunting her past and the whole 'retro-
spective' she creates (while writing/drawing, she is
already dead, maybe orpheic). Especially in the foreplay,
showing us her pre-history, the viewpoint is that from of
an angel (Franziska?). But also in the more 'vivid'
main part and the raw epilogue, our viewpoint remains
distant, fleeting, cursive, as sliding through this
life, only passing by: Death has already touched us and
we can only make ourselves useful by reading and feeling with toned/composed intensity/depth what Charlotte
had decided to write/draw down and pass on while she
flared up in a singular series of lucid moments.

Hence the transparancies: the figures are opaque,
shifting, unsertain, restless, made of gouache on
paper. They have no hardened bodies, existing only
out of mood colours. The bold words give them life,
the transparant overlays bearing the sometimes joyful calligraphic texts – dancing and melodic – do
not recreate the veil that Charlotte seemed to be
aching to break but give clarity and a strong sense
of temporality – despite the morbid repetitions and
death time always 'now', always present – to the
dreamy images underneath. The autographic overlays
tend to give the opaque characters and surroundings
what they lack: a voice, a mind, a personality, a

certain sense of clarity and definite eloquence: at
last, the dead, the mumbling, the unheard are ~~giving~~
being given a voice and not only an appearance (ever
fleeting). Knowing that surviving and becoming a married
woman and a mother would be an ongoing disaster, C.S.
preferred to sacrifice herself, following the insights
of her former lover/beloved A.W./A.D., to artistically
change hereditary misery into golden songs for man-kind?
"And I would almost like to say 'amen'."
"Take good care of this, this is my life."

> At last the girl became the
> Madonna herself, Redemptor at
> once, not giving life to a child
> but to a golden Singespiel made
> of opacities and transparancies,
> un-filtering tragic fate to offer
> in-sight, truth (?), luminosity...

(I do not know of any other verbo-visual narrative that
has been composed with a self-soothing humming at its
base, resulting in a semi-autobiographical Testament
that is to be read and viewed closely but maybe 'heard'
as well, listende to, and probably brought on stage
or to the screen - which all happened. In the beginning
there was... sound?)

> But what about the girl?

She remains. She angelically survives in multiplicity:
the many lives and stories, the untold words and tragedies
the unseen scenes that had to be invented (dead bodies),
the many losses suffered but not knownof, those endless
moments and situations C.S. existed of, as a compact,
utterly silent being (how to utter what one only feels
bluntly and sharply but doesn't know of), had been re-
ordered, translated, told, sequenced, visualized and
playfully dramatized... sung in a manuscript we can
watch, hear and read. It exists and is beeingtransmitted.

C.S. has un-folded the many layers she almost
mutedly consisted of. She made the book a song,
her unravelled and re arranged, exquisitely eloquent,
portable and transferrable body (celestial and
inherently multimedia). For all her sufferings and
her atrocious end, she - the girl - became a book.

> What is a human in the end?
> What is a woman, what is a girl?
> We'd love to live and yet we die
> and all we know of life we hear
> from others at the start.

S.C.

German Citations in the Graphic Essay

In his graphic essay Sébastien Conard quotes Charlotte Salomon in German. Below you'll find the English translations of those citations which are taken from Salomon, Charlotte. *Life? or Theatre?: a selection of 450 gouaches*, translated by Leila Vennewitz. Taschen, 2017.

p. 193

> Like young girls when they begin to draw (as the 16-year-old girl explained to me), if they are in a dull mood dark colours flow from their brush. But if they are happy, the brush makes red and yellow dots. I saw the proof in two pictures given to me by another young girl. There, I found out that in many young girls there is a certain resemblance to one of our great philosophers, Nietzsche, who in several of his poems reveals this same "yellow-dotted" naiveté of the soul that is touched. My hopes, therefore, lie with the future souls of young girls. (453)

p. 194

> "I'm busy night and day, no time to rest or play. Come in, come in!" (244)
> "I'd like to have Death and the Maiden, too. That's the two of us." (370)
> "One day people will be looking at us two." (463)
> "I belong thus to those who say: 'Two souls dwell in my breast'." (307)

Notes

1. *Charlotte Salomon in close-up*, curated by Mirjam Knotter, 13 March–22 November 2020. See https://jck.nl/en/node/4209.
2. https://www.theparisreview.org/fiction/2264/the-virgin-suicides-jeffrey-eugenides

Chapter 11

Developing a Style of Her Own: *Mophead* by Selina Tusitala Marsh (2019)

Marine Berthiot

This chapter highlights the contribution of girls' comics in art history, as Selina Tusitala Marsh challenges the racist and sexist stereotypes of Polynesian girls propagated by nineteenth-century painters like Paul Gauguin, and by contemporary European art historians whose discourse on Pasifika muses is imbued with colonial remnants. Marsh's commitment to the well-being of the Pasifika community in Aotearoa New Zealand also permeates her aesthetics, which adapts Samoan storytelling devices to interact with her young readers and gives visibility to the cultural trauma she experienced while at school in the 1980s.

In 2010 Selina Tusitala Marsh wrote an article entitled "The Body of Pacific Literature" in which she outlines the ethics of her own teaching and writing practices. She mentions the Spoken Word Poetry workshops organised in Manukau, South Auckland, by Youthline, an association that undertakes preventive work against suicide, especially amid teenagers from Māori and Pasifika origins. Suicide is often referred to as a pandemic in the context of Aotearoa New Zealand. Young men of Māori and Pacific descent are particularly at risk (Ministry of Health). By organising poetry competitions within an area of Auckland decried for its social segregation (Grbic, Ishizawa and Crothers 35), Youthline offers a stage for youth from minority groups to be heard in their own words, in their own rhythms and in idiolects that challenge the primacy of standard English. As a poet and as a teacher, Marsh stresses the importance of care and dialogue as the basis of her ethical commitment towards her community and towards New Zealand literature. In this regard, her graphic memoir, *Mophead* (2019), could be considered a gift to Pasifika youth.

> If, as [Albert] Wendt has argued since decolonisation began in the Pacific from the 1960s, "self expression is a pre-requisite of self respect" (Wendt 60), how might the body of Pacific writing in Aotearoa New Zealand influence that other impressionable, vulnerable body of Pacific youth? What role do I, as a university teacher and researcher of that literary body, play in the healing, restoring, renewing, and invigorating of that other body? (Marsh, 2010, 1)

Marsh has previously explored the autobiographical mode in poems and in essays. In her graphic memoir, mostly addressed to children, she focuses on the damaging impact school bullying and racism had on her self-esteem while growing up. She especially investigates the detrimental power verbal abuse can have on girls, particularly for coming-of-age Pasifika girls enrolled in the New Zealand curriculum. After trying to assimilate and becoming invisible to her classmates' mockery, she decided to assert herself and her own style via the medium of poetry. As an adult, Marsh connects this teenage posture of rebellion to a long series of firsts that she has been collecting as an adult: she was the first Pacific Islander to receive a PhD in English Literature at the University of Auckland in 2004, the first Pacific Islander to become a Commonwealth Poet in 2016 and the first female Pacific Islander to be elected Poet Laureate of New Zealand from 2017 to 2019.

With *Mophead*, Selina Tusitala Marsh participates in the history of New Zealand comics and art history, as the story is centred on a Pasifika girl heroine, is written by a woman author-artist from the Pasifika community and is addressed to children of ethnic minority backgrounds, especially Pasifika children. For the purpose of this chapter, I analyse the way Selina Tusitala Marsh adapts the conventions of the graphic memoir to testify to her girlhood trauma for a child audience. At first, I will study *Mophead* as a limit case in reference to Leigh Gilmore's work on girls' and women's testimonies of trauma. I will then focus on the fact that Marsh writes to render her community visible. Finally, I will analyse Marsh's aesthetic representations of Pasifika girls' bodies.

Mophead as a Limit Case

Since the 1980s, graphic memoirs, also called "autobiographics" (Gilmore and Marshall, 2019a, 6), have been an innovative multisensory medium to tackle the telling of traumatic experiences, as it allows artist-writers to circumvent restrictive definitions of trauma as unspeakable and unrepresentable (Caruth). As meaning is conveyed through a complex combination of images and words, readers are engaged to interact with the story and interpret it in multiple ways (Burger 2). Marsh seems to apply Lynda Barry's comics methodology, developed in *What It Is* (2008) and *Syllabus* (2014), and based on an aesthetic experience aimed "to recover the experience of drawing as a child" (Frangos 6). By adopting a "childish" drawing style and a child's language – at least in the depiction of her childhood trauma – Marsh questions racial stereotypes persisting in schoolyards with the very means of communication a child would use. She also adapts the conventions of autobiographical texts to the Samoan literary heritage. As Martina Wagner-Egelhaaf notes in her "Introduction: Autobiography across the World, Or, How Not to Be Eurocentric", "one has to keep in mind that the Western notion of autobiography as a written form of self-expression foregrounding the individual cannot automatically be applied to South Pacific native cultures" (687). In this sense, Marsh's graphic memoir insists on the development of the protagonist as a relational being and as a member of the Samoan diaspora.

Speaking Out against School Bullying

Drawing her younger self (**fig. 1**) as a scapegoat requires measures and frames to be read and believed, as Marsh challenges traditional assumptions of girls as "voiceless" (Gilmore and Marshall, 2019b, 40; Mitchell 93). Inversing letter colours on page 1 – using a white font upon her black hair – Marsh leads us into her own version of her school years, a world where words stand out by their size, their colour, their font and their written form, as their letters sometimes are composed of hair.

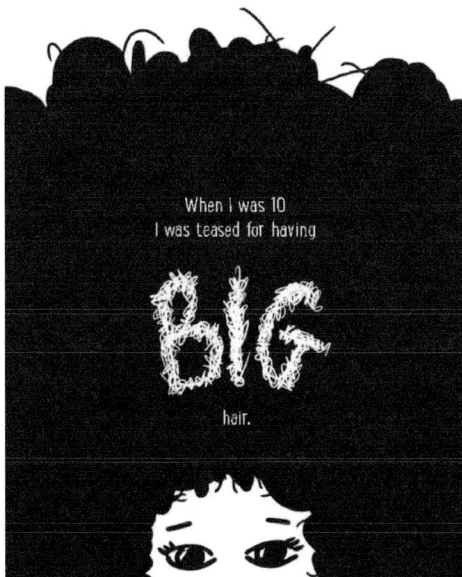

Called names with overt racist undertones, such as "Mophead", "Fuzzy-Wuzzy", "Golliwog" and "Pippi Blackstocking" (n.p.), young Selina tried several solutions to escape from discrimination: she cut her hair, and she tamed her hair to look smoother, but assimilating into the mainstream did not heal her pain. As shown in the following passage employing short and simple words mirroring a child's vocabulary and logic, the

Figure 1 S. T. Marsh, *Mophead*, n.p. Reprinted with permission from S. T. Marsh, *Mophead* © Auckland University Press, 2019.

girl had internalised the racist comments: "I was tall, skinny and brown like the mop in our garage. It smelled like old socks. [...] Being called Mophead made me feel bad" (n.p.). Criteria often associated with becoming a fashion model (height and slimness) are here the cause for self-debasement. Young Selina's self-esteem was at its lowest, as she compared herself to a smelly mop and perceived herself as "bad". On the contrary, her Pākehā (New Zealanders of British descent) classmates had the power in this unequal relationship, as they were the "good" ones, those who were on the right side of history, and policing the school environment. Wang and Collins note that "traumatic events in early life can have a fundamental impact on later life self-esteem and the ability to over-come difference. Experiences of racially infused bullying in childhood [...] are something that [...] can have long-lasting effects on socializing" (2787). As a victim of racism, young Selina is always drawn alone, isolated in her garage, the target of insults or at the end of a line of students. The only time she is surrounded is by her family. School becomes synonymous with isolation and suffering, while at home the young Marsh undertakes a series of enjoyable exploits, regaining her equilibrium through imaginative play, as the change of colour palette suggests.

In this context, I posit that *Mophead* can be read as a "limit case". Leigh Gilmore (2001c) defines this form of life-writing as "testimonial projects", which "constitute an alternative jurisdiction for self-representation in which writers relocate the grounds of judgment, install there a knowing subject rather than a sovereign or representative self, and pro-duce an alternative jurisprudence about trauma, identity, and the forms both may take" (143). Rippl et al. clarify that limit cases "self-consciously si[t] on the fence between fiction and non-fiction" (7), an interpretation Isabelle Somé confirms (229). Limit cases therefore borrow auto-fictional tools. Olga Michael notes that the use of auto-fiction in graphic memoirs is particularly apt to express girls' trauma, as this device allows author-artists to "visually and verbally capture the often silenced narrative of girls' working through and surviving different forms of abuse" (121). *Mophead* is thus a rewriting, a selection of chosen moments, at the exclusion or occlusion of others, such as the conspicuous absence of Marsh's siblings. In addition, Marsh's drawing style exaggerates the voluminousness of her hair compared to the hairstyle she had on the photographs displayed at the end of the narrative. The power of her childhood imagination is also shown as border crossing. Her young I-con[1] attracts readers' attention and sympathy with her round face, simple features and inquisitive eyes. Her simplifying self-portrait thus implies that her story could be that of other people too. Scott McCloud defines this technique as "amplification through simplification". For him, "[b]y stripping down an image to its essential mean-ing an artist can amplify that meaning in a way that realistic art can't" (n.p.). As a result, young readers can identify more easily with the events the heroine goes through.

Juxtaposing episodes of her life at home with the way she was compelled to behave at school, Marsh highlights the multiplicity of her selves from an early age, insisting on her capacity to adapt, adjust and survive in a hostile environment. The medium of the graphic novel therefore provides her with visual and literary means to testify about the life-shattering experience of school bullying and racism, which could be considered litigious if expressed in another form like a non-fictional essay, for example (Gilmore, 2017, 4). The childish figure of young Selina conveys the emotional impact verbal abuse had on her when, for instance, Marsh draws a self-portrait of her younger self by zooming in on her doodled hair and cutting her mouth off-frame. The girl's sadness is expressed in her eyes, as she is wearing her classmates' nickname for her, "Mophead", in big red capital letters on top of her hair like a thorny crown. This image conveys the pain young Selina experienced when she was stigmatised. It also highlights the fact that the schoolgirl was disempowered by her fellows' racist comments, as her voice is metaphorically silenced by the absence of her mouth. Young Selina is therefore a character young readers can feel empathy for because Marsh adopts children's haptic drawing style and doodles to tell her girlhood trauma. As Alissa Burger notes, graphic memoirs are "an ideal fit for encouraging students to consider perspectives other than their own, gain insight into the world around them, respond with empathy, and increase their capacity for social understanding" (7). *Mophead* thus reads as a testimony which converts its young readers into acting against discriminations. It is yet worth noting that Marsh does not fall into the trap of depicting the child as a conventionally innocent person, perhaps because she is too much aware that this association of ideas is "a racialized construct" as Gilmore and Marshall (2019a, 5) remind us. They claim that "girls of color in the American context of slavery have never been seen as innocent – either sexually or politically" (5). In the Pacific, Tamasailau Sua'ali'i (78) explains that Indigenous girls have been othered, exoticised and eroticised by colonists, and colonial literature and art proliferated this idyllic image of Pasifika girls and women as sexual objects. By desexualising her younger self, presented as an androgynous stick figure, Marsh circumvents stereotypes of lascivious Pacific Island girls and gives her past self a credibility that she would perhaps have been denied had she drawn herself with curves.

Empowering Victims with a Sense of Humour

To allow readers an insight into her story of abuse, Marsh employs a vast array of techniques which ritualise the passage into her past and into trauma. Before the story per se starts, plunging us into what she endured from age ten, readers encounter adult Selina on paper, in miniature, having run a long distance on an uneven path over a red-ochre background. The choice of a bleed (an image which spreads beyond panel borders and across two pages) is significant, as it is not used in a traditional way: we would expect the depiction of a spectacular event with this choice of frame. Yet here she represents herself as a marathon runner – not as a poet – and playing with perspectives over a flat reddish background. Over the next pages, the miniature poet's I-con further displays her skills as an entertaining figure, doing a cartwheel and finding her balance over the logo of Auckland University Press. This intervention on the part of her "avatar" (Klepper 442) around and inside the traumatic telling of her childhood first accompanies her younger self in "a gesture of care", showing readers – as in a mirror effect – the path to ethical witnessing (Gilmore and Marshall, 2019a, 111). Her presence as a witness and as a guardian of the testimony that she protects from the edges shows readers – themselves witnesses in a mirror effect – that, as in narrative therapy, Marsh has formulated an alternative story to cope with the derogatory discourse that was imposed on her. Michael White and David Epston, the founders of narrative therapy, an Australian- and New Zealand-based form of therapy, explain this process as "the externalization of the problem-saturated story" (16). By distancing herself from "the dominant story" told by her classmates, young Selina was empowered to convey her own perspective: "as persons become separated from their stories, they are able to experience a sense of personal agency; as they break from their performance of their stories, they experience a capacity to intervene in their own lives and relationships" (White and Epston 16). By inserting her humorous avatar and her adult self-portrait as caring figures of authority, Marsh shows reader-witnesses the way into ethical empathy, transforming mockery into self-parody, racism into an ode to difference and self-pity into self-esteem.

When she entertains the audience with gymnastic prowess and exhortations to the public, Marsh represents her adult self as a *Tusitala* (in Samoan: "storyteller"). By doing so, Marsh adapts Samoan *fāgogo* literary techniques into her graphic novel. She indigenises the Western literary medium of comics, which was imported in Aotearoa New Zealand from the United Kingdom at the beginning of the twentieth century and the United States from the 1940s onwards (Bollinger 2). Marsh re-enacts the figure of the *Tusitala* whose mission is "the telling of legendary tales in Samoa which are often accompanied by dances and songs" (Baisnée 114–115). When taking the form of bedtime stories (McMullin 220), *fāgogo* is "interactive" (Gin 605) as storytellers adapt their telling to their audience. In *Mophead*, the audience is composed of children and is given centre stage when adult Selina answers their questions at a "Writers in School" session. Marsh therefore endows her graphic novel with a pedagogical power, which is further explored in the Teachers' Notes that she designed to guide elementary and secondary school children in their readings and interpretations of *Mophead*. Drawing herself as a *Tusitala* dialoguing with "real-life" intradiegetic readers thus reflects the audience response Marsh expects extradiegetic readers will have. When she presents her *tokotoko* (in Māori language: "a carved Māori walking stick", n.p.) to the class, an anonymous student (readers only see their backs, and their silhouettes are in the shade) repeats "A wa-wa-wa-wat?" (n.p.) The reaction of the child reveals surprise at hearing a Māori word in a conversation held in the English language. The student's unfamiliarity with Te Reo Māori (the Māori language) also reveals a certain arrogance some Pākehā can have regarding the language and culture of the Indigenous people of New Zealand. The child does not formulate a complete question to inquire about the word he or she does not understand, nor does the student use the interrogative pronoun "what". As a result, the child's reaction is derogatory, which implies a certain feeling of superiority on the part of the Pākehā child, having fun at a Māori word as, in a similar way, kids used to mock young Selina for her Pasifika heritage. As a *Tusitala* Marsh does not reprimand the child but instead tells her audience the story behind the Poet Laureate's emblem of power. She draws in miniature the ceremony she attended when she received her *tokotoko* at a *marae* (a meeting place in Māori culture), situating it on top of the geographic outlines of New Zealand's islands and above a collection of *tokotoko*. In this image, Marsh encapsulates the biculturalism of New Zealand society, depicting the poetry ceremony in a Māori village, close to the city of Auckland whose skyscrapers, including the iconic Sky Tower, symbolise the Anglophone world. Marsh's *tokotoko* is unique, as its shape recalls the *fue*, the oratory emblem of "Samoan talking chiefs" (n.p.). Her *tokotoko* therefore inserts Samoan literary traditions at the heart of New Zealand literature and culture, in-between Māori and Pākehā customs. The presence of Te Reo Māori words, but also Samoan, Tongan and Rarotongan words inside *Mophead* is reinforced by the addition of a glossary at the end of the book, entitled "Upu: Words" (n.p.). There, Marsh also draws a performing Samoan orator in the style of drawings found in bilingual textbooks for children. Her drawing is explained with labels in both Samoan and English to highlight the various emblems of power *Tusitala* wear when they perform in front of an audience. By drawing a series of mises en abyme of the reader-writer/audience-teller relationship, and by communicating in both official languages of Aotearoa New Zealand and in Samoan, Marsh decolonises the graphic memoir by testifying to her girlhood trauma in a "stor[y] in the style of *fāgogo*" (Moyle 29). By playing with her own image, with literary conventions and expectations, Marsh highlights that she is now the one with the power to make other people laugh, not at her own expense, but to relieve the audience from past and shared trauma. Marsh's adult I-cons therefore embody her multicultural experience of Samoan, Māori and Anglophone literatures, giving agency to her past scapegoated "I", and refusing victimisation.

The cheeky comment Marsh's mini avatar formulates in the paratext, "She also drew me" (n.p.), mocks Philippe Lejeune's autobiographical pact, as she ostensibly and irreverently establishes a difference of identity between the writer's "I", the narrating "I" and the drawn characters' "I"s. Lejeune claims that

> an autobiography (a story telling the life of its writer) is based on a common identity of name between the writer (as he appears on the book cover with his name), the narrator of the story, and the character of whom he speaks.[2]

Several problems arise in this definition. Not only does Lejeune's formulation exclude women writers (as the masculine pronoun implies that the writer shall be male); it also implies that the writer's self is unique and unchanged from birth to death. This essentialist understanding of the self (Anderson 4) is debunked by Marsh, who mischievously plays with Western understandings of identity. Valérie Baisnée notes that "Marsh decentres the 'I' by multiplying the imaginary locations of its enunciation and its figures, displacing the centrality of the English language by inscribing alterity in it to avoid mimicking the western 'I'" (108). This comment, formulated to describe the poems in Marsh's debut collection *Fast Talking PI* (2009), can be applied to *Mophead*. By adapting Samoan literary techniques into her graphic novel, Marsh destabilises Western representations of Pasifika girls who have been victims of trauma. The rupture survivors recognise between their past and present selves following traumatisation (Gilmore, 2011, 158) is expressed in the multiplication of her selves, drawing some young, some old, some small, some tall. Marsh's avatars can take the protean shapes of a mini *Tusitala*, a gigantic poet full of *mana* (in Te Reo Māori: power, charisma), a desperate child and a resilient student in a non-chronological manner. She therefore insists on the resourcefulness of her different selves to recover from traumatic experiences, and she connects this resourcefulness to the precolonial literary traditions of Samoa.

Multicultural Life Writing

Mophead can also be read as a multicultural comic. Frederick Luis Aldama notes that "author-artists of color talk about real, biographical experiences living at the margins of xenophobic society informing their comics as much as they talk of the influence of fiction, film, and art" (2). Even if Marsh recognises that she is an exception within New Zealand's Pacific Island minority groups, as she could climb the social ladder and become a role model for her nation, because she comes from a minority, her graphic life-writing runs the risk of being interpreted as a form of "ethnic autobiography". For example, Betty Ann Bergland differentiates between autobiography (mainly from White men from the Western world) which celebrates one individual's life, and ethnic autobiography which "constructs a life and a community" (87). The problem with this definition lies in the fact that Marsh (2010, 4) could be "tokenized" as *the* Samoan poet of New Zealand, an idea that she vigorously debunks. The New Zealand Pacific Islander community expanded rapidly after the Second World War when immigration from the Pacific was encouraged to replenish the workforce, and again after the Immigration Act 1987, which opened the borders of New Zealand to targeted workers whose skills were needed, and not to specific nationalities. In this second wave, Samoa was one of "the ten countries of origin with the largest numbers of migrants" (Collins 7). In the 2018 census, Pacific Islanders represented

8.1 per cent of the New Zealand population (Stats NZ/Tatauranga Aotearoa, 2019, n.p.), composing the third largest minority, after Māori (16.5 per cent) and Asians (15.1 per cent). To this day, Pākehā remain the majority ethnic group with 70.2 per cent. The term "Pacific Islander" hides a multiplicity of cultures, languages and origins, which make of their community a heterogeneous group (Tawake 161; O'Donnell 3). Moreover, mainstream perceptions and constructions of Pacific Islanders in the media can be negative in New Zealand. Collins, for example, denounces "the establishment of stratifications within migrant populations" (84), leading the majority of Pacific Islanders to be perceived as "low-skilled" and less valuable than other ethnicities like Pākehā and Asians who would be regarded as "high-skilled" (84). In this context, *Mophead* gives visibility to the prejudices suffered by her community.

An Ode to Difference

An ode to difference is nothing new in New Zealand literature. In *To the Is-Land* (1982), the first volume of an autobiography later adapted into the film *An Angel at My Table* by Jane Campion (1990), Janet Frame already comments on her school years in these terms:

> I did not think of myself as original: I merely said what I thought. Yet an acknowledgement of an apparent "difference" in my thinking seemed to fit with the "difference", as I thought it to be, of my life at home [...]. I came to accept the difference, although in our world of school, to be different was to be peculiar, a little "mad". (112–113)

Janet Frame's school years, too, were marked by "difference" due to her working-class background. Her aspiration to become a poet was counterbalanced by self-deprecation and low self-esteem. She was aware that what her private life (poverty, patriarchy, her brother's uncontrollable epileptic bouts, but also her mother's poetic aspirations) made her stand out and sound discordant in the normative public sphere. When Selina Tusitala Marsh emphasises the idea of "difference" in her subtitle ("How Your Difference Makes a Difference"), in her motto ("But we're not made to be the same") and in the dedication to her book ("For those who stick out"), she self-consciously transforms *Mophead* into a kind of self-help manual. As a métisse, she refuses to deny her Samoan and Tuvaluan heritage. As a member of the Pasifika community, she rejects assimilation into Pākehā mainstream culture. When she tried to wear the invisibility cloak of the "mimic man" to escape from bullies, Marsh was constraining herself. As Homi K. Bhabha notes, the mimic man, or should I say here "the mimic girl", "is the effect of a flawed colonial mimesis, in which to be Anglicized is emphatically not to be English" (87). This idea of a distorted reflection is represented in *Mophead* when Marsh draws the word "same" twice in a mirror image (n.p.). As a result, the reflected word appears underneath the original and in a light grey, not in black. As the word is reflected, its letters are reversed in a graphic style which deforms them, as if written in a foreign alphabet. Marsh's visual description of her experience of assimilation denounces the fact that she was accepted by her Pākehā peers only when she had given up on her Pasifika identity markers. In the 1980s the school system in New Zealand was still focused on assimilating children into mainstream Pākehā culture. Bicultural policies were nascent, and children who were neither Pākehā nor Māori had to abide by the dominant Pākehā education system, which was adapted from the British school curriculum (Lee 50). Cultural and linguistic differences were thus overlooked, even effaced via school "streaming" policies. Wang and Collins explain that "[s]treaming involves placing students in different classes based on academic performance, which often results in ethnic gradients and school-based segregation" (2786). The education system therefore perpetuates ethnic inequalities, as Māori and Pasifika children are often channelled into vocational degrees, which bars them from attending university courses, accessing more prestigious professions and earning better incomes (Sibley and Ward 701; Ioane et al. 430). Education is therefore critical in levelling social inequalities, and, in this system, Pacific Islanders are at the intersection of several discriminating factors. Janet Wilson notes that "perpetuation of the socio-economic and racial inequalities of colonialism through low-skilled labour has led to negative depictions of Pacific diasporas" (149). In this sense, the testimony Marsh gives of her years of being bullied at school and of the assimilating practices performed is revelatory, as it renders these racist deeds public.

With *Mophead*, Marsh reclaims Pasifika cultures, arts and creativity from colonial mimicry. After meeting with a poet during a "Writers in School" visit, young Selina rejects the idea of becoming an "honorary White" and explores instead the possibilities offered by Black and Indigenous cultures from around the world. She starts writing, as readers witness her entry into poetry in a drawing where her hands are shown writing the word "different" without a pen, as if ink came out of her hands by magic (n.p.). Her own voice stands out from the crowd, coloured as it is in red ochre, and she stops wearing the school uniform like the other pupils, preferring to go to school barefoot. Asserting her cultural singularity, rebellious teenage Selina pays a tribute to her heroines in a drawing where her mini avatar is multiplied, and shown reading several books simultaneously. This thirst for knowledge is further symbolised by the pile of books precariously stacked, and on which her mini avatars have climbed to get a better look. On Marsh's wall of honour are inscribed the names of second- and third-wave postcolonial feminists, African American abolitionists, civil rights activists, African American women writers, Polynesian queens, anti-nuclear activists from the Pacific and Commonwealth poets. Marsh therefore inscribes her *ars poetica* in a non-Western and non-patriarchal literary and political tradition which is not limited to and by Pākehā lore. It is worth noting that no New Zealanders, whatever their ethnicity, are present in this list. In her autobiography, *From The Centre: A Writer's Life* (2021), Patricia Grace, who is a Māori novelist, short-story writer and the author of numerous children's books, explains that when she grew up, there were no Māori hero/ines to identify with. For her, "*[i]f there are no books which tell us about ourselves, but tell us only about others, that makes you invisible in the world of literature. That is dangerous*" (n.p.). Marsh, like Grace, notes the invisibility of her community in the New Zealand's artistic and literary scenes of her childhood, compelling her to find hero/ines abroad, in the Pacific and in the United States. By sharing her idols with her readers, Marsh not only challenges the stereotypical image of the compliant girl as "apolitical" and "passive" (MacDowell 205, 213), but she also gives New Zealand children and teenagers from minorities a mine of discourses with which they can identify and experiment. Rebecca M. Marrall reminds us that

> the content of graphic novels – particularly those that explore cultural narratives – offers students both an opportunity to become more aware about diversity while promoting inclusion for students who are members of historically underrepresented groups (249).

In her quest for difference, Marsh therefore gives visibility and credibility to her community's cultural trauma. By staging her younger self interacting with Black and Indigenous cultures, Marsh shows child readers a tolerant and open-minded Pasifika heroine whom they can relate to and imitate.

Wild versus Same and Savage

Ron Eyerman defines cultural trauma as "a dramatic loss of identity and meaning, a tear in the social fabric, affecting a group of people that has achieved some degree of cohesion" (2). After more than half a century of settlement in Aotearoa New Zealand, Pacific Islander communities have contributed substantially to the history of their nation. However, their portrayal in the media has long been disparaging. Sarina Pearson notes that

> in a country where advertising executives once openly defended the fact that "there are more dogs shown on commercials than there are Māoris [*sic*] and Polynesians" (Scott 84), and television executives routinely asserted that ethnic minorities fail to rate, the change in New Zealand's mediascape has been dramatic. (29)

Marsh's childhood trauma can be read as a synecdoche of a wider trauma which affected the Pasifika community as a whole. Marsh (2010, 3–4) once lamented the relative invisibility of the body of a Pacific literature in New Zealand and connected it to the high rate of suicide amid the youth of the Pacific Island community. For her, writers from this community should continue to participate in the creation of New Zealand's "imagined" nation to help children grow up with positive images of themselves. Her interpretation of nationalism reflects the heterogeneity of her community. Readers can notice that there are only two panels with closed borders in the whole graphic novel. They each correspond to her parents' origins. Instead of representing her family line with a tree, Marsh gives a childish explanation of the reason why her hair is so voluminous. She explains DNA with drawn maps of her maternal and paternal countries, describing their hair in calligraphic words and argues that her ancestors' hairstyles have contributed to her messy mop. Adopting a child's logic, Marsh attacks borders, frames and genetic discourses to praise freedom of speech. By writing about her personal trauma, she participates in the writing of the New Zealand nation, beyond its bicultural frame, as she herself is of "dissemi-nat(ion)ed" descent, from a history of multiple migrations.

The Pacific Island population is today the youngest on average in New Zealand, compared to the other ethnic groups. "The median age was 23.4 years for the Pacific ethnic group, 25.4 years for Māori, 31.3 years for Asian, and 41.4 years for European." (Stats NZ/ Tatauranga Aotearoa n.p.) Their increased visibility in the media has been quite creative, as Michelle Keown (44) and Janet Wilson (151) note, especially in TV shows, TV series, films, cartoons, performative poetry and theatre. It is thus in a more open-minded mediascape that Marsh publishes *Mophead*, even if, as Pearson shows, "[g]reater visibility […] does not necessarily translate into greater youth empowerment" (29). Marsh's choice to employ the word "wild" ten times in *Mophead* to qualify the power of poetry is therefore significant, as she does not want to fall into the colonial clichés of the "noble savage" nor of the Indigenous "eco-warrior" comic books often tend to reproduce (Aldama 7; Benson-Taylor 11). Associating wildness with Pacific Island women poets from Tonga, Samoa, the Solomon Islands, Vanuatu and Hawai'i, she rejects colonial and patriarchal discourses on Pasifika women and girls. This is best illustrated when, accepting her hair as it is, young Selina frees herself from social expectations and social constraints. In a series of actions, readers can attend the liberation of the teenage girl. It starts with the word "tied", drawn with imprisoned hair, and it ends with the word "wild", in red capital letters roaming in a bleed over a background of loose black hair that looks like doodles. The letter T in "tied" has the shape of a cross, as if Marsh was hinting here at the part played by Christian missionaries in the control and the shaming of girls and women's bodies from the Pacific. For Rawiri Waretini-Karena, "European powers used religion as a tool to justify enslavement, murder, and genocide on a global scale that devastated Indigenous cultures" (698). Young Selina's rebellion is, in this context, partly directed at colonial representations of Pasifika girls' bodies.

Aesthetic Representation of Pasifika Girls' Bodies

Abram Fox encourages critics and teachers to incorporate comics into the study of art history as comics can echo fine arts (91). Sean P. Connors also includes comics and graphic novels into art history (24) because these media procure a certain "aesthetic pleasure" (26). On top of being a testimony of pedagogical value, I argue that *Mophead* can be read as a counterpoint to the European art which was produced in the Pacific during colonisation. In this final section, I discuss the ways Marsh's drawing style challenges colonial styles of art exoticising Pacific Islanders and eroticising girls and women into black Venuses. Finally, I discuss how the inscription of *Mophead* into the history of New Zealand comics can empower Pasifika girls.

Challenging Colonial Art

In two poems published in her first collection, *Fast Talking PI*, Marsh (2009) overtly attacks Paul Gauguin's representations of Pasifika girls' bodies. In "Guys like Gauguin", she accuses the French artist of paedophilia and of having perpetrated the myth of the Pacific as "an erogenous zone/corporeal and sexual/emotive and natural" (45), as opposed to the north, which symbolises reason, civilisation and power. In "Two Nudes on a Tahitian Beach, 1894", the speaker who is one of the nude models throws verbal abuse at the painter: "Gauguin,/you piss me/off" (49). She then describes how Gauguin forced her to get undressed for the sake of his painting, orchestrated her position and facial expression, and compelled her not to move while her girlfriend next to her condemns Gauguin for his lecherous thoughts. In her monograph on Gauguin, Françoise Cachin highlights the fact that, before travelling to the Pacific, the painter had a pre-existing conception of Polynesian beauties inspired by Pierre Loti's idyllic texts on Tahiti (128, 142). As evidence, she displays "Soyez mystérieuses" [Be Mysterious], a carving from 1890, which was created in Brittany with a model from this region, and yet the White girl is as dark-faced as a Tahitian nude. Gauguin was attracted to a Romantic and orientalist discourse figuring Pasifika women as "mysterious", ungraspable and unaltered by Western's so-called "civilisation" – as opposed to the idealised state of nature Westerners projected onto Pacific Islanders. It is, however, worth noting that some art historians like Françoise Cachin continue to propagate constructs of Pasifika girls as exotic, without challenging this racist and sexist discourse. For example, Cachin describes Gauguin's Tahitian girl models in this way: "it is their placid strength, their dolent animal weight which make their beauty"[3] (146). Cachin thus perpetuates the colonial portrait of Pasifika girls as languid, Venus-like and yet animal-like, therefore of a lesser humanity than European girls. Cachin then focuses

her attention on Teha'amana, a Tahitian teenager with whom Gauguin had sexual inter-
course:

> with little Teha'amana, a pure Polynesian girl, the Tehura of his tales, he finally
> tasted for the first time the Edenic rest and the simple pleasures which he had
> imagined from Europe. With this new peace, and the company of the teenage
> girl who will be, of all his conquests, the most beloved of his vahines and models,
> Gauguin started a period of intensive work which lasted almost a year.[4] (153)

It is clear from this passage that Cachin, but also Geoffroy-Schneiter in her 2017 edition
of Gauguin's *Ancien culte mahorie* (69), are complicit with the reproduction of colonial stereotypes, as Gauguin is portrayed as a concupiscent explorer seeking sex with underaged
Pasifika girls as if this behaviour is the accepted norm. Mishuana Goeman explains that
"colonialism is not just about conquering Native lands through mapping new owner-
ships, but it is also about the conquest of bodies, particularly women's bodies through
sexual violence, and about recreating gendered relationships" (33). This is revelatory of
the power inequality at stake in Gauguin's paintings and of the Western erotic fantasies
he projected onto Pasifika girls that he himself called "savage" (Huret, quoted by Geoffroy-Schneiter 65[5]). In this context, Selina Tusitala Marsh's role as a poet, as a spokes-
person for her community, and as a graphic artist, comes as a counterpoint to colonial
perspectives on Pasifika girls' bodies which persist in twenty-first century European art
history. Marsh's drawing style develops her own perspective on her own body, and decolonises Pasifika girls' bodies as represented in colonial art.

For depictions of her childhood, Marsh uses a palette of four colours only: black,
white, pale pink and red ochre, refusing the luxurious palettes of Gauguin's oil paintings and watercolours. In his graphic biography of Gauguin, subtitled "*l'autre monde*" [the
other world], Fabrizio Dori is inspired by the Tahitian paintings in his choice of colours,
rehearsing colonial visual tropes in his mimesis of Gauguin's drawing style, symbolic
forms and vivid palette. On the contrary, in *Mophead*, all Marsh's characters are white, the
colour of paper, whether they are Pākehā, Māori or Pacific Islanders, echoing the aesthetic
choices made by Witi Ihimaera and Tina Makereti when they edited a collection of short
stories from Māori and Pasifika writers and artists under the title *Black Marks on the White
Page*. In this collection, Indigenous authors from New Zealand, Australia and the Pacific
indigenise the English language and participate in the decolonisation of Pacific literature through their art. The fact that all the characters are drawn white – except for Barack
Obama's avatar – can be surprising and could be misconstrued as an aesthetic technique
to whiten ethnic differences. Yet Marsh's drawings teach child readers that ethnicity is not
visible as an exterior attribute like skin colours, but a cultural, linguistic and social experience of belonging to one or more communities. In this sense, Marsh abides by the defini-

tion of ethnic groups implemented in New Zealand censuses as "New Zealand is unique in having methodically measured multiple, self-ascribed ethnic identities since 1986" (Didham and Rocha 590). As a result, Marsh gives Pasifika characters "identity markers" (Lewis 46). She especially uses red ochre to colour flower necklaces and hair accessories such as bougainvillea flowers, and to distinguish her own voice from other people's. As a mode of expression, red is especially linked to Pasifika characters and art in *Mophead*. Marsh also decorates the clothes Pacific Islanders wear with Pasifika traditional patterns. Moreover, neither young Selina's I-con nor her mini avatars are represented in a passive, indolent or erotic attitude. The little girl breaks conventions in the role plays she imagines herself in, and with the mythic figures that she recognises as hers. When she pretends to be a horse rider, she looks like a witch mounted on a broom. When she studies literature at university, she identifies with the gorgon Medusa, to whom Hélène Cixous dedicated an ode to women writers' emancipation, and which Marsh draws escaping from the book she is reading. Represented as an ethereal creature whose hair is composed of snakes, the gorgon is a "wild" mythic female character whose hairstyle does not conform to any patriarchal norm, like Marsh's. As Aldama notes, "comic books are a particularly good medium to overturn denigrating stereotypes" (18), and Marsh's *Mophead* offers a counter discourse on Pasifika girls' bodies, actions and thoughts beyond the frame of colonial exoticism.

Inscribing *Mophead* in the History of New Zealand Comics

The world of New Zealand comics is today particularly productive and varied (Bollinger 8). Yet, in his encyclopaedic *New Zealand Comics and Graphic Novels* (2012), Tim Bollinger includes the bibliography of only one writer-artist of Samoan descent, Mat Hunkin. Marsh's decision to write a graphic novel centred on her experience as a Pasifika girl therefore stands out in the New Zealand comics scene. Many women design comics in New Zealand, like Li Chen (2021) famous for her *Extra Ordinary Comics*, Indira Neville (2010) with her comics *100 School Demons* and Sarah Laing (2016) known for her graphic memoir *Mansfield and Me*. Although women artists are still a minority in comics publishing, they reach a wider readership than superhero comics, mostly read by White males (Aldama 5). As Anna Jorgensen and Arianna Lechan argue, "[b]y assuming that 'girls just didn't read comics', it was easy for comic book creators to ignore this large group of readers" (267). Women writer-artists from minorities therefore open the market to women and girl readers, and to cultural groups who are often not visible in their own terms in mainstream comics. David DeIuliis, for instance, states that "the cartoonists themselves are cultural gatekeepers in the sense that they project images within the comics that affect racial perceptions and associations" (239). The story Marsh tells is empowering for girls from minorities as young Selina evolves from an anti-hero to a paragon of New Zealand literature, asserting her community's rights and the voices of Pasifika women poets and leaders. When she is depicted as "a damsel in distress", she is not rescued by a male super-hero, but by herself after a meeting with a bohemian poet. Her tale is therefore a story of female emancipation and girl power, the kind of narrative which was traditionally absent from comic books.

When telling her school bullying experience, Marsh mentions the emotional impact it had on her, yet she devotes more panels to her recovery from trauma. She notably emphasises the power of poetry when used as a coping technique, making of *Mophead* a graphic *Künstlerroman*. Marsh depicts her initiation into poetry from her school years to her consecration with literary prizes and performances in front of figures like Queen Elizabeth II. The *Künstlerroman* is "a traditionally male genre" which "relegate[es] [women] to the secondary functions of mother, mistress, and muse" (Hamelin 3). Yet Marsh feminises and decolonises this genre by staging herself as a female poet, not as a Pasifika muse. Marsh uses the storytelling potential of graphic novels (Connors 11; Bessette 2) and their connection with oral literature to initiate children into poetic language. *Mophead* can be read by a child on her or his own, but can also be read out loud to a child by a parent, an educator or a caring figure. Its frequent use of monosyllabic words such as "bad", "tall", "thin", and their repetitions inside the text shows that *Mophead* could potentially be read by a beginner reader. In this context, poetry is presented as a liberating language, mixing both words – written and told – and images. Young Selina's first encounter with "Sam the Poet" is translated in a bleed. Sam's voice is materialised escaping from his mouth as a breath of fresh air onto which the poetic line, "They know the way a mountain laughs" (n.p.), is metamorphosing into a picture of a laughing mountain. The poet's words move the children's imagination into visualising a natural element as a living being. Contrary to Western science, poetic power thus gives children access to Māori cosmology which considers mountains as ancestors (Roy n.p.). Marsh's apprenticeship into poetry is visible and audible in her use of rhymes, of an ornate handwriting to reflect her inner thoughts, in her readings of Pasifika women poets and in her depiction of herself drafting her first collection of poems on a sketchbook. In the very last page of her graphic *Künstlerroman*, Marsh has replaced Sam the Poet in her ability to change children's minds with her poetic words. Her iconic red words, addressed to a Pākehā boy, travel a double-paged drawing thanks to the movement of her *tokotoko*, whose threads recall Sam's breath of air, and the Māori symbol of the *koru*, a spiral design found in the wild in silver ferns, and used to represent the return back home. The poem she is offering the child is in fact *Mophead*, as its first words are "When I was 10…", repeating the incipit of her memoir. Marsh therefore plays with the potential of "comics reading as a socially and culturally mediated activity" (Connors 16) when she associates the *Tusitala*'s storytelling skills with poetry, her graphic memoir with a poem and the Samoan literary heritage with a New Zealand literature honouring its multiculturalism and multilingualism. Marsh therefore initiates children into poetry via the comics medium and empowers them with its freeing and healing potentials.

Conclusion

With her graphic memoir, Marsh explains how she developed a poetic voice of her own by rewriting an alternative discourse to the one imposed on her by school bullies. By researching the poetry of Pasifika women and reading postcolonial feminists, she asserted her own vision of what it means to be a "fast talking PI". *Mophead* therefore highlights the cultural trauma experienced by the Pasifika community in New Zealand due to colonisation, racism and segregation. Writing the trauma that she experienced at school in the form of a graphic memoir does not heal Marsh as its ramifications are deeply rooted in the colonial history of Aotearoa New Zealand. The circular construction of *Mophead* can liberate a certain tension accumulated throughout the book. When young Selina is depicted as a scapegoat, the insults are spread onto the pages, but without visible enunciators. This device places readers in the abusers' shoes. On the contrary, when Marsh encounters famous political figures, she draws herself as an observer and she situates herself off-screen, inviting readers to share her thoughts and viewpoints. During her final encounter with a Pākehā boy who mocks the *tokotoko*, Marsh is plunged again in the trauma of her school years, as the boy associates the symbol of her poetic power with a mophead. Now in a position of power due to her age, her occupation and her cultural capital, she decides to educate the boy by telling him the story of *Mophead*, repeating her testimony one more time. The circular composition of her text can thus be interpreted as a playful device gently turning the bully into a fool. However, it can also reflect the vicious circle of racism into which ethnic minority groups feel trapped. This ambivalence pervading the end of Marsh's graphic *Künstlerroman* thus produces a bittersweet tang to the text, which prevents cathartic interpretations of her trauma telling. Reading *Mophead* can yet teach children tolerance, as it does address prejudicial attitudes in a show and tell way which is adapted to and interactive with its audience.

Acknowledgements

I would like to thank the main supervisor of my thesis, Professor Michelle Keown, for her support and her advice on the first version of this chapter.

Notes

I would like to thank the main supervisor of my thesis, Professor Michelle Keown, for her support and her advice on the first version of this chapter.

1. In this article, I use the words "I-con" and "avatar" as synonyms. The term "I-con" (which could mean "with myself" in this context) echoes Leigh Gilmore's concept of an accompaniment offered by the adult self towards the younger traumatised self. The term "mini avatar" specifically refers to Marsh's miniature self-portraits which participate in the creation of comic relief in her graphic narrative.

2. My translation for: "[l']autobiographie (récit racontant la vie de l'auteur) suppose qu'il y ait identité de nom entre l'auteur (tel qu'il figure, par son nom, sur la couverture), le narrateur du récit et le personnage dont on parle" (23–24).

3. My translation for: "c'est leur force placide, leur poids d'animalité dolente qui font leur beauté" (1988, 146).

4. My translation for: "avec la petite Teha'amana, Polynésienne pure, la Tehura de ses récits, il va enfin goûter pour la première fois le repos édénique et les bonheurs simples dont il avait, d'Europe, imaginé les délices. Avec cette nouvelle paix, et la compagnie de l'adolescente qui sera, de toutes, la mieux aimée de ses vahinés et de ses modèles, débute pour Gauguin une période de près d'un an de travail intensif" (1988, 153).

5. This quotation is by Jules Huret, in "Paul Gauguin devant ses tableaux", *L'écho de Paris*, 23 February 1891.

Bibliography

Aldama, Frederick Louis. "Multicultural Comics Today: A Brief Introduction". *Multicultural Comics. From Zap to Blue Beetle*. University of Texas Press, 2010, pp. 1–25.

Anderson, Linda. "Introduction". *Autobiography*. Taylor & Francis, 2011, pp. 1–16.

Baisnée, Valérie. "'I'm Niu Voices': Selina Tusitala Marsh's Poetic Re-Imagining of Pacific Literature". *Commonwealth Essays and Studies*, vol. 41, no. 1, 2018, pp. 107–117.

Benson-Taylor, Melanie. "Indigenous Interruptions in the Anthropocene". *Publications of the Modern Language Association of America*, vol. 136, no. 1, Jan. 2021, pp. 9–16. https://doi.org/10.1632/S0030812920000139. Accessed 1 June 2022.

Bergland, Betty Ann. "Representing Ethnicity in Autobiography: Narratives of Oppression". *The Yearbook of English Studies*, vol. 24, 1994, pp. 67–93.

Bessette, Lee Skallerup. "We're All YA Now: A Review of Graphic Novels for Children and Young Adults". *The Comics Grid, Journal of Comics Scholarship*, vol. 8, no. 2, 2018, pp. 1–6, https://doi.org/10.16995/cg.124. Accessed 1 May 2022.

Bollinger, Tim. *New Zealand Comics and Graphic Novels*, edited by Dylan Horrocks. Hicksville Press, 2012.

Bhabha, Homi Kharshedji. "Of Mimicry and Man". *The Location of Culture*. Routledge, 1994, pp. 85–92.

Burger, Alissa. "Introduction". *Teaching Graphic Novels in the English Classroom*, edited by Alissa Burger, Springer, 2018, pp. 1–8, https://doi.org/10.1007/978-3-319-63459-3_1. Accessed 1 May 2022.

Cachin, Françoise. *Gauguin*. Flammarion, [1968] 1988.

Caruth, Cathy. "Unclaimed Experience: Trauma and The Possibility of History". *Yale French Studies*, 79, Literature and the Ethical Question, 1991, pp. 181–192.

Chen, Li. *Extra Ordinary Comics*. 2021, https://www.exocomics.com/. Accessed 1 June 2022.

Cixous, Hélène. "The Laugh of the Medusa", translated by K. Cohen and P. Cohen. *Signs*, vol. 1, no. 4, Summer 1976, pp. 875–893.

Collins, Francis. L. "Legislated Inequality: Provisional Migration and the Stratification of Migrant Lives". *Intersections of Inequality, Migration and Diversification*, edited by Rachel Simon-Kumar, Francis L. Collins and Wardlow Friesen. Palgrave Pivot, 2020, pp. 65–86, https://doi.org/10.1007/978-3-030-19099-6. Accessed 1 July 2022.

Connors, Sean P. "Designing Meaning: A Multimodal Perspective on Comics Reading". *Teaching Comics Through Multiple Lenses: Critical Perspectives*, edited by C. Hill. Taylor & Francis, 2016, pp. 11–28.

DeIuliis, David. "Culturally Gatekeeping the Black Comic Strip". *Black Comics: Politics of Race and Representation*, edited by Sheena C. Howard and Ronald L. Jackson. Bloomsbury Academic, 2013, pp. 239–250, https://doi.org/10.5040/9781472543424. ch-014. Accessed 1 July 2022.

Didham, Robert, and Zarine L. Rocha. "Where You Feel You Belong: Classifying Ethnicity and Mixedness in New Zealand". *The Palgrave International Handbook of Mixed Racial and Ethnic Classification*, edited by Zarine L. Rocha and Peter J. Aspinal. Palgrave, 2020, pp. 587–604, https://doi.org/10.1007/978-3-030-22874-3_31. Accessed 1 May 2022.

Dori, Fabrizio. *Gauguin, l'autre monde*. Sarbacane, 2016.

Eyerman, Ron. "Cultural Trauma and Collective Memory". *Cultural Trauma: Slavery and the Formation of African American Identity*. Cambridge University Press, 2009, pp. 1–22, https://doi.org/10.1017/CBO9780511488788.001. Accessed 1 May 2022.

Fox, Abram. "Exploring the Art in Sequential Art". *Graphic Novels and Comics in the Classroom: Essays on the Educational Power of Sequential Art*, edited by Carrye Kay Syma and Robert G. Weiner. McFarland & Company, Incorporated Publishers, 2013, pp. 91–100.

Frame, Janet. *An Angel at my Table*. Virago, [1982, 1984, 1985, 1989] 2008.

Frangos, Mike Classon. "Swedish Norm-Critical Comics and the Comics Pedagogy of Lynda Barry". *The Comics Grid, Journal of Comics Scholarship*, vol. 11, no. 1–3, 2021, pp. 1–18, https://doi.org/10.16995/cg.4042. Accessed 1 July 2022.

Gauguin, Paul. *Ancien Culte Mahorie*. Gallimard, [1892] 2017.

Geoffroy-Schneiter, Bérénice. "Les paradis perdus de Paul Gauguin". *Ancien Culte Mahorie*. Gallimard, 2017, pp. 61–75.

Gilmore, Leigh. "Introduction. The Mark of Autobiography: Postmodernism, Autobiography, and Genre". *Autobiography and Postmodernism*, edited by Kathleen M. Ashley, Leigh Gilmore and Gerald Peters. University of Massachusetts Press, 1994, pp. 3–18.

—. "Introduction". *The Limits of Autobiography: Trauma and Testimony*. Cornell University Press, 2001a, 1–15.

—. "Represent Yourself". *The Limits of Autobiography: Trauma and Testimony*. Cornell University Press, 2001b, pp. 16–44. https://www-jstor-org.ezproxy.is.ed.ac.uk/stable/pdf/10.7591/j.ctv3s8p46.5.pdf?refreqid=excelsior%3Aca86178ae77d07fe-2671291f47ecb2f0. Accessed 1 May 2022.

—. "Conclusion: The Knowing Subject and an Alternative Jurisprudence of Trauma". *The Limits of Autobiography: Trauma and Testimony*. Cornell University Press, 2001c, pp. 143–148, https://www-jstor-org.ezproxy.is.ed.ac.uk/stable/pdf/10.7591/j.ctv3s8p46.10.pdf?refreqid=excelsior%3Aca86178ae77d07fe2671291f47ecb2f0. Accessed 1 May 2022.

—. "Witnessing Persepolis: Comics, Trauma, and Childhood Testimony". *Graphic Subjects: Critical Essays on Autobiography and Graphic Novels*, edited by Michael A. Chaney. University of Wisconsin Press, 2011, pp. 157–163.

—. "Introduction: Tainted Witness in Testimonial Networks". *Tainted Witness. Why We Doubt What Women Say*. Columbia University Press, 2017, pp. 1–25.

Gilmore, Leigh, and Elizabeth Marshall. "Introduction: Witnessing Girlhood". *Witnessing Girlhood. Towards an Intersectional Tradition of Life Writing*. Fordham University Press, 2019a, pp. 1–11.

—. "Gender Pessimism and Survivor Storytelling in the Memoir Boom Girl, Interrupted, Autobiography of a Face, and Nanette". *Witnessing Girlhood. Towards an Intersectional Tradition of Life Writing*. Fordham University Press, 2019b, pp. 38–62.

Gin, Steven. "Towards an Electronic Fāgogo: Lani Wendt Young's Telesā Series and Social Media". *Journal of Postcolonial Writing*, vol. 54, no. 5, 2018, pp. 601–613, https://doi.org/10.1080/17449855.2018.1524914. Accessed 1 May 2022.

Goeman, Mishuana. "Introduction: Gendered Geographies and Narrative Markings". *Mark My Words: Native Women Mapping Our Nations*. University of Minnesota Press, 2013, pp. 1–40.

Grace, Patricia. "'I Never Found Myself In A Book': Patricia Grace on the Importance of Māori Literature". *The Guardian*, 30 Apr. 2021, n.p., https://www.theguardian.com/world/2021/may/01/i-never-found-myself-in-a-book-patricia-grace-on-the-importance-of-maori-literature. Accessed 1 May 2021.

Grbic, Douglas, Hiromi Ishizawa and Charles Crothers. "Ethnic Residential Segregation in New Zealand, 1991–2006". *Social Science Research*, vol. 39, 2010, pp. 25–38.

Hamelin, Christine. "Gender Mapping Genre: Studies in Female Künstlerromane from Canada, Australia, and New Zealand". Unpublished PhD diss., Queen's University, 1994.

Ihimaera, Witi, and Tina Makereti, editors. *Black Marks on the White Page*. Random House New Zealand Vintage, 2017.

Ioane, Julia, Ian Lambie and Teuila Percival. "A Review of the Literature on Pacific Island Youth Offending in New Zealand". *Aggression and Violent Behaviour*, vol. 18, no. 4, 2013, pp. 426–433.

Jorgensen, Anna, and Arianna Lechan. "Not your mom's graphic novels: Giving girls a choice beyond wonder woman". *Technical Services Quarterly*, vol. 30, no. 3, July 2013, pp. 266–284. https://doi.org/10.1080/07317131.2013.785779. Accessed 1 May 2021.

Keown, Michell. "'Can't We All Just Get Along?': bro'Town and New Zealand's Creative Multiculturalism". *Moving Worlds*, vol. 8, no. 2, 2008, pp. 44–58.

Klepper, Martin. "Autobiographical/Autofictional Comics". *Handbook of Autobiography/Autofiction*, edited by Martina Wagner-Egelhaaf. De Gruyter, 2019, pp. 441–445, https://doi.org/10.1515/9783110279818-058. Accessed 1 June 2021.

Laing, Sarah. *Mansfield and Me*. Victoria University Press, 2016.

Lee, Jenny Bol Jun. *Jade Taniwha: Māori-Chinese Identity and Schooling in Aotearoa*. Raukati Ltd, 2007.

Lejeune, Philippe. "Le pacte autobiographique". *L'autobiographie*. Gallimard, 1974, pp. 13–46.

Lewis, Mark. "Illustrating Youth: A Critical Examination of the Artful Depictions of Adolescent Characters in Comics". *Teaching Comics Through Multiple Lenses: Critical Perspectives*, edited by Crag Hill. Taylor & Francis, 2016, pp. 46–58.

MacDowell, Paula. "Girls' Perspectives on (Mis) Representations of Girlhood in Hegemonic Media Texts". *Girlhood Studies*, vol. 10, no. 3, Winter 2017, pp. 201–216.

Marrall, Rebecca M. "Multicultural Education through Graphic Novels". *Graphic Novels and Comics in the Classroom: Essays on the Educational Power of Sequential Art*, edited by Carrye Kay Syma, and Robert G. Weiner. McFarland Company, Incorporated Publishers, 2013, pp. 245–250.

Marsh, Selina Tusitala. *Fast Talking PI*. Arc Publications, [2009] 2012.

—. "The Body of Pacific Literature". *MAI Review*, vol. 1, 2010, pp. 1–6.

—. *Mophead*. Auckland University Press, 2019. E-Book.

—. *Teacher Resources on Mophead*. Auckland University Press, 2020.

McCloud, Scott. *Understanding Comics: The Invisible Art*. HarperCollins, 1993.

McMullin, Dan Taulapapa. "The Fag End of Fāgogo". *Narrative Culture*, vol. 6, no. 2, 2019, pp. 216–228.

Michael, Olga. "Graphic Autofiction and the Visualization of Trauma in Lynda Barry and Phoebe Gloeckner's Graphic Memoirs". *Autofiction in English*, edited by Hywel Dix. Palgrave Studies in Life Writing, 2018, pp. 105–124, https://doi.org/10.1007/978-3-319-89902-2_6. Accessed 1 July 2021.

Ministry of Health/Manatū Hauora. "Suicide Facts: Data Tables 1996–2016". 28 Nov. 2019, https://www.health.govt.nz/publication/suicide-facts-data-tables-19962016). Accessed 1 May 2021.

Mitchell, Claudia. "Charting Girlhood Studies". *Girlhood and the Politics of Place*, edited by Claudia Mitchell and Carrie Rentschler. Berghahn Books, 2016, pp. 87–103, https://www.jstor.org/stable/j.ctt14jxn16.10. Accessed 30 Sept. 2018.

Moyle, Richard. *Fāgogo: Fables from Samoa*. Auckland University Press, 1981.

Neville, Indira. *100 School Demons*. 2010, https://indiraneville.wordpress.com/. Accessed 1 July 2021.

O'Donnell, David. "'Spiritual Play': Ritual Performance and Spirituality in Samoan Theatre". *PotR*, 2015. https://www.otago.ac.nz/performance-of-the-real/otago666945.pdf. Accessed 30 Sept. 2018.

Pearson, Sarina. "Persistent Primitivisms: Popular and Academic Discourses about Pacific and Maori Cinema and Television". *Journal of the Polynesian Society*, vol. 122, no. 1, 2013, pp. 21–44, https://doi.org/10.15286/jps.122.1.21-44. Accessed 1 May 2021.

Rippl, Gabriele, Philipp Schweighauser and Therese Steffen. "Introduction: Life Writing in an Age of Trauma". *Haunted Narratives. Life Writing in an Age of Trauma*, edited by G. Rippl et al. University of Toronto Press, 2013, pp. 1–18.

Roy, Eleanor Ainge. "New Zealand Gives Mount Taranaki Same Legal Rights as A Person". *The Guardian,* 22 Dec. 2017, https://www.theguardian.com/world/2017/dec/22/new-zealand-gives-mount-taranaki-same-legal-rights-as-a-person. Accessed 1 May 2021.

Scott, Mark. "Whitewash: The Acceptable Image in Television Advertising". *Between the Lines: Racism and the New Zealand Media*, edited by Paul Spoonley and Walter Hirsh. Heineman Reed, 1990, pp. 84–89.

Sibley, Chris G., and Colleen Ward. "Measuring the Preconditions for a Successful Multicultural Society: A Barometer Test of New Zealand". *International Journal of Intercultural Relations*, vol. 37, no. 6, 2013, pp. 700–713.

Somé, Isabelle. "L'écriture autofictionelle: une odyssée libératrice". *Cliniques méditerranéennes*, vol. 1, no. 91, Jan. 2015, pp. 229–242, https://www.cairn.info/revue-cliniques-mediterraneennes-2015-1-page-229.htm. Accessed 27 May 2021.

Stats NZ Tatauranga Aotearoa. "2018 Census Population and Dwelling Counts". 23 Sept. 2019. https://www.stats.govt.nz/information-releases/2018-census-population-and-dwelling-counts. Accessed 13 May 2021.

Sua'ali'i, Tamasailau. "Deconstructing the 'Exotic' Female Beauty of the Pacific Islands and 'White' Male Desire". *Women's Studies Journal*, vol. 13, no. 2, Spring 1997, pp. 75–94.

Tawake, Sandra. "Transforming the Insider-Outsider Perspective: Postcolonial Fiction from the Pacific". *The Contemporary Pacific*, vol. 12, no. 1, Spring 200, pp. 155–175.

Wagner-Egelhaaf, Martina. "Introduction: Autobiography Across the World, Or, How Not To Be Eurocentric". *Handbook of Autobiography/Autofiction*, edited by Martina Wagner-Egelhaaf. De Gruyter, 2019, pp. 683–688. https://doi.org/10.1515/9783110279818-087. Accessed 1 May 2021.

Wang, Bingyu, and Francis Leo Collins. "Becoming Cosmopolitan? Hybridity and Intercultural Encounters amongst 1.5 Generation Chinese Migrants in New Zealand". *Ethnic and Racial Studies*, vol. 39, no. 15, 2016, pp. 2777–2795.

Waretini-Karena, Rawiri. "Colonial Law, Dominant Discourses, and Intergenerational Trauma". *The Palgrave Handbook of Australian and New Zealand Criminology, Crime and Justice*, edited by Antje Deckert and Rick Harris. Palgrave Macmillan, 2017, pp. 697–709.

White, Michael, and David Epston. *Narrative Means to Therapeutic Ends*. Norton & Company, 1990.

Wilson, Janet. "Transnational Movements: Australia, Canada, New Zealand, South Pacific". *The Oxford History of the Novel in English: Volume 12: The Novel in Australia, Canada, New Zealand, and the South Pacific Since 1950*, edited by Coral Ann Howells, Paul Sharrad and Gerry Turcotte. Oxford University Press, 2017, pp. 142–157, https://doi.org/10.1093/oso/9780199679775.003.0012. Accessed 1 May 2021.

Conclusion

Eva Van de Wiele

The essays in this volume problematise the term 'girl', and distance themselves from the discomfiting use of a definite article, as suggested by Mel Gibson (Chapter 1) and Martha Newbigging (Chapter 2). Many of the chapters unpack personal or fictional experiences that indicate tensions between ideological and lived identity, between child and adult, between girl and boy. It is not a coincidence that these discussions focus on words and wording(s), since linguistic practice informs social practice and vice versa (according to Fairclough's critical discourse analysis). As enjoyable as it might be to discover that there are girls comics, that feeling of recognition or excitement might be instantaneously accompanied by embarrassment, as Gibson argues, because of negative or limiting cultural constructions around girlhood and girls' popular culture.

Girls may want to read a panoply of comics[1] but might not find or might be denied access to a wide range of comics genres or forms. Gibson unpacks accessing comics as a girl and indicates different forms of gatekeeping in the British comics industry since 1950. Bedroom culture or girls' bedrooms as alternative cultural domains (McRobbie and Garber 1976) is an important topic Gibson touches upon. Rightfully, she points out that the genre of comics culturally prescribed for girls, such as DC Thomson's *Bunty*, was not available to her through the comic bookshop but worked through subscription and was delivered to readers' homes. While boys were welcome guests in the comic bookshop, girls were less so (or otherwise seen as "trespassers") and expected to devote themselves to their "own" material in other geographical spaces. The two scholars interviewed by Michel De Dobbeleer (Chapter 9) confirmed Gibson's insights, as their comics reading was built on the domestically available family series featuring male protagonists. Sylvain Lesage also discusses the rarity of comics for and on girls, as a consequence of which they are largely ignored by comics historians creating gaps in our understanding of both female artists and readers (Chapter 5). Moreover, the embarrassment around comics also sticks to the medium itself, as Katrien De Graeve and Sara De Vuyst remember how their entourage stated that they needed to take out "real" books from the library too. This "double" embarrassment (the former related to gender, the latter to the medium itself) can result in forced amnesia on the part of girl readers, not remembering their girlhood reading in adulthood. Martha Newbigging's visual essay (Chapter 2) uses self-characters[2] to reactivate memory that might have been lost or discarded. Newbigging references cartoonist and educator, Lynda Barry, for her thoughts on how we hold, retrieve, and draw images as signifiers of memory and meaning making. Barry notes,

> I believe making lines and shapes and coloring them in can still help us in the way it helped us when we were kids. When we used paper as if it were a place rather than a thing. A place where something alive can happen through motion [...] Drawing is one of our oldest ways of working things out. (223)

Drawing is also a way of working things out and an ethical act for Ali Fitzgerald, an American artist working in Berlin, as María Porras Sánchez describes (Chapter 3). Fitzgerald offered comic workshops in refugee shelters. Her redrawing of several girl refugees' testimonies harbour, according to Porras Sánchez, not only a way for Fitzgerald to connect with them but also to make their stories visible from a non-hegemonic perspective to readers. Other comics "draw" portraits of girl refugees, by allowing them to literally voice their experiences and to express their personality, through first-person narration like Gulia Pex's *Khalat* or *Escape from Syria* by Samya Kullab and Jackie Roche. Turning what is invisible into visible matter, both drawn and in words, is key in many of these chapters. Sometimes the opposite is true, as Aswathy Senan shows through her analysis of Toms's Malayali series *Bobanum Moliyum*, the ten-year-old twin brother and sister, change from being devices to appeal to readers in a domestic setting (1960s) to emblems of political and social critique (1970s) to disappearing by the 1980s when the comic strip had completely morphed into a political cartoon (Chapter 8).

The question whether girls need to see themselves represented in order to sympathise with the characters is an intricate one or might miss the point. On the one hand, as De Graeve and De Vuyst and Gibson state, girls can empathise with protagonists of all ages, genders or races. On the other, however, symbolic annihilation, not seeing oneself represented, might have led girls to stop reading comics or to feel embarrassed about reading specific kinds of comics. The invisibility of minorities can be socially determined, or related to racial segmentation, such as that of Māori and Pasifika people from New Zealand. Marine Berthiot's discussion of Selina Tusitala Marsh's *Mophead* gives a manifold description of cultural references and phenomena discussed in Chapter 9 such as the "male gaze" in her analysis of the poetic comic and graphic memoir (Chapter 11). Comics artist Selina Tusitala Marsh describes in *Mophead* stages of self-acceptance, talking about how she first tried to assimilate or render herself invisible before she spoke up for herself. Again, discourse analysis is a vital research tool, as Berthiot acknowledges the woman artists' memory of the effects and affordances of words uttered against girls. Especially the repetition of invisibilities and of stereotypes root problematic ideas into children's minds so that girls perform their girlhood (stereo)typically and are commented solely upon their looks, even when drawn by women. By aiming her work particularly at (Pasifika) children, through a way of drawing described by Lynda Barry from *What It Is*, and *Making Comics* to *Syllabus*, Tusitala Marsh undoes stereotypes and creates a positive, poetic reading experience for her readers.

Other cultural constructions around femininity discussed in this volume oppose the female as grotesque or unhappy when confronted by masculine hegemony. However, British 1960s comics magazines for girls and young women offered an alternative to motherhood and marriage, by visualising girls that went on holidays, indulged in sporty leisure activities or moved to the city to be employed, as Joan Ormrod shows (Chapter 7). Ormrod evinces how these representations are linked to the aesthetic categories of "cute" and "zany" as described by Sianne Ngai: the former, a leisurely girl; the latter, a labouring girl. Unsurprisingly, magazines such as *Mirabelle*, which promoted the active female body, were criticised for tying girlhood to consumerism. For girlhood studies, such magazines signal a multimedial and cultural change in the representation of girlhood from the 1960s in the UK. Contemporaneously, the child magazine *Pif Gadget* reflects social changes in France as mixed reader audiences were targeted discussing gender roles when those roles were actually changing (Chapter 5).

Newer comics series from general publishers have been "feminising" their main characters to remediate male dominance. The girl-and-her-dog comics series *Margot & Oscar Pluche / Sac à Puces* discussed by Benoît Glaude (Chapter 6) features a girl protagonist in a more traditional family strip and addresses newer themes, but Glaude shows that contemporary series retains stereotypes such as typical female traits by graphically reproducing those stereotypes (Johnson). Another example of contemporary comics with child protagonists, are nostalgic, multimedial incarnations of series such as the one discussed by Senan. Toms's *Bobanum Moliyum* series plays on readers' nostalgic memories to market a series and its cross-writing potential to speak to everyone's child within (Chapter 8).

Comics are thus to be considered as cultural stations, in the sense that these works read and observed are as formative in people's lives as their education and training, as the technological developments and value systems they are confronted with and embedded in (notion of David Bolt, see Gibson's Chapter 1). They take up a "role in the lives of many girls – to represent the female experience and instill cultural mores" (Danziger-Russell 31). They also constitute readers' selves. Comics do this through both media: language and words. Glaude has convincingly demonstrated how comics scholars can investigate verbal interactions in comics quantitatively to understand characterisation. Gibson, Ormrod and Berthiot have shown that discourse analysis is key to lay bare societal changes and social influence through language. Moreover, many contributors to this volume discuss the format and the way in which readers encounter the comic. It determines their agency upon and their feelings about the object. Gibson sought out superhero comics in floppies, cycling to different shops, patiently building a collection of her own, against the disapproval or smirk of male comic bookshop owners and customers. Floppies were also objects she shared with her father, even though he cut out some pieces of the pages for his scrapbooking. This form of male, adult control over the child's comics reading is comparable to Michel De Dobbeleer's reading out comics to his children, "chaperoning" their understanding by revising politically incorrect or outdated ideas and terms (Hatfield and Sanders, 460).

Of course, the reader is not necessarily passive and can opt for oppositional reading. Sylvain Lesage has given proof of such reader reactions by close reading gender roles in Jean Tabary's series *Corinne et Jeannot*, showing the constant breaking of the fourth wall and linking it to polemic editorials and vigorous discussions among readers in the correspondence of the communist comics magazine *Pif Gadget* (Chapter 5). Even when a male artist like Jean Tabary replaces the asymmetric male–female relationship by its exact opposite, the dominated male, or when discussions are actually marketing devices, readers' reactions testify that the results are not necessarily negative and that readers wish to change representations in favour of a more convincing equilibrium of power.

The visual essays in this volume, JoAnn Purcell's drawn account of her daughter (Chapter 4), Martha Newbigging's visual essay on queerness (Chapter 2) and Sébastien Conard's tribute to Charlotte Salomon (Chapter 10), fruitfully engage with manifold ways of being "girl" and of telling one's or another's story. Drawings such as Newbigging's contrast normative representations and open up to representations of the girl self with agency, strength, risk-taking and venturing out with independence. Drawing comics is their method to witness these non-normative behaviours that actively resist the constraints of expectation. Similar to how Newbigging claims significance to show/tell a counter-narrative, JoAnn Purcell claims room for her daughter's non-normative sense of time. Instead of theorising about the concept of crip time (Robert McRuer, Alison Kafer and Ellen Samuels), Purcell draws and describes the actual lived experience of a mother and a daughter coping with time constraints and how comics making, can make "time to take care". The singularity of a disability and of growing up as an adolescent girl become clear through the drawings on and the being of Simone, while the experience of motherhood is evident from Purcell's direct unerasable lines on the paper. Joanne's daughter is a girl moving to high school. The contrasting line between girlhood and womanhood or motherhood is visualised in words and collaged images by a man, Sébastien Conard. His essay draws the memory of Charlotte Salomon, Holocaust victim, who drew her girlhood. Her peculiar (not sequential, nor mutational), multimodal graphic memoir, *Life? or Theatre?*, is a testimony to the horrors of the Second World War. Conard's essay is an act of remembering and acknowledging this girl/woman's gesture. One of many girls on the verge of motherhood, this transformation was stopped by brutal extermination. By capturing her "self", her face in "stamps" on the typewritten paper, Conard imprints the likeness of the artist on his homage. An homage that resulted from a visit to a museum exhibition in her honour. His text works through repetition, multilingual citations and referencing to what *Mädchen* might mean in German.

All authors and artists have put the comics' manifold genres and formats into cultural perspective. As Lesage has importantly indicated, one of the reasons for the asymmetric construction of the ninth art canon is that "the conditions of conservation and access are much easier for mixed publications than for specifically female publications" (105). Volumes such as these, I hope, can remediate that.

Notes

1. Kimberley Reynolds states: "There is a noteworthy contradiction between what girls actually read, the prohibitive rhetoric which laid down what they ought and ought not to be reading, and what in fact it was tacitly accepted that girls read" (92–93).
2. Martha Newbigging prefers the term "self-character" to "avatar" because it has more intimate associations, as opposed to the "coldness" of an avatar.

Bibliography

Lynda Barry, *Picture This*, Drawn & Quarterly, 2010.

Danziger-Russell, Jacqueline. *Girls and Their Comics: Finding a Female Voice in Comic Book Narrative*. Scarecrow Press, 2013.

Hatfield, Charles and Sutliff Sanders, Joe. "Bonding Time or Solo Flight?: Picture Books, Comics, and the Independent Reader". *Children's Literature Association Quarterly*, vol. 42, no. 4, 2017, pp. 459–486.

Kafer, Alison. *Feminist, Queer, Crip*. Indiana University Press, 2013.

Lesage, Sylvain. "Discussing Gender in a Communist Comics Magazine: *Corinne et Jeannot*, 1970", In Dona Pursall and Eva Van de Wiele (Editors), *Sugar, Spice, and the Not So Nice: Comics Picturing Girlhood*. Leuven University Press, 2023, pp. 70-88.

McRobbie, Angela and Garber, Jenny. "Girls and subculture". In Stuart Hall and T. Jefferson (Editors), *Resistance through rituals: Youth subcultures in post-war Britain*, Hutchinson, pp. 209–223.

McRuer, Robert. *Crip Theory: Cultural Signs of Queerness and Disability*. New York University Press, 2006.

Samuels, Ellen. "Six Ways of Looking at Crip Time". *Disability Studies Quarterly*, vol. 37, no. 3, Summer 2017, https://dsq-sds.org/article/view/5824/4684. Accessed 12 October 2022.

Afterword
Picturing Girlhood

Julia Round

As a girl, woman, daughter, mother, aunt and sister, I often think about these gendered roles and labels. I occupy them all at different times but have seldom felt like I fully understand how exactly they fit me, whether they suit me or how their priorities, expectations and restrictions should map onto the thinking "I". At the start of my academic career I think perhaps I viewed many of the theories and ideologies around gender and the female as abstract ideas: with little bearing on me as an individual, on my own life and tastes. But as my research has developed and cohered around certain areas, I've found myself repeatedly encountering and exploring ideologies of the female and feminine. For example, within Gothic studies, where they may appear as victim, as writer, or as Other; within comics studies, where they may be marginalised or fetishised; and within children's literature, where they are often lessons, or symbols, stereotypes and archetypes.

The Comics Picturing Girlhood event was a wonderful space to explore these ideas, bringing together international scholars with diverse backgrounds and experiences to reflect on the forms of girlhood they had encountered and the ways these have been depicted, received, categorised and responded to. As the articles in this collection have stressed, it is not only girlhood and its representations that are shaped by material, historical, intersectional and cultural expectations. Our engagement with these depictions and the ways we feel able to interact with them are also subject to these pressures. And our relationship to our own memories of girlhood (whether taken from personal experiences or our perceptions of another's) are also reshaped by these encounters: building a complex web of intertextual and multimodal associations and creating different understandings and interpretations of a concept that is already deeply variable and constantly shifting. Girlhood itself is an unstable category that changes and is interpreted differently across generations (Gibson 2008) but our engagement with it is just as fluid.

The conference call for papers suggested four main areas that researchers could address: genre and categorisation, representations of girlhood, emotional impact and response, and practice and interactivity. The first of these invited us to consider the historical and social contexts of popular stories and the categories of girlhood and its stories that have arisen. What genres have been felt acceptable, and what historical, social and economic preferences inform this? The papers published here certainly demonstrate the familiar patterns that stories of young girls might fall into, for example, as María Porras Sánchez explores in a discussion of refugee narratives. But Porras Sánchez also offers analytic suggestions for how reductive treatments can be avoided, and how characters can be given wider and more plural possibilities. The potential of girls' texts to reshape understandings is also apparent in Joan Ormrod's discussion of the British comic *Mirabelle*, which draws attention to the way that textual aesthetics can (literally) reshape expectations: giving characters agency that perhaps prefigures significant political movements. Comics are shown here to have unexpected potential, as their multimodal capabilities allow word and image to be disconnected, creating clashing discourses and speaking to multiple audiences simultaneously, as Aswathy Senan's discussion of the Malayalis strip *Bobanum Moliyum* also demonstrates. Other work presented at the event but not published here also speaks to these themes, such as Nicoletta Mandolini's exploration of the ways that Ana Caspão's *Fundo do nada* (2017) uses the concept of abjection to reframe the traditional coming-of-age narrative as a macabre experience, and Alison Halsall's analysis of the feminist recasting of the scouting story in *Lumberjanes* (2014–2020).

Just as important, perhaps, are the genres and categories that girls are excluded from, as Mel Gibson discusses in her chapter "It's *the* girl!", based on her keynote talk. Gibson uses her own memories of childhood embarrassment and feelings of exclusion from the comics genres that she loved to reflect on the ways these acts can shape professional behaviour and self-image. This adds a valuable temporal dimension to the discussion, demonstrating how adult readers are encouraged to leave behind particular texts and drawing attention to the ways girlhood is cast in these titles and framed in their paratexts: as a small space, full of embarrassing memories, to be remembered with humour and treated with self-deprecation. Gibson also extends this argument to the professional sphere, pointing towards similar feelings of doubt and inadequacy around certain research methodologies, such as auto-ethnography. I was struck by the significance of this point, which exposes a self-perpetuating hierarchy within research fields where certain methods are valued more highly than "messier" alternatives.

This leads me to the question of gatekeeping – who does this excluding, and why? Gibson's discussion links this power with seniority and patriarchy, but other papers within the conference spoke to different angles, such as Charlotte Johanne Fabricius's discussion of *The Unstoppable WASP*, which explored the comic's central figure of a white girl as gatekeeper of access and opportunity. We might also think about privileged representations of girlhood as gatekeeping figures – which images are made most central and what qualities do they embody? This leads me to the second question of the conference call for papers, which asked researchers to consider what the representation and embodiment of girlhood looks like in comics, with a particular focus on how comics might make visible marginalised identity categories (both in diegetic characters and their real-life creators). These themes are sensitively and convincingly explored here in Marine Berthiot's analysis of Selina Tusitala Marsh's autobiographix *Mophead*, which centralises a Pasifika girl heroine and reclaims her from discourses that have discriminated, abused, othered, exoticised and eroticised this figure. Berthiot shows how many facets of the comics medium contribute to this and, vitally, how the comic assimilates Western formats into Indigenous narrative tropes – inverting this power imbalance. The question of who speaks (and therefore of who has control) is also explored by other work in this collection. Sébastien Conard's graphic essay considers the powerful voice within Charlotte Salomon's *Life? or Theatre?* and the multiplicity of female experience it conveys. JoAnn Purcell reflects on her own comics creation, and how this process allowed her to recognise "crip time" – enabling recognition of her daughter's agency and challenging normalised myths around notions such as progress, pace, trajectories and closure. Purcell's comics allow her to recognise crip time alongside her own experiences: making the contrast explicit and forcing her to reflect on her own responses to this.

Emotional impact and response was the third area suggested by the conference call for papers, asking delegates to consider emotionally loaded representations of girls such as the coquettish, nymphetic, cute or grotesque, and their impact on readers. The papers herein stress the importance of recognising the personal and using it as a strength. For example, Berthiot notes that autobiographix like *Mophead* can sidestep the notion of trauma as unrepresentable. Gibson and Purcell both emphasise the way that auto-ethnography can expose unexpected points of tension and contrast, and the importance of reflecting on the assumptions that underpin not just our research subject but also our methodology. The creative work published here also foregrounds the importance of recognising and enabling emotive expression. Glaude and Lesage both focus on popular series for children and their reception. Glaude studies the readership of the fifteen albums of the Franco-Belgian *Margot et Oscar Pluche / Sac à Puces* (1990–2009). Lesage deals with *Corinne et Jeannot*, a comics series published in the French communist magazine *Pif* in the 1970s through looking at the way the series constructs gender roles and how the abundant readers' letters respond to those.

The final conference theme focused on practices and interactivity, asking how girls use their comics, and how they might be encouraged to act as more than just readers. Again, the graphic essays herein constitute a form of response to this question, as creative responses that use comics to express and sustain complexities. My own research into letters pages in the British girls' comic *Misty* has also found that readers often responded creatively to the comic's stories: for example, by sending in creative work or making imaginative connections with their own lives (Round). Martha Newbigging's "Looking for Queerness" most clearly articulates the positive and affirming qualities of creative response: positioning drawing as a practice of reasserting that can counteract the type of mass forgetting or fake memories that Gibson's work points towards.

Taken together, these pieces offer a valuable insight into the potential of narratives of girlhood to disrupt assumptions and allow marginalised and under-recognised voices to reclaim control. The vast potential for political statement – even in the most unlikely of places (as Senan notes) – is recognised as part of this. My own keynote talk at the conference (not collected here, as it will form the basis of a chapter in the forthcoming *Edinburgh History of Children's Periodicals*) discussed the depiction of supernatural possession in British girls' horror comics as an act with unexpected and political connotations. Far from being a straightforward enactment of passive obedience, possessed girls in these comics often retain their agency, as their possession enables them to negotiate historical trauma. Activity and passivity become blurred concepts here.

Similarly, I find myself reflecting on the tension between movement and stasis that emerges from many of these discussions. Girlhood is often described as a transient or liminal state (Armitt; Georgieva), and many of these papers observe that girls are "transient beings" (Porras Sánchez). But alongside this is a stasis and stagnancy that underpins representation and ideology. For example, Senan points out that the *Bobanum Moliyum* characters are stuck aged eleven, De Dobbeleer indicates that the children in the Flemish *familiestrip Jommeke* will forever remain ten and Porras Sánchez cites Bauman in discussing the "frozen transience" of refugees, as "an ongoing, lasting state of temporariness" (46). Rather than debating which is most true, perhaps (as with many other aspects of girlhood) we are better acknowledging the contradiction and characterising girlhood as "a perpetually transitory state of time" (Lemaster n.p.). Maybe what is important is not the progression of its rites of passage, initiations and conventions, but the ebb and flow of power that underpins these. Who speaks, who has agency, who reflects and responds – and what cultural assumptions and emotions shape these processes? The voices here demonstrate the potential impact of these questions, as the analyses offered go far beyond the pre-established character types and processes mentioned in the introduction. They demonstrate new possibilities for the depiction and reception of plurivocal, dissimilar girls and will undoubtedly provide a vital grounding for future research in this field.

Bibliography

Armitt, Lucie. "The Gothic Girl Child". *Women and the Gothic*, edited by Avril Horner and Sue Zlosnik. Edinburgh University Press, 2017, pp. 60–73.

Bauman, Zygmunt. *Liquid Times: Living in an Age of Uncertainty*. Polity, 2013.

Georgieva, Margarita. *The Gothic Child*. Palgrave Macmillan, 2013.

Gibson, Mel. "Nobody, Somebody, Everybody: Ballet, Girlhood, Class, Femininity and Comics in 1950s Britain". *Girlhood Studies*, vol. 2, 2008, pp. 108–128.

Lemaster, Tracy Wendt. "Girlhood and the Feminist Imaginary in Twentieth-Century Transatlantic Women's Literature". Unpublished PhD diss., University of Wisconsin-Madison, 2012. https://depot.library.wisc.edu/repository/fedora/1711. dl:WPTWJ5ZTKMDCL8G/datastreams/REF/content. Accessed 28 July 2021.

Round, Julia. *Gothic for Girls: Misty and British Comics*. University Press Mississippi, 2019.

About the Authors

Marine Berthiot is a PhD student in English Literature at the University of Edinburgh. Her thesis deals with "Rewriting Girlhood Trauma in New Zealand Literature" and is supervised by Professor Michelle Keown. The purpose of her research is to study the impact of genres on the representations of trauma experienced by female characters in their childhood.

Sébastien Conard is an author, artist, art teacher and researcher. He holds a PhD in the Arts, concerning word, image and narrative in the graphic novel and the historical avant-gardes (LUCA-KULeuven 2016). He teaches theory and practice within the fields of graphic storytelling, illustration, printmaking and graphic design at KASK Ghent School of Arts and LUCA Brussels. He recently edited and curated *Post-Comics, Beyond Comics, Illustration, and the Graphic Novel* (KASK and het balanseer, 2020).

Michel De Dobbeleer is a Slavist, classicist and Italianist. He has published (and organised international seminars/panels) on comics adaptations of East European classics, (ultra)minor comics from the Balkans, siege and other comics chronotopes, "real" and alternate history in comics, graphic children's poetry, comics translation and on spin-offs of popular comics series. Currently he focuses on *The Adventures of Jommeke* [De belevenissen van Jommeke], confronting its title hero, his friends and their twentieth-century Flemish context with the child-related (sub)topics and concepts at stake in the COMICS project.

Mel Gibson has been working with children, young people and comics since the mid-1980s when she started work as an Outreach and Children's Librarian in Gateshead Public Libraries, UK. This continued through that career and into her later academic one. She is currently working on UK histories of libraries, comics and graphic novels as well as the content of contemporary graphic novels, especially titles aimed predominantly at girls. These interests both link with her interest in women's memories of their childhood comic book reading, as shown in her book *Remembered Reading* (2015).

Benoît Glaude is a researcher at Ghent University and a visiting lecturer at UCLouvain, Belgium. He has published several books about French-speaking comics, including his PhD on comics dialogues (*La Bande dialoguée*, 2019), as well as a volume on novelisation in children's literature (*Les Novellisations pour la jeunesse*, coedited with Laurent Déom, 2020). His current research focuses on literary mediations of comics, adapted into novels, audiobooks for youth, children's picture books, etc., as observed from an extensive collection of French-language comics magazines (the Alain Van Passen Collection in the Ghent University's Faculty Library of Arts and Philosophy).

Sylvain Lesage is an associate professor in History at the University of Lille. A member of the IRHiS (CNRS) research team, he specialises in book history, media studies, with a particular interest in comics. His PhD dissertation provided the material for two books: *Publier la bande dessinée. Les éditeurs franco-belges et l'album* (2018) and *L'Effet livre: métamorphoses de la bande dessinée* (2019). He also co-edited with Gert Meesters a book dedicated to the magazine *(À Suivre),* which played a key role in the history of the French-language graphic novel *(À Suivre). Archives d'une revue culte* (2018). He's finishing a book dedicated to the history of the transformation of French comics into a "ninth art" (*Ninth Art. Bande dessinée, books and the transformation of Mass Culture*, 2022). More on https://pro.univ-lille.fr/sylvain-lesage/

Martha Newbigging is a multidisciplinary artist with practices in illustration, comics and animation. They have illustrated over a dozen children's books, and their animations have been screened internationally. They teach illustration in the School of Creative Arts & Animation at Seneca College in Toronto and have facilitated many arts workshops for children and youth in both school and community settings. They hold a BFA from OCAD University, and a Bachelor of Education and Masters of Environmental Studies from York University. Their current practice-based doctoral research focuses on autobiographical drawing and critical pedagogy.

Joan Ormrod is a senior lecturer in Film and Media BA Hons in the Faculty of Arts and Humanities at Manchester Metropolitan University. Her research explores gender and representations in comics. Her books include *Wonder Woman, the Female Body and Popular Culture* (2020) and co-edited collections *Superheroes and Identities* (with Mel Gibson and David Huxley 2015) and *Time Travel in Popular Media* (with Matt Jones, 2015). She is currently researching UK romance comics and girlhood and published preliminary research "Reading production and culture UK teen Girl comics from 1955 to 1960", in *Girlhood Studies* (2018). She edits Routledge's *Journal of Graphic Novels and Comics* (http://www.tandfonline.com/toc/rcom20/current) and is one of the organising team for the annual International Graphic Novels and Comics Conference.

María Porras Sánchez is an assistant professor at the Department of English Studies, Universidad Complutense de Madrid. She has formerly taught at Aberystwyth University and Universitat Oberta de Catalunya. Her main research areas are graphic narratives, cultural translation and postcolonial and transnational literatures in English language. She combines her teaching and research with her work as a literary translator. She has coedited, with E. Sánchez-Pardo and R. Burillo, *Women Poets and Myth in the 20th and 21st Centuries: On Sappho's Website* (2018). Her last work to date is a critical edition and translation of *Headscarves and Hymens: Why the Middle East Needs a Sexual Revolution* (2018), by Mona Eltahawy.

JoAnn Purcell holds a PhD in Critical Disability Studies at York University where she combined her background as a visual artist and registered nurse and created comics alongside disability and difference. She is the current and founding programme coordinator of Illustration at Seneca College and occasional contract faculty at York University. She was instrumental in the creation of the award winning Animation Arts Centre and coordinator in the early years. She held the interim position of Chair of the School of Creative Arts and Animation in 2019. As faculty she teaches drawing, painting, colour theory, art and illustration history and a seminar class in Comics and Social Justice. She has years of hands-on experience as a visual artist, animator and visual effects artist and previously in psychiatric nursing.

Dona Pursall is a PhD student of Cultural Studies and Literature. Her research is part of a wider European project seeking to piece together an intercultural history of children in comics. Through a historical exploration of UK humorous comics (*Beano*, *Dandy*), her research considers children, childhood, imagination, mischief and culture within the context of social unrest and political change. Dona was awarded The Sabin Award for Comics Scholarship in 2021.

Julia Round's research examines the intersections of Gothic, comics and children's literature. Her books include *Gothic for Girls: Misty and British Comics* (2019, winner of the Broken Frontier Award for Best Book on Comics), *Gothic in Comics and Graphic Novels: A Critical Approach* (2014) and the co-edited collection *Real Lives Celebrity Stories* (2014). She is a Principal lecturer at Bournemouth University, co-editor of *Studies in Comics Journal* and the book series *Encapsulations* and co-organiser of the annual International Graphic Novel and Comics Conference. She shares her work at www.juliaround.com.

Aswathy Senan is coordinator at the Research Collective, Delhi, India. She is also a writer, translator, researcher and social activist. Her PhD thesis titled "The Comic Strip of the Kerala Everyday: Bobanum Moliyum, 1957–2014" (University of Delhi, India) studies the comic strips published in Malayalam periodicals, focusing on Bobanum Moliyum comic strip. She has worked as an editor of comic strips and graphic narratives and also contributed to and edited publications on gender and media.

Eva Van de Wiele is a postdoctoral researcher at Ghent University, working on the haptic sections within children's comics magazines of the Van Passen Collection for the ERC project Comics. Her doctoral thesis focused on the spread of (inter)national comics in early Italian *Corriere dei Piccoli* and Spanish *TBO* (and its girl supplement, *BB*) and the way these periodicals edutained, loyalised and commodified their child readers.

Index

T